In Stockmen's Footsteps

Jane Grieve's story of her childhood in rural Australia, her subsequent travels and her pivotal role in the establishment of the Australian Stockman's Hall of Fame, will resonate with all Australians, especially those whose family story is firmly bound to the Australian bush and its heritage.

—Tim Fairfax, AM

In Stockmen's Footsteps

JANE GRIEVE

Foreword by
Jack Thompson, AM

ALLEN&UNWIN
SYDNEY · MELBOURNE · AUCKLAND · LONDON

Allen & Unwin
Sydney, Melbourne, Auckland, London

83 Alexander Street
Crows Nest NSW 2065
Australia
Phone: (61 2) 8425 0100
Email: info@allenandunwin.com
Web: www.allenandunwin.com

Cataloguing-in-Publication details are available
from the National Library of Australia
www.trove.nla.gov.au

ISBN 978 1 74331 099 1

Internal design by Darian Causby
Map by Darian Causby
Set in 12/18 pt Goudy Old Style by Midland Typesetters, Australia
Printed and bound in Australia by Griffin Press

10 9 8 7 6 5 4 3 2 1

*This book is dedicated to Barry Hall, Senior English Mistress,
the New England Girls' School, Armidale*

FOREWORD

Jack Thompson, AM

There are many ways of being an Australian. Jane Grieve's memoir *In Stockmen's Footsteps* is her own delightful tale of what 'being an Australian' has meant to her.

There is no doubt that Jane's double connection, by direct descent to two immigrants on the First Fleet in 1788 (one above decks, one below), is a fairly compelling statement of colonial Australianness.

Jane Grieve's love of our 'wide brown land' mirrors my own. It is this connection, through the Australian Stockman's Hall of Fame and Outback Heritage Centre in Longreach, Central Western Queensland, that has brought us into the same orbit—Jane's with her pivotal role in the establishment of the Hall of Fame during the decade leading up to its opening in 1988, and mine through the role I have played in its more recent Indigenous Heritage Program.

The iconic Australian identity R.M. Williams features strongly in both our personal stories.

Much of my own love of the bush, and indeed bush skills, was learned from the time I spent with Aboriginal stockmen in the Northern Territory as a teenager in the fifties. During that incarnation I was kitted out in the inevitable R.M. Williams bushman's gear, avidly poring over the R.M. Williams mail order catalogues that were an integral part of outback station life.

I developed an abiding respect for the enormous contribution of Aboriginal stockmen and women towards Australia's outback prosperity. It was a partnership and an era that has largely disappeared, and was on its last legs at the time when I worked in the Territory. With its demise went a rich history of lifestyles, skills and stories.

The Australian Stockman's Hall of Fame's Indigenous Heritage Program has so far collected over 200 precious oral histories, photographs and artifacts from the Kimberley to the Cape.

Jane's romantic inclinations led her as a young woman to seek this world. This book tells of her time spent during the last days of horseback mustering on large outback properties in North Queensland, days when station properties were home to small communities of people who each contributed to the life of the station from the kitchen to the stockyards.

As a woman, her role was blurred and encompassed both domains. Like all Australians who lived 'out west', her R.M. Williams boots and Akubra hat were a fundamental part of her everyday attire.

There is much between the lines in this intriguing memoir of a post-Second World War country upbringing. These years represent a time in Australia's history about which little has been written. It was a time of restoration, when those whose lives had been turned upside down by cataclysmic events worldwide wanted nothing more than to live quiet lives. They raised their large families in a time of burgeoning prosperity that had seemed an impossible dream in the recent Depression years; they stoically papered over the wounds left by two world wars.

This is the story of a woman raised by a young couple who had both seen active war service. Jane was the fourth of five daughters.

She grew up with her feet firmly connected to the rich blacksoil of Queensland's Darling Downs, while the romantic notion of 'further out' was firmly etched into her consciousness through books and the tales of her elders.

It was a fertile field for her later achievements.

With warmth, wit and clarity Jane takes the reader through the processes of her life—from its very origins, which led (seemingly inexorably) to her inevitable meeting and productive partnership with like-minded people.

Born in 1953, Jane has lived through a time of enormous cultural change in Australia. Her vivid and often poignant recollections of her rural childhood in the 50s will resonate with anyone who lived through this era. Likewise the upheaval of the 60s and 70s with its 'free love', travel and defiance of cultural mores, which so defined all of us who lived through it.

When the opportunity arose to 'make a difference', especially as it related to the subject which was closest to her heart, Jane grasped it with both hands and devoted ten years of her life to it.

This is a great story, told with freshness and candour through the eyes of one of its central figures, of the creation of an important national Australian monument.

—Jack Thompson, AM

CONTENTS

N

Darwin
Oenpelli

The Kimberley

Broome

Tennant Creek

NORTHERN
TERRITORY

TROPIC OF CAPRICORN

Alice Springs

WESTERN
AUSTRALIA

SOUTH
AUSTRALIA

Nullarbor Plain
Eucla

Ceduna

Sorrento
Rottnest Island   Perth

Great
Australian Bight

AUSTRALIA

0   200   400   600   800 Km

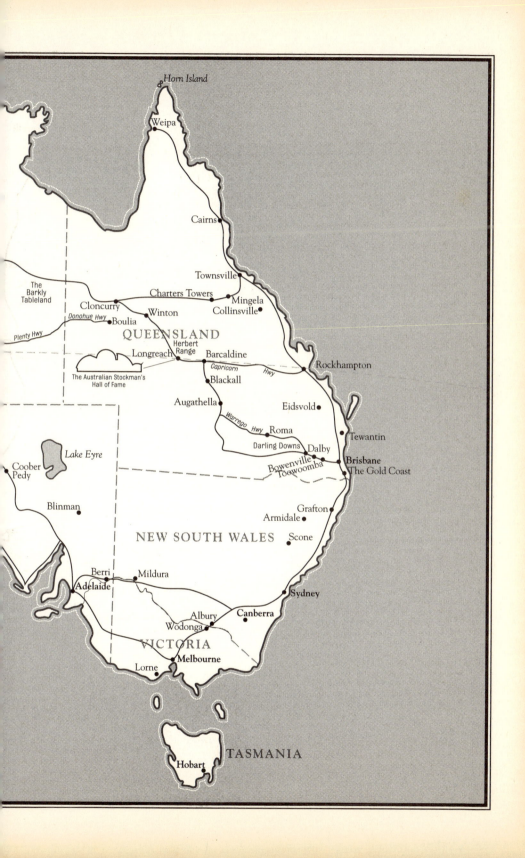

The Men Who Try and Try

I was never a great believer
in the things that men call luck
For it takes hard downright digging
ere the vein of gold be struck.

Dame Fortune may be fickle
but none of us can deny
She loves to lay her treasures
at the feet of those who try.

I've read the records closely
and I've watched life's battles too
It's taught me one good lesson
which I pass on to you.

Fate cannot build a barrier
so rugged or so high
That it cannot be surmounted
by those who try and try.

And when in life's grand procession
of people that pass on by
I'll raise my hat the highest
to those who try and try.

— Joseph Benjamin Cummings

It's the morning of 29 April 1988, Australia's bicentennial year.

Shuffling nervously, we form a receiving line inside the entrance to the Australian Stockman's Hall of Fame and Outback Heritage Centre at Longreach, on the Tropic of Capricorn in outback Queensland. Our line-up, a welcoming party, constitutes a select group of people hand-picked for our social importance, and our involvement in the establishment of this great memorial to Australia's pioneering past. In that order.

This is one of only a handful of major bicentennial projects.

Ranald Chandler, board member since the project's instigation, and his wife Jenny are the first in our small line-up. Dr Jean Battersby is the chair of the Australia Council. I am the project's executive director, its unseen primary administrator for the past ten years. Jean, Jenny and I wear smart outfits which include, naturally, silk stockings, hats and pearls. I am thin and anxious. My nerves are shot to pieces after a decade spent behind the scenes husbanding an eclectic collection of high-minded men and women, scions of Australian business, art and society, through the many seemingly insurmountable hurdles which have had to be negotiated to make this $14-million miracle rise in stone out of the dust of a 100-acre paddock on the edge of town.

'I'm going to cry,' I say to Jean, out of the corner of my trembling mouth. I am, I really am. This surely cannot be happening! But then, so many incredible things have come to pass in the last ten years that this is just one more, the greatest, in a series of impossible steps to success.

'No, you are NOT!' hisses Jean in reply. 'She's just an ordinary person; quite ordinary. And not an intellectual.'

I know Jean has said this only to shock my ragged nerves. But, for me, without a doubt the Queen—Queen Elizabeth II, to whom I pledged *allegiance daily as a schoolchild at the Bowenville State School many years before—is one of the most hallowed and extraordinary women in the world.*

I have been in her presence once before. On that January day, 34 years earlier, it was my grandfather as chairman of Jondaryan Shire, near Toowoomba, who was escorting the new young queen to meet a similar milling crowd of adoring subjects in nearby Oakey. Today it is the Longreach Shire chairman and chairman of the Australian Stockman's Hall of Fame, Sir James Walker, who accompanies the royal party from the airport across the road to the entrance steps of our magnificent building.

I can see through the glass doors that the huge crowd has grown into a colourful cast of thousands waiting expectantly for the arrival of the royal party. Their plane has landed. Somewhere out there are my fiancé Robert, my mum and my proud sisters who have travelled with me the 1100 kilometres and ten years' travail to witness my day of glory.

They have nursed me to this point as, battered and war-weary, I stumble to the finishing post of the greatest endurance ride of my life. Dad is not here to witness my big day. He died nine months ago; we are all still shocked and grief-stricken. I have no doubt that he is with me in spirit.

The doors open and in they come: the Queen, the Duke of Edinburgh, the Prime Minister Bob Hawke, Queensland's Premier Mike Ahern, shire chairman Sir James Walker.

One by one we take their hands and welcome them; acknowledge their congratulations. Ours is an impressive achievement, there is no doubt about that. From an idea planted by American David Briggs in artist Hugh Sawrey's mind in 1974, carried forward by an indomitable R.M. Williams, and brought into being by a group of determined Australian leaders, we now stand proudly on the substantial slate floor of a once-impossible dream—the Australian Stockman's Hall of Fame and Outback Heritage Centre.

CHAPTER 1

MY SKIN

'You ARE a funny girl. You actually look HAPPY!'
—Kathleen Mylne (my grandmother) to
Kathleen Paull (my mother) on the occasion of my
birth on 17 March 1953

We all come from somewhere. It stands to reason that, lonely as it might be inside your own skin at times, none of us exists in isolation at least in terms of our origins.

A particular family history accounts for how I came to be me. The broader story of my life, therefore, would not exist without the input of a great many people both past and present. Those people danced in and out of my life from before its very beginning, in fact and in second-hand tales. They blessed me with and bequeathed to me their stories, their attitudes and their actions. If I can honour them, then that for me is a good outcome.

With this in mind, I now make my best endeavour to commit my story to paper.

My grandmother's words were an inauspicious start. But I was completely and blissfully unaware that being the fourth daughter of a son-less couple was any sort of impediment whatsoever—and, as Mum did not disclose them to me till I was 53, by which time it no longer mattered, I did what any self-respecting baby boomer would do and just got on with it. I was given the gift of a life, to make of it what I would. Forcep-propelled, I came into the world paddling and just kept right on doing so.

Unaware I may have been of my grandmother's misgivings about my gender, but my family left no time apprising me of the minutiae of my two-year-old sister Tina's tantrum on leaving the viewing window where, according to the mores of the times, I was upon request (by a piece of paper with the words 'Baby Paull' written clearly in Dad's neat hand) held up for critical public examination behind a substantial pane of glass that protected the sensitivities of the newborn-babies' ward in the Southport Hospital on the Gold Coast.

Tina wanted to keep looking at the monkeys. Dad wanted to get home and hand his tribe of fidgeting little girls back to our grandmother, Norn. I, meantime, a born claustrophobe, was no doubt fully engaged with fighting the constraints of the copious papoose-like swaddling in which babies were tightly wrapped in those days. Meanwhile, somewhat hairless and inert, I had unwittingly misrepresented myself at the very outset and taken on the role of family jester without doing anything except just being me.

It was hard to be taken seriously from that point on. Especially as the monkey image was reinforced a couple of years later when I slipped under the restraining rail at David Fleay's Zoo, also on the Gold Coast, in order to get a closer look at the monkeys.

I had hair issues, which didn't worry me much, except that on this occasion one of the monkeys reached through the bars of its cage under the pretext of accepting my proffered peanut, and grabbed me by my bird's-nest hair with a grip that would not be deterred from its grim purpose of adopting me.

I was not happy. Nor, incidentally, was David Fleay. The situation was eventually brought under control but not without a lot of unfortunate comparisons.

Despite this, it would not be a stretch of the imagination to say that I grew into quite an adorable child; but then, most children are. I was a stick insect. Food did not interest me at all and mealtime with its sedentary disciplines and tinned peas even less so. Little did I know that I was extraordinarily fortunate in that I was offered, and often successfully coaxed, cajoled or threatened into actually eating part of, three good meals every day, with home-killed mutton and home-milked cream, homemade butter and ice-cream, and homegrown vegetables (in between the tinned peas).

What interested me most was the custom of the day which was the taking of morning and afternoon tea with sugary home-cooked cakes and biscuits. The bought biscuits were, of course, kept in a special tin for the grown-ups, high on a shelf in the large pantry which they thought I couldn't access but which I did, often. Monkeys are nothing if not nimble.

I mentioned that the stick insect which was me had hair issues. Mum's penchant for pudding-basin haircuts wasn't a great help, but out there on our farm on the Oakey Creek her options were limited. I had fine, straight black hair which defied management; what small hope it had, such as regular brushing, the person underneath the hair furiously fought against. The result was a bird's-nest arrangement which my sisters regularly, loudly, inspected for birds' eggs and regularly, loudly, regretted finding none.

At the age of five I decided to take matters into my own hands with the kitchen scissors. The resultant hairdo grew straight up for what seemed like years, and is still remembered fondly as 'Jane's sticky-up piece'.

There was one occasion when a simple, fun mudfight with my playmates at the farm got out of hand. I fear I must have lobbed a low throw because Greg, in the mysterious way of boys who can be driven into vengeful spurts of energy by things that happen roughly below the belt, suddenly went into a frenzy of throwing sloppy, sticky black mud at the back of my retreating head. By the time I reached home and the safety of Mum's apron, the multiple layers had set like clay. From being a simple, manageable bird's nest with possibilities of retrieval, my hair had become a semipermanent fixture. I still remember sitting sobbing in the concrete laundry tub while Mum worked frantically against the drying properties of Darling Downs mud, desperately trying to sort the hair from the huge clay pot which was irrevocably stuck to the back of my head.

The lack of meat on my bones gave an angular appearance to my backside. For years it was understood that I had a hairpin-bend behind, and no one wanted to have me sitting on their knee because I was indeed a very angular and lively little package.

My hairpin bend betrayed me on more than one occasion, the most notable being when, at the age of seven, I had disobeyed the cardinal rule about going down to the creek without a grown-up. Dad, outraged, was chasing me to deliver the punishment. That day I discovered that I had some speed about me, because despite the fact that Dad held the 120-yard hurdles record at the Southport School from 1933 until 1946, I was gaining ground.

Disinclined to stand like a man to receive my punishment with the razor strop, I skittered from room to room with Dad in hot pursuit. Miscalculating the layout of the house I reached a dead end in the sitting room, whereupon I leapt into an armchair and buried my head down into the cushions like an ostrich.

Needless to say, ostrich-like, my hairpin bend betrayed me and took the punishment on my behalf.

I was eventually brought home to Bowenville from the Southport Hospital but not before Mum had had the mandatory ten-day bed rest in hospital with her tummy firmly bound to aid in the return of her erstwhile youthful figure. My three siblings got their pet monkey and a nurse called Hilary was installed at our home, a 1000-acre farm called Yarrabin on the dead-flat Darling Downs, to look after it.

I was given regular, four-hourly feeds from a titty bottle. Every time she had a baby, Mum, recently discharged from the army and its draconian rules and disciplines and authoritarian figures of which she was one, mindlessly obeyed the current Baby Nurse who insisted with the best will in the world, and based on her nanny training, that something dreadful would happen if baby was suckled anything other than four-hourly. (What? She might get fat when she turned 50? Hell, it happened anyway!)

Consequently, baby would wake and cry; Mum, her breasts engorged and spurting, would head for the cane cradle, and nurse, firmly snatching up the squalling bundle with an air of superior knowledge and absolutely the best of intentions, would cluck her tongue and say, 'Now, Mother, another 2½ hours to feed time'.

Conversely, baby would cry herself into a deep, dissatisfied sleep from which it was absolutely essential (based on the same dictum) that she be woken up to feed on the dot of four hours since the last go.

By which time all parties had lost interest.

The spurting breasts eventually dried out and were replaced with formula but not, I venture to suggest, without a substantial amount of pain, disappointment and heartache.

It could be said that having such a regulated approach to life from the very beginning must have had a profound effect on me. Perhaps, therefore, I have Nurse Hilary to thank for my strong sense of the importance of being reliable.

While living on the banks of the Oakey Creek at Bowenville in South East Queensland presented some logistical challenges in terms of access, communication and household appliances, it wasn't too bad. Not too bad at all. We kids loved it. We did, after all, live in a comfortable house. We each had a bed—mine on the sun verandah near my sister Tina's, with whom I also shared a dressing room. And, let's face it, household appliances were not of great consequence to us; they were mostly Mum's domain. Many were not invented at that time, which made what might seem like disadvantages these days completely irrelevant.

The world into which I came wide-eyed—in the cane ironing basket, balanced on the back seat of the family's Vanguard, with my three older sisters in various changing locations throughout the car according to whim and dictate during the long, bouncing trip home from the coast—was a world of Hope. Little did I know it, but it was hot on the heels of a global event that offered not much hope at all: the Second World War.

The shadow of these cataclysmic times hung over our lives. Our parents bravely did their utmost to protect us from the memories that must surely have encroached not only on their dreams but many of their waking thoughts.

But while this was undoubtedly the case, they most certainly managed to present us with a reality which included their unequivocal acceptance, the security of knowing that our home was our castle and our family our refuge, and a binding and unquestioning love for each other.

There are little snippets of evidence of a hidden history that pique our interest; but our questions are deflected, and met with shrugs, and laughed off by grown-ups who turn their faces away.

Like the two silk-lined boxes left open in the glass-fronted hall cupboard among other untouchable treasures, bright multicoloured ribbons issuing from the tops of one cross-shaped and one star-shaped silver medal. Dad's medals: a Distinguished Flying Cross and an American Silver Star.

Like the bits and pieces in the trinket box we get to go through on rainy days and which our children after us are similarly offered in a bid to manage restless energy.

There, among the strings of cheap beads and pairless shank earrings and discarded small ornaments, there's a small leather box, velvet- and silk-lined. It contains three large silver buttons. Their sheen still sparkles despite the passage of time.

The cursive script printed into the silk fabric of the lid reads 'By Appointment—Hamilton & Inches, 88 Princes St, Edinburgh'. The buttons are embossed with a crown over a map of Australia, and the words 'Australian Military Forces' around the circumference.

A similar little box is from 'Hardy Bros. Ltd, Jewellers & Silversmiths, Australia' and contains three brass buttons with exactly the same design as the silver ones. And there is any number of curved brass brooches, about 2 inches long, with nothing but a cut-out of the word AUSTRALIA in bold letters, as well as one or two rising-sun badges with a double-shank attachment.

What place do these forgotten trinkets have on a farm on the Darling Downs? Thrust unceremoniously into an old shoebox and put among the toys, it's as if they are nothing more than bright shiny objects for the fleeting amusement of children.

In a lead-lined cedar trunk in the garage is a treasure-trove of inanimate objects. Unlike the trinket box, this is a forbidden place; a secret place.

When opened, stories ooze out of it and dance into the shaft of light that straggles down through cobwebs from the high, grimy window above. They clasp the dust motes and whirl away dancing into the rafters as if to say, 'Thanks for setting us free!' They challenge us to hear them speak with voices muted by time and neglect, their words left unspoken for so many years that the emotions they would have conveyed, if set free earlier, have ceased to be relevant.

But they are relevant. Despite the best efforts of their progenitors, our progenitors, those emotions work their way into the psyches of whole families. They evidence themselves in periods of deep silence, fraught with tension; in occasional raised voices; in the discreet clinking of bottles in garages; and most especially in the inexplicable solemnity of Anzac Day.

CHAPTER 2

MY FATHER'S SKIN

Peter McCallum Paull 7/10/1917–10/7/1987

POSSIBLE EPITAPH
If I must die because of war
This earth will take my body back,
Absorbed within the universal law.
The small 'I have', the vast 'I lack'
Will be as one. The atom 'me'
Will merge within the great 'I am'
And what will be will be,
For all man's strife to blast and damn.
　　　　　　　　　　　—Paddy McCallum

It does so validate one's Australianness, having a convict ancestry.
　　Dad's mother Eileen brought with her McCallum name a double connection to the First Fleet in 1788—one above decks in William Balmain, third surgeon on board the *Lady Penrhyn*, who lent his name to the Sydney suburb of Balmain; and the future mother of his children, Margaret Dawson, at 15 one of the youngest convicts aboard.

Margaret was below decks en route to Norfolk Island, her life catapulted into an uncertain future with a seven-year sentence for the heinous crime of stealing clothing from her employer.

Their son William, who took his paternal grandmother's name of Henderson and also became a doctor, married the daughter of another convict, Thomas Rose, who arrived on the *Barwell* in 1798. As Thomas Rose's crime is deeply interred under multiple layers of time and tight-lipped generations, and Thomas himself respectably clothed in a purported relationship to the Duke of Mons, we can safely assume that his crime was very mild, and vaguely noble. He became a success in the colony and (according to family lore) lent his name to another well-known suburb of Sydney, Rose Bay.

The name 'Rose' has come down through the generations as a middle name because of its attachment to a fabled inheritance in Chancery. My sister Sally got the name, but none of us got the inheritance.

In 1856 two of Dr Henderson's daughters married the identical twin McCallum brothers, horse traders fresh out from Oban in Scotland with a clean slate. Thus the name McCallum came down the line to us through Dad and has embedded itself in my son Jock. It carries to him a rich history of seven preceding generations of Australians, the maximum possible number of years of modern Australianness.

For an Australian of Caucasian descent, you can't go back further than the First Fleet.

The rest of Dad's heritage is a blend of Scots and Cornish, with a refugee from a family of devout Bristol Quakers thrown in for good measure.

They all spread out in this land of opportunity, becoming miners, landholders, newspaper editors, businessmen, local mayors and members of parliament, squatters and horse traders.

Horses were the primary mode of transport in early European Australian settlement. They were a very valuable commodity, highly prized, the skills associated with their husbandry greatly valued, and the horses themselves often acquired at any cost.

To this end there were horse traders, and then there were horse traders, as they say. The kind of horse trading Ned Kelly and his brothers indulged in was nefarious and clothed with a certain retrospective glamour; but it was not respectable. Dad's maternal forebears the McCallums, despite the closely guarded secret of the convict ancestors brought into the family by marriage, were horse traders of a different ilk. Indenters, they were high-flyers in the lucrative business of supplying Waler horses as remounts for the British cavalry in India.

On Dad's paternal side, my great-grandfather William Paull gave his occupation as 'squatter' on his marriage certificate. You can't get much more true blue than that, although William wasn't born here. No, he was born in Redruth, Cornwall, and came out in 1873 as a tin miner to a dot on the map called Blinman in South Australia to take up the management of a tin mine there.

What a shock he must have got when he saw the place! But he got on with mining the tin, and stuck it out long enough to receive a lovely gold watch inscribed with gratitude from the citizens of Blinman in 1877.

He obviously decided that being a squatter was a better way to get ahead, although buying Cowarie Station on the lower Diamantina in South Australia, near Lake Eyre, was to take on the Australian outback at its extreme edges.

Like so many of his ilk, Great-grandfather William's outback bachelorhood lasted well into his 30s. The prospect of living at Charters Towers in North Queensland must have sounded more attractive to a potential bride, and Great-grandmother Margaret

Christie married him in Melbourne and moved north with him in 1884.

William took up the management of a goldmine in Charters Towers. The Towers was a gold town of fantastic wealth. In an era when the success of a community was measured by the number of its pubs, Charters Towers boasted a spectacular 40 pubs within its town limits, serving a population of 25 000 thirsty souls. To be fair, the pubs offered much-needed accommodation for the many single men who flocked to the promise of its mining wealth. As well, they yielded the dual function of providing a social life on the same premises.

So great was the prosperity of this region that Charters Towers was one of the few Australian cities that boasted its own stock exchange. It was outside that stock exchange, in Gill Street, that my great-uncle Lyell Paull was struck on the head by the shaft of a Cobb & Co coach. He survived, but suffered epilepsy for the rest of his life. While this story may seem irrelevant, I believe it's worth mentioning because I have always felt that if fate decrees that one had to acquire a ghastly lifelong complaint, being hit in the back of the head by the shaft of a Cobb & Co coach was one of the more romantic ways of doing so.

Great-grandfather William Paull established a family culture of community and public service. He took a leading role in the civic life of Charters Towers. He was mayor twice, and became the member of parliament for Dalrymple in 1905. One of his four sons, my grandfather Alan, followed suit as chairman of the Jondaryan Shire many years later. After him, Alan's son Peter (my dad) gave years of service to the committee of the Toowoomba Royal Show, ten of those years as its president.

In 1907 William Paull left the north for the last time, and took his family to Bowenville. There he bought the farm where, 46 years later, I began my life.

Alan, or Garg as we knew him, regaled his wide-eyed grandchildren with the story of how he was so delicate when he was born that he had to be carried around on a velvet pillow for the first few months of his life at Charters Towers. We stared at him aghast each time he told us that story; imagining him in this way seemed to belie the richness of his long and very full life.

Strangely, despite his long Australian heritage, Dad was born in England, at Woking, Surrey, on 7 October 1917. In a twist of inverted colonialism, his father Alan (even though he was born Australian) answered the clarion call to war when Mother England—somewhat oppressively—beckoned.

Newly wed to Eileen McCallum, nonetheless Alan enlisted, in 1915, in the 26th Battalion, Australian Infantry Forces (AIF), and went off to France and the Western Front. He fought at Pozières Ridge in 1916; at Messines Ridge in Flanders in 1917; and at Villers-Bretonneux in 1918. A noble contribution indeed, from which he returned home with lungs damaged by gas, a scar on his buttocks from where he had removed a piece of deeply embedded shrapnel himself with a pair of tweezers, and a fragment of bullet permanently lodged in his ribs.

My grandmother Eileen had followed him to England and stayed with relatives in Surrey, providing her husband with a place of comfort on furlough and, as it eventuated, to recover from his war wounds.

I never met Dad's mother. She was a beautiful goddess in family mythology. This was in part because she was indeed beautiful, but also because she never suffered the ignominy of growing old.

It was Eileen's history that was the most deeply embedded in Australia's colonial era, and offered some choice tidbits from that tough but romantic time. Her sister Paddy McCallum, my maiden great-aunt, was the keeper of the stories by the time I came along. She dispensed them liberally to those of us who were interested . . . even the secrets of the convict forebears that were considered shameful and spoken of in hushed terms, if at all.

One of Paddy's family tales was that of the courageous life of her grandmother Janet Nairn. Janet set off from Dunfermline in Scotland in the 1850s with her father and a cargo of horses with which to establish their financial security in the new colony. On the sea voyage her father died from the effects of a horse bite; Janet arrived in Australia destitute and alone. How terrified she must have been, yet how brave, since she prevailed and lived a long and fruitful life here. At her gruesome end she had a cancerous breast removed without anaesthesia.

There are light moments of wry humour in the oral history that Aunty Paddy bequeathed to us. The McCallum one involved my great-grandfather John McCallum, the indenter and horse trader who became the commercial editor of the *Argus* in Melbourne.

One day in the 1860s he called to visit his identical twin, Malcolm. At the top of the stairs he reached out his hand and spoke a greeting to his brother; only to find that he was addressing his own reflection in the hall mirror.

The familial faux pas to which I relate the most, however, involves my maternal grandmother Kit. She was shopping one day in David Jones in Brisbane when she saw a woman walking briskly towards her.

'Oh, heavens,' she said to herself as she tried desperately and unsuccessfully to recall the woman's name (something that resonates with me most horribly). 'I know that woman, I know that woman—what on earth is her name?'

Her panic was unfounded. It was her own reflection in the mirror.

While one of the joys of being Australian is freedom from the constraints of class and snobbery which so bind nations with an older heritage—Mother England being the worst—Dad's christening certificate has afforded his family some magic moments of reflected glory. None was more so than when his parents (by that time he had a stepmother Eleanor, our to-be grandmother Norn) enrolled him as a boarder at the Southport School.

It was as elite a school as Queensland offered in 1929 and the enrolment officer was more than a little conscious of that fact. Dad was hamstrung by having to confess that he came from a small place called Kaimkillenbun, not a particularly grand address and one that suggested by virtue of its remoteness the absence of regular Christian worship. The bursar waved a dismissive hand and said somewhat censoriously, 'Has the boy been christened?' whereupon my grandfather was able to reply, 'Yes, he has actually. In Westminster Abbey.'

It was one of those moments.

My grandfather Alan's war as a lieutenant in the Australian army was every bit as terrible as one reads about.

Unlike my father who never spoke about his war, Alan (or Garg) did want to talk about his war experiences to us kids; all the time. Rather ignobly, in the way of children, we avoided his stories; they were awful. One invariably made him cry, which was excruciatingly embarrassing for us.

This particular story was about an occasion when the trenches were so waterlogged that they were a bog; in desperation my grandfather and the other soldiers stacked the bodies of their dead comrades to use as a means of negotiating their way along the mud. There were no other materials for the purpose.

We switched off and our eyes glazed over when he started on about names of foreign places where he fought, the trenches and how awful it was. He was shot in the back and he didn't want us to think that was because he was running away; there was just no way to avoid the bullets and shrapnel going everywhere. And the bullet was still in there because when they tried to take it out, they were afraid he would be paralysed if they kept digging for it. And that was why, if we were staying the night with Norn and Garg, we must understand that if we heard him yelling out in the darkness it was because of the morphine he had to take to ease the pain. It made him not himself.

Our eyes bulged at this point, and Norn was always hovering with a look on her face that begged us to listen and understand.

I often wonder how he felt when, having gone through all he did in the war to end all wars, carrying his bullet for the rest of his life as a grim reminder, his only precious son was obliged to put himself in the line of fire at the same age he had been. What a dreadful irony!

Dad was raised to be a farmer. He had a jump-start, though, when his war came to steal away his youth: he already had a pilot's licence. He immediately joined the Royal Australian Air Force (RAAF) as a flying instructor.

Dad took a couple of dunkings in 'the drink' in the name of war, but escaped serious injury each time. He carried external scars to his nose and arm, and about those he consented to explain to us their origins.

The internal scars were harder to dig out of him.

Dad served as a flight officer at Horn Island in Torres Strait as he progressed through the ranks in the air force. He ended up as a wing commander of 462 Bomber Squadron at Foulsham in Norfolk, England.

While of course those years brought a wealth of experience and worldliness into his life, not the least being that he befriended the

English relations who had made a home for his parents at the time of his birth, that experience was gained at the cost of six years of his youth, and a lifetime's indelible memories.

Dad, naturally enough, didn't see it that way. He just did what they all did. He did his duty and did not count the cost.

I sit on the ungainly feet of my beautiful, handsome father lying prone on the kikuyu lawn at Yarrabin, and, grasping his bony knees, cling on for grim death.

Squealing, I feel myself hoisted high into the air, higher and higher, till I hang upside down, my clinging arms and Dad's restraining hands all that are keeping me from spearing into his chest.

I hang suspended for a moment and feel Dad rocking backwards and forwards as he gathers momentum for the final movement. Then with a mighty thrust and a 'there you go, Jo-Poker!' he flings me into a somersault behind his balding head, and I roll in a shrieking ball to the foot of the verandah steps.

In no time I am back up again and round the other side under the athol pine, queuing behind my big sisters for another go at being a bag of wheat on the bagloader.

'Enough—enough!' says Dad, trying to sit up. Hero, the family dog, has somehow insinuated himself into the queue and is leaping about excitedly, his sharp claws and clumsy feet playing havoc with any bare skin.

'No! Me, me too!' cries my six-year-old sister Tina, and she is grasped in her turn and flung in a shrieking tangle of arms and legs near the front steps. Hero follows her over, spots Mum sitting calmly on the Adirondack chair on the verandah, watching her little family at play. He wags his tail fiercely at the sight of her. Tina squeals again and rolls away as the recalcitrant tail whips her around the ears, its owner intent only on attracting the attention of the one person in the family who is impervious to his charms. He's not

allowed up the stairs and into her domain; Mum can take or leave him and he knows it.

'No more bagloaders now,' says Dad firmly. 'We'll lie quietly and look out for Sputnik for a while.'

We lie as quietly as we can with an excited dog in attendance, licking our faces and jumping back at once when he is pushed away. Someone throws a tennis ball as far away as possible and that gets rid of him for a minute or two.

'What will we see, Dad?' asks Tina, Dad's special little pal.

'Just a light, like a tiny little star, only it will be moving. Wait; what's that? Look! There it is! There's Sputnik! See it moving along up there, through the stars? That's Sputnik! That's a spaceship! Come and look, Mum. We can see it!'

And sure enough, moving silently through the welter of tiny stars that stand starkly against the velvet blackness of the pristine Darling Downs night sky is a tiny dot of light.

It's just a couple of days short of Dad's 40th birthday, October 1957.

CHAPTER 3

MY MOTHER'S SKIN

Kathleen Ruth Mylne (Lop) 11/01/1922

THE WHITE HOUSE ON THE HILL
When I go a-sailing on lovely Moreton Bay
I can see my own house from very far away;
So white upon the hill top it glistens in the sun
It looks as if it watches me, and smiles to see the fun.
The wind is always changing on restless Moreton Bay,
But my house on the hill top stands watching all the day;
And when I climb the hill again and leave the sea below
I'll find my mother waiting there to welcome me, I know.
                              —Kathleen (Kit) Mylne

William and Jane White came first. Protestant Irish, driven by frustration with life in Ireland, conveyed with the help of an immigrant's fare to Sydney on the *Royal Consort*. Drawn by the hope of a new life, they endured that somewhat tautological cliché, a 'difficult sea voyage'.

Their baby daughter Emily had survived their long and arduous trip along with her brother Ernest, but died soon after their arrival in

November 1840. The family was heartbroken. Jane gave birth to my great-grandmother Helena just one month later. She and her older brother Ernest were christened on 17 March 1844, 109 years to the day before my own birth.

Australia expected them to work hard; they did. They eventually prospered as squatters on an enormous holding, Beaudesert Station in South East Queensland. The remains of a set of my great-great grandfather William's cattle yards were still standing beside the Nerang River in the 1950s, a silent reminder of how recent were our pioneering days.

William White made his mark on the fledgling state of Queensland by virtue of his achievements, undoubtedly, but also by fortuitously arriving at a time of beginnings. He was a founding member of the Queensland Club; he was appointed to Governor Bowen's first Queensland upper house, its Legislative Council.

His one surviving daughter, Helena (Lena), ended her days in Brisbane in 1922 as Grannie Mylne, a formidable matron in a mob cap, well satisfied, I have no doubt, with having raised six children despite being widowed at the tender age of 37.

The father of Lena's children, my great-grandfather, was a Scotsman, the first Graham Mylne. Graham left the British Raj, in which by the age of 25 he had reached the rank of captain, to take over the property Etonswill (as in *Pickwick Papers*), which his three colonial brothers had established on the Richmond River near Grafton in New South Wales. They and his two sisters had been drowned in the wreck of the *Duncan Dunbar* off Sydney Heads in August 1857.

Graham's 'Cawnpore Letter' to his cousin Charles Kinloch that year is a treasured family artefact now in the keeping of the fourth Graham Mylne. In it he describes in vivid detail, in an attempt to camouflage his grief, his involvement in the siege of Lucknow—but eventually breaks down into a heartbreaking exposé of his despair at learning, while reading a newspaper on a train in India, of the loss of his family.

That first Graham Mylne meticulously kept diaries that recorded the whole of his 17 years in Australia and much of his time in India as well. He died in 1876 at the age of 42 from a stroke brought on by the sheer stress of his enormous workload. The distances he travelled by horseback, in the dray, in his sulky, and the condition of the roads he traversed are beyond what we can possibly imagine nowadays.

His tenacity, ability and courage defy belief. He still managed to give public service to his adopted land through 14 months' representation on Queensland's Legislative Assembly from 1867.

On his passage to Australia from London in 1859 on the P&O 'screw' ship *Malta*, Graham met and befriended Governor George Bowen. They became lifelong friends and business partners with the purchase of Amby Downs at Roma, in South West Queensland, where my grandfather was born eight years later. The district where I grew up almost a hundred years later was named for Governor Bowen—Bowenville.

How they all struggled to gain a foothold and stamp their British way of life on this land! For better or for worse—and now we can see the whole picture and it is not necessarily a comfortable one—they did what it took to insinuate themselves and their beliefs here.

William's lasting legacy (his cattle yards at Nerang have long since made way for a suburban morass) was the construction of Lota House at Manly on Moreton Bay, near Brisbane, in 1863. Four generations of his family subsequently lived there. My mother was born upstairs in January 1922 and called Lota home until she married and moved to the country with Dad in 1946.

Indeed that house, Lota, now the hub of a retirement village but still standing sentinel over the bay and looking across to Stradbroke

Island from my grandmother's bedroom window as it always has, is (if a white person can lay claim to such a thing) my Dreaming Place. I spent much of my happy childhood there in the bosom of my greater family, with some or all of the 18 grandchildren who make up my generation of our branch of William and Jane's descendants.

I still go there sometimes. I wander into the chapel, which was once the billiard room, a separate little house full of wonderful smells, mystery, allure and hiding places. We were allowed in there sometimes if we were quiet and well-behaved little children. The sun would stream in through the curtains above my grandmother's window seat, and the dust motes would dance in that strip of sunlight right down to the satin cushions, and we tried to catch them with our chubby little fingers. But they were hard to catch.

Sometimes we were allowed to get the ivory mahjong pieces out of their lead box and look at the different pictures on them.

But we were never allowed to touch the top of the billiard table.

But mostly, when I visit Lota nowadays, I like to sit quietly on the verandah alone and look out over the bay to Stradbroke Island that I once understood was faraway England—no one disabused me of this illusion.

I feel them all around me, my people—William with his big beard and bigger voice, his hot Irish temper and kindly ways; his Jane, for whom I was named, who only lived there a short while before she died, and whose image looks solemn wearing a voluminous satin crinolined dress in a photograph in the hallway.

In my mind's eye Captain Graham Mylne, the first, walks quickly past with his soldierly step as, hat in hand, he courts the daughter of the first household—'My Lena' as he lovingly refers to her in his diary. The weight of the loss of his four siblings in the wreck of the *Dunbar* is still etched in his demeanour. He does not know it, but a second, third and then a fourth Graham Mylne will seek and find love and comfort within these solid walls.

Then Grandaddy shuffles past, the second Graham Mylne—an ancient old man when I knew him, too old to tell me about his extraordinary life . . . his childhood here at Lota where he and his brother Tom came to live with Grandfather William after his father died; sailing on the bay, using his grandmother Jane's petticoat as a sail; being sent by ship to Sandhurst Military Academy in England when he was just 15, and learning conversational French in Blois and German in Dresden while he waited to be old enough to do the Sandhurst entrance exam (which he passed fifth out of 900 candidates); his adventures in the British Army in India, and the scarlet-fever epidemic there that almost killed him; his time at the Boer War with the Australian 6th Imperial Bushman Regiment where the young English vet declared all their beautiful Australian Waler horses to have strangles (they didn't) and ordered them shot, which they duly were, and Grandad never got over it.

He loved his horses, and was, they say, a fine horseman. Born in the saddle. But I never knew that side of him, or in the days when he managed Collins White Pty Ltd and the family's outback Queensland properties Eulolo, Strathfield and Glenormiston from his office in Mary Street, Brisbane.

In my mind's eye Mimi, or Kit, his buxom Scottish wife and my grandmother, the hank of keys on the belt that disappeared into the folds of her ample tummy jingling and twinkling in the sun, emerges from the shuttered French doors and bustles around all us wee ones on the front verandah overlooking the bay. Lily the cook comes out and carefully places a wicker tray laden with fine china and tea in a silver teapot and scones and Nice biscuits on the round outdoor table for our morning tea, while we try to be good and not jiggle, and stretch our necks to see if perhaps Lily has put some Iced Vovos on the biscuit plate, too, a reward for 'good' children.

I think of Kit's circuitous journey to end up here in hot old Queensland married to Grandad, after a childhood spent playing in the heather in the highlands of Scotland. Her special book for her family describes being allowed, with her sister Lily, to peep over the balcony at the Perth Hunt Ball. The dancers in full highland regalia wear 'the most beautiful appurtenances and lace ruffles kept for great occasions from the Jacobite days'. And in the 'vast ballroom, they dance eightsome reels formed the whole length of it—the wonderful dancing of them, and the brilliance of the whole scene a sight never to be forgotten'.

I can't help but contemplate how easy my life has been in comparison with all of theirs, but how mundane, too. I imagine the feelings of Kit's mother, Nessie Nicholls, as she stood with her two prettily-dressed little daughters at the wharf in Portsmouth to meet their daddy Jasper, the sea captain, to be told he had died of yellow fever in South America many months before. The black-edged admiralty letter dated 8 November 1889 that arrived some months later is another of our family treasures.

I see Kathleen, or Lop—my pretty, laughing little mum—coming home to Lota House in her Australian Army Medical Women's Service (AAMWS) uniform in 1944 during the war. My grandfather had secreted enough cyanide tablets for each family member—and some to spare—in anticipation that Lota would be at the forefront of a Japanese invasion from the sea.

Sometimes Mum brought the handsome Peter Paull, the air force pilot, home with her on the train for a brief leave weekend. My grandmother commented in her diary that Peter was a lovely boy but far too young, far too immature. For what? For being in charge of a massive aeroplane flying out into the night over Germany? For making up crew lists then, the next day, scratching out names, crossing off whole crews, having to write the dreaded letter to their families—'I am sorry to have to advise you . . . did not return . . . fate unknown . . . grave concerns'? My father wrote beautifully, but he never got over the need to write those awful letters.

I know all their voices through their various writings and my mother's and aunts' tales. I see little Jane, the youngest of the children, tousle-haired and untidy despite Nanny's best efforts at scrubbing me way too hard with the towel after bathing me with my sisters in the huge, claw-footed bathtub upstairs. It's 1958 and I am straddled monkey-like along the lowest branch of the Queensland nut tree out the front of the big house, reaching down to my cousin Tim Mylne, one of the white-haired 'Snowies' who share my identical DNA through different parents.

That nut tree provided us kids with endless hours of adventure, endless pockets of sweet nuts that required cracking on the cement lid of the huge underground tank outside Lily's kitchen. The lid's small indentations held the hard nuts steady under our imprecise assaults with hammer and rock, as we played and giggled and banged our way through the tough outer shells to the treasures within.

Oh, what tales, what stories, if only that old house could speak!

We gather round the piano in the Yarrabin dining room.

We have cleared away the remains of our meal from the old mahogany McCallum dining table, only the lace tablecloth and the pair of silver Lota candlesticks still in evidence. The washing up will happen later.

I, aged five and the smallest of the four little girls, sit under the table on the red rattan matting and pick earnestly at a loose piece of its straw fabric that I have been working on for some time.

Teacher hovers at Mum's shoulder as she searches through the music books in the seat of the piano stool. Teacher's wife Mrs Collins sits at the table still, proudly nursing her cherished baby John, a late-life miracle she has managed to carry to full term—unlike all the others.

Dad sits at his place at the head of the table, waiting.

I look into the forest of legs that waves and shifts in front of the piano, trying to see what progress is being made, hoping the music sheet Mum gets out will include 'Gigi', my favourite. Impatient, my attention turns to running my small fingers up and down the grooves etched into the turned table legs, my chewed fingernails meeting no resistance against the comfortingly smooth sensation of the burnished, dark-brown wood.

I hug the timber table leg, relishing the full-bodied, familiar smell of furniture oil, my bladder bursting with excitement. Waiting is not my strong point. But I have to wait. Mum has to find the music book she wants. Then and only then will the music start.

Suddenly Mum says, 'Ah! Here we are!' and with a swift motion pulls out a couple of songbooks and whips them onto the piano. Then she snaps down the lid of the piano stool, sits down and after a certain amount of fussing and page-turning, begins to play.

'Nobody knows de trouble I see—Nobody knows my sorrow!' we all sing with varying degrees of knowledge of the words according to our ability to read. I marvel that there is a grown-up anywhere in the world who seems to understand the concept of trouble, since grown-ups are usually (in my limited experience) its judges, rather than those who suffer its effects. But as Mum has often explained, those poor old Negro slaves had much to be troubled about.

The Negro spirituals are too sad to be my first choice but I love them anyway, for the fact of the family singing together round the piano and Mum, the central figure, being so vibrant and alive.

I love the way Mum comes to life when she plays the piano. Her face *flushed, she laughs aloud and shakes her pretty head and tut-tuts when she misses a note, humming a few bars of song and playing chords with her left hand while her right hand shuffles the pages. While she finds her place again, the big kids Sally and Prue do their best to keep the tune afloat while the deep voices of Teacher and Dad underscore our childish trebles.*

Then Mum decides it's time for a change of pace. I watch the light shining on her soft, unblemished skin as she switches to another sheet of music. It seems an eternity until she settles herself down, making a few feints at the piano and stretching her fingers while Prue holds the top corner of the music book, ready to turn the page.

The music of Rogers and Hammerstein fills the room and I give a shout of delight. Mum's elbows pump and her hands dance along the keyboard as, laughing, Tina and I dance with each other in our pyjamas, singing at the top of our voices 'The Night They Invented Champagne'.

The music spills out through the French doors onto the darkened front verandah. It weaves its way through the oleander bushes that border the inside of the white garden fence around the Yarrabin garden and, to the surprise of the sleeping koalas in the gum trees that line the driveway, floats unfettered out into the great silence of the Darling Downs night.

CHAPTER 4

UNION

The wedding was happy and delightful—no wedding could have been sweeter with the families and so many friends with us. The bride and bridegroom were both radiant and Loppy looked sweet in her white frock and blue flowery little 'funny' hat. Lennons did the party perfectly. The cathedral—scene of so many little dramas in my Queensland life—was peaceful beautiful and great as always. Gentle Mr Nominson officiated. The boys were all splendid in their parts, Sandy giving the bride away. Peter looks and is beautiful.

Perhaps the nicest touch for us was that after the party, without changing her frock, Kathleen and Peter and I all drove home to Lota, to Daddy, in bed, and looking very frail. Then all the others came and we had tea and wedding cake and lots of fun. Finally they left us and Loppy in her pretty rust coloured dress and queer little pretty straw 'half hat' was carried shoulder high and put on top of the car and driven off by Peter. It was all so happy and simple and unconventional.

Kathleen's wedding, January 28 1946

—Extract from the diary of my grandmother,

Kathleen Mylne

My four sisters and I were the product of city lass meets born-and-bred country boy.

Their love, starting out as the hero-worship of a young girl for the stroke of the Southport School's First Eight, developed possibilities when they were both by chance playing support roles at the society wedding of mutual friends.

It blossomed in the theatre of war and survived the vicissitudes of separation and distance to culminate in a quick decision to tie the knot at St John's Cathedral in Brisbane on 28 January 1946.

Dad looked handsome, as he always did, in his air force uniform. Mum looked gorgeous, as she always did, in a natty lilac hat which then took up residence in the very large hat section of her wardrobe.

Dad was 28; Mum was 24. The previous six years, the greater part of what might have been their carefree youth, but was not, had been taken up with war. It must have seemed to them that peace and love were a grand substitute for the massive role each of them had been obliged, by virtue of their place in time, to play in it.

They went on the train to Tewantin for their honeymoon, where they stayed at the Tewantin Hotel. There, Dad discovered that he was an unwitting card sharp; he also discovered that he was not a compulsive gambler, because he threw in a poker hand of four aces to save their skin.

They had teamed up with some other hotel guests to have an evening's card-playing. Dad was enjoying a spot of luck, nicely rounding off his good fortune in securing the hand of his beautiful bride. His luck went on and on, the pairs and threes seeming to have a magnetic attraction to his hand, and relations with their new friends started to become a little strained.

That's when he threw in the four aces. It seemed the most sensible thing to do in consideration of the tic that was beginning to take on a life of its own in his opponent's cheek. He later regretted it, though, from the safety of years. But he never had much of a taste for poker after that.

After Dad was demobbed from the air force they moved to the Darling Downs, where they took up a portion of my grandfather's farm near Bowenville. They called their farm Yarrabin, an Indigenous word meaning 'tall white gum tree'.

Not long after Mum and Dad married, Mum's brother, Sandy Mylne, married Dad's sister, Margaret—thus dudding us out of a full set of cousins but, fortunately for all of us, taking up another portion of my grandfather's farm so that all three families lived as close neighbours for the first six years of my life. Both young couples started to have babies in parallel, creating a lovely family enclave with eight children of matching ages as playmates overseen by our doting Paull grandparents, Norn and Garg. My fourth sister, Nicola, was born many years later.

In 1955 there was a polio epidemic. We wondered why Dad took to carrying Mum to the toilet (or, as we called it, the 'dum') at nights. Her feet were stiff and sore.

Mum was trained as a physiotherapist so she had a more than rudimentary grasp of matters medical, and a pragmatic approach to illness. But still, they held the awful truth with its dire implications at bay until it could be ignored no longer.

One night when my sister Sally was eight she woke up to find our grandmother Norn in the room. 'Everything is all right; just go back to sleep,' she said. It had been raining, the road was a bog and our house isolated by flood. Sal looked out the window and saw lights on the other side of the flooded creek. A tractor; an ambulance. The next morning, Mum was gone.

She didn't come back for many months.

Dad's childhood and consequent persona were defined by one terrible event. When he was a little boy of five, his adored mother, the beautiful and much-loved Eileen, died. Eileen had just given birth to her second child, my aunt Margaret, in Toowoomba. Weakened by the birth, she succumbed to the effects of being inadvisedly inoculated for diptheria. The doctor recommended this new medical procedure while she was in town giving birth, as country people did not come to town often.

Dad was utterly traumatised by his loss.

One can only imagine his reaction to the prospect of losing the second primary female figure in his life. Add to that the acute awareness that he had four little daughters who needed the love and care of their mother, and one can only surmise that it must have been a truly ghastly time.

Aunty Paddy McCallum, the redoubtable Gladys and maiden sister of Eileen, was a nurse, and came and shared our enforced isolation with us while Mum languished in an iron lung in the isolation ward at the Toowoomba General Hospital.

My second birthday was spent in isolation at Yarrabin. Aunty Paddy was a somewhat draconian nursemaid but she tried; she tried. She organised a birthday party at which the invited guests were pillows dressed up and seated around the McCallum dining table. Dad wore his dinner suit to add an aura of pomp to the occasion. Aunty Paddy made her trademark awful ice-cream with lumps of undissolved gelatine, set in the kerosene fridge in a tin ice-cube tray.

I became 'her' baby. When exhorted, with a pat on her chest to indicate to whom she was referring, to say 'Paddy', I patted her chest and said 'Pat Pat'. So Pat Pat she became to me, and her love of her family, literature and the bush took root in me also.

Mum recovered fully. Her bout of polio was spread throughout her whole system, rather than localising and irrevocably traumatising just her spine, as it did so many who were less fortunate. While Mum was in isolation she heard the news that a vaccine had been developed. Polio had been vanquished—in Australia at least.

I worshipped my beautiful sisters. Sally, the oldest, was clever and confident and funny and my protector. Prue, who came next, was a carbon copy of Dad's lost mum Eileen. Completely unconscious of her magnetic charm, she was athletic and capable and could do everything. Everybody adored her.

The third girl, Tina, was the true girl in a clutch of girls. She dreamed of fairies and looked after all the dolls and spent hours swinging on the swing, singing and chatting to her 'friends', her shapely little legs pumping gracefully as she swung higher and higher till we feared she would go right over the top. Tina wore petticoats and loved her dresses so much that she often put them all on at once.

In contrast, I hated dresses and refused to wear them. I tried very hard to be the missing boy, not the least because I sensed that boys had much more fun lives than girls from beginning to end. I had no precedent for the anatomical implications in a house where the one boy, Dad, was (understandably) excruciatingly modest, and never even left the lavatory seat up, which might have given me a clue.

I never succeeded, anyway. But I prided myself on being a 'tomboy'.

My sister Nicola was born when I was nine. Her life took a different course from ours as she was raised virtually as an only child. Like my other sisters she, too, was beautiful and clever and became a model and an actress when she grew up.

*

With our four Mylne cousins across the creek there was never a lack of brainpower to think up games. Cops 'n' robbers was the most popular. The big kids got the important jobs that involved guns and ambushes and arrests; the little kids got supporting roles that often included spending time in 'jail'. Space was never an issue, and our games rambled so lavishly through the house and the sheds and the workers' quarters out the back that often some of the participants would not be seen until the cowbell was rung to call us all back into the house for afternoon tea.

Our uncle, Sandy Mylne, had grown up at Lota House with Mum, of course, and spent his childhood sailing on Moreton Bay. He had served with the Royal Australian Air Force (RAAF) in fighter planes in North Africa during the war. Our grandmother's anguished diary entries during that time, written in fountain pen in her beautiful Edinburgh hand, are some of the most evocative pieces of writing that I have read.

The photograph of him she had slipped into her diary, a fresh-faced boy standing on the wing of an aircraft, belies the tasks he was obliged to perform as a fighter pilot. Tasks that, I know, haunted him on his deathbed 42 years after the end of the war.

Uncle Sandy was an extraordinarily clever man. He could make anything and always had a current hobby happening. Once he mastered it, or won all the available trophies, he moved on to another. His last was knitting; he could turn a sock heel like no other.

When we were young, he took to boatmaking. In the shed on his next-door property, Birrageela, he built two magnificent canoes, the *Gay Lady* and the *Blue Bear*. The *Gay Lady* had a centreboard, a mainsail and a jib—the sails stitched by Uncle on an industrial sewing machine, and perfectly set up with all the ropes and guys and rigging in miniature. Two sets of paddles provided for contingencies, such as either a lack of wind or a lack of sailing skill, or getting ourselves out of a tricky situation brought about by some involuntary inertia or a man overboard in the Oakey Creek. The *Blue Bear* was a smaller sailing craft but the two of them were quite sufficient for all of us to crowd on and sail up and down the Oakey Creek like the seafarers and pirates we became.

The Mylnes moved to town life in Toowoomba when I was six; our grandparents Norn and Garg moved to the Gold Coast soon after. So our immediate world shrank in terms of family, although Norn and Garg's beach house in Britannia Avenue at Broadbeach was a regular haven for everybody. And, in the way that life has, change brought us new neighbours, the Prentices, who bought our grandparents' property Carn Brae. Then in time they sold to the Hirsts with their three little girls Philippa, Mary and Wendy. They became our firm friends.

As we grew up we were allocated household tasks according to a round roster Mum made out of cardboard and turned every day. Four little girls, four daily tasks . . . burning the rubbish; feeding the chooks; drying the dishes; filling the coke scuttle for the Aga stove.

Although I bemoaned the lack of real adventure in my childhood life—nothing burnt down, I never broke my arm, my parents did not divorce (well, nobody's parents divorced—but still)—in retrospect my parents created for us, out of the rubble which was the war, an idyllic and carefree childhood.

And I had my imagination, in which I rescued Roy Rogers from the clutches of a wild band of Red Indians and nursed him back to health in my tiny two-man tent with a scene of an Indian village imprinted on the sides.

*

Christmas 1957, Carn Brae, the home of our Paull grandparents on the Oakey Creek at Bowenville. It's hot as hell and the grown-ups are indoors getting things ready.

We kids have been sent outside to play. There are eight of us—our white-haired cousins the Mylnes (whom Mimi our other grandmother calls 'the Snowies' for obvious reasons), and us, the dark-haired Paull girls. Between us we are never short of ideas for play.

Barefoot, we leapfrog on the lawn. Leapfrog turns into horse races when the littlest ones can't quite make the leap over high backs.

The Carn Brae lawn is pricklier than our kikuyu one at Yarrabin. All in all they have more prickles at Carn Brae than we do at Yarrabin, even though it's just across the creek and upstream a bit. They have khaki burr like we have, but bull's heads too. And bull ants that bite. You have to watch out at Carn Brae.

But still, our grandparents' garden is full of wonders. A grapevine runs the length of a trellis on the south side of the house, where the kitchen is. Our grandfather has painstakingly trained the kookaburras to come and take meat from one of its posts.

The kitchen garden is full of fruit trees and carefully tended vegetables. The strawberry patch holds a special attraction for small children.

The pink berries on the pepperina trees out the back near the machinery shed have a particular smell when crushed that always, for the rest of my life, reminds me of my grandparents. And the pepperina trees themselves, although their bark is rough on tender young legs, have nice low branches that invite young climbers like Tim and me into their arms; Tim, of course, going higher than me but not much. And only because he is 18 months older and that much bigger.

And, of course, you have to get across the bull's head burrs to be able to climb them. But there are ways and means. Sometimes Tim even gives me a piggyback.

The old long-drop dumpty outside the wire back fence isn't used much these days—there's an inside lavatory now on the back verandah near the jackaroo's room—but its solitary wooden house, leaning at a bit of a crazy angle from lack of attention, is an occasional destination for Tina and me in company with one of the braver big kids. You have to run the gauntlet of possible snakes and spiders. And the ubiquitous prickles. Then, nervously, and feeling rather as if you want to do a wee yourself, you peer with hushed awe into the darkness which is all you can see when you lift the wooden lid.

'A baby fell in there once,' my cousin Tim, fount of all knowledge and impossible tales, has told me. 'No, they never got them out; they couldn't get them out because the hole in the dumpty seat wasn't big enough. Anyway, it's too deep. They just drownded in all the poo.'

The horror of it! Still down there, no doubt a skeleton by now.

The lawn where we are now playing looks out through the antbed tennis court to a bend in the Oakey Creek. Majestic river red gums wave their bounty of azure leaves at the blue summer sky. The windmill turns lazily, creaking, the tail crashing occasionally against its constraints as small eddies of wind catch it and throw it aside.

The grown-ups come out onto the verandah—our grandmother Norn, my mum and dad, Aunty Margaret and Uncle Sandy. 'You can come up now,' they call. We tumble up the stairs, agog with excitement and expectation. Father Christmas is about to arrive.

A tray is set out with homemade biscuits, Christmas cake and eight cups of Norn's world-famous homemade ginger beer—retrieved from the pile of recycled beer bottles fermenting Norn's ginger beer plant in the woodshed out the back. These occasionally blow up with a horrible bang that takes with it our dreams of fizzy soft drink. But this time they have made it safely through to Christmas.

We are exhorted to be quiet. Insofar as we are able to according to our age and temperaments, we are. Only the big kids notice that Garg is strangely absent.

Father Christmas appears in the doorway. A collective gasp is heard. Small hands clamp over open mouths. I hide behind Mum, peering with enormous eyes around her skirt.

'Ho ho ho,' says Father Christmas in a muffled voice that is surprisingly like Garg's. The beard is cottonwool, but there is no need for padding to create the portly tummy. For a few seconds silence reigns with the magnitude of the moment. Then all hell breaks loose.

Father Christmas takes his place behind the tin slippery slide on one corner of the verandah. There, calling the name of each child as he does so, he dispenses one by one eight gifts from a pillowcase slung over his shoulder.

CHAPTER 5

YARRABIN

Mum had been raised by a nanny to a life that included a cook and a laundress and a housemaid and not much awareness of household drudgery. Dad's family were country-bred. The women were capable, pragmatic and utterly self-sufficient. They ran households like clockwork. The care of their family's needs was their undisputed role. They had recently been through a Depression which added thrift and improvisation to their myriad competencies.

Our grandmother Norn, and her mother, whom we loved dearly but called Mrs Rutledge because of the step-nature of our relationship, took Mum under their wings. They taught her that routine was the first rule of survival as a country housewife.

On Monday you lit a fire under the burnished copper wash tub in the laundry and did the washing by stirring everything in a great, hot soup with a long pine stick, scrubbing the clothes on a wooden washing board, squeezing out the moisture using a hand-turned wringer, and hauling it bit by bit in the wheeled wooden clothes basket out to hang on the prop clothesline. On Tuesday you dealt with the huge pile of ironing you had hauled in the evening before. You damped everything down, adding starch to the damping water, and lifted the lid on the Aga stove where you put the Mrs Pott's irons on to heat on the top plate. On Wednesday you cleaned the house, dusting and sweeping and oiling and burnishing and polishing. On Thursday you baked, and on Friday you drove the 50 kilometres to town if necessary—but since the mailman delivered our groceries in a giant cardboard box to the huge mailbox at the front gate, the going-to-town routine was not always taken up.

The Aga stove needed to be fed its coke from the coke scuttle. The kerosene fridge needed its wick trimmed, whatever that meant, and for its light to be kept burning, according that mysterious force of nature that created cold out of heat. The drinking water was cooled in a heavy canvas bag hanging from a rafter at the back steps, creating water of a delicious smell and taste that forever meant 'home'.

Mum's tasks, and indeed our lives, were performed without the luxury of an electric fan in the torrid heat. Our bathwater—such as it was, supplied from the rainwater our roof captured in two 1100-gallon tanks and carefully husbanded to last until the next rain—was heated in a chip heater beside the bath.

There was no shower. Just a bath. We kids shared the bathwater, if not the bath. I was usually last because of my habit of adding a discreet wee to the mix. I could never understand why this annoyed my sisters so much.

We heard the news, and listened to the Kindergarten Hour on the ABC, on a battery-powered wireless. Our flickering lights were powered by a 32-volt generator up in the shed that Dad turned on in the evenings, and in time other implements evolved that were able to take advantage of this simple power source—the most notable being a simple washing machine which took over the onerous demands of the washing copper.

Our telephone contact was via a party line. The exchange lady at the Bowenville post office, Mrs Gilbert, answered in response to one long ring and connected our calls (measured in three-minute increments punctuated by 'three minutes—are you extending?') from one exchange to the next until she reached the number we wanted.

The three parties on our party line were able to ring each other at will—unless, of course, someone else was already using the line. Our number was 1-3K: the morse code long-short-long ring series brought us to the phone. The Mylnes were 1-3R: short-long-short. Our grandparents were 1-3D: long-short-short. One short ring meant 'I've finished'.

It was completely infra dig to listen in to anyone else's phone call, although stories abounded of people on other lines who did. One example goes something like this: Party A says to Party B, 'I would tell you, but I know that old bitch Mrs X always listens in.' An indignant snort, and Mrs X interjects, 'I do NOT!'

In due course the march of progress made its way to the Darling Downs. In 1963 I went to the Tallebudgera School Camp on the steam train from Toowoomba. I cried with homesickness and did not remove my underpants for the entire ten days in case someone saw my bottom. The parrots at the Currumbin Bird Sanctuary did a group poo which completely coated me, resplendent in a fluffy pink angora cardigan, with sloppy guano. And I got my first kiss, a very chaste one, from Des Baartz, in spite of or perhaps before the poo incident.

When I arrived home, encrusted with salt and sunburn, the tall, wire-draped timber poles which had begun their inexorable march west through our property like pilloried giants had started to discharge their bounty at our place: 240 volts replaced the small, noisy generator in the shed. Through that transformer box on the pole near the back gate, our lives, too, were transformed . . . none more so, I venture to speculate, than Mum's.

A beautiful baby sister, Nicola, had also become part of our family by that time; Tina had a real baby to fuss over. I was disappointed that the much-touted 'surprise' we were to get in October 1962 was a sister and not a pony. The two big kids, Sally and Prue, had gone off to boarding school in Armidale. Our family's shape was changing and now our lifestyle changed dramatically, too, as electrical appliances slowly made their way into our home.

Television. The very snappy model our family acquired was not in a huge ugly wooden box that dominated the room, but sat as a separate heavy TV monitor on a base with four smart legs. It brought us grainy black and white images from a repeater station at the faraway Bunya Mountains. Our lives were infiltrated by American ideology. Our games changed from the British-inspired cops 'n' robbers to the wild west and cowboys 'n' indians.

'Eeeeh, Ceesco!' 'Eeeeh, Pancho', my childhood playmate Johnny and I called out to each other, twirling our six-shooters, walking with bow legs.

Our perception of the war also developed an American bias.

Mum, perhaps divining how this device and its prototypes would come to dominate all our lives so completely, strictly monitored our TV watching time. She referred to it as the 'idiot box'.

But Pandora's box had been opened.

By this time, Johnny, our workman's son, had become my main playmate, our family dynamics having so drastically changed (not the least by my having been usurped as the cherished baby).

While Tina and Jenny, Johnny's twin, played dollies and girlie games, John and I made a fearsome duo outside. Nothing was safe from our attention. We climbed, chopped, chased and created. We toted cap guns on our hips. We leapt Indian-style onto the pony, Topsy. Johnny brought endless inspiration for adventure from his glamorous Helidon cousins, who must have been holy terrors.

He arrived home once from the Helidon cousins' place with a

tomahawk ('tommy hawk') and together we had hours of pleasure destroying the (very tall, which rendered our activities invisible) core of a crop of silage Dad had inadvertently planted near the house. We created a wonderland of Indian paths and hiding places, and no one thought to question where we were disappearing off to every afternoon.

We 'borrowed' Johnny's father's tobacco and climbed into the anonymity of a huge river gum down at the creek, and were happily puffing on newspaper durries when the branch broke and threw us 15 metres to the unyielding ground below in a tangle of flailing legs and arms and bare torsos and my black hair and Johnny's blond hair and broken branch and twigs and gum leaves.

We chased birds with the box of Saxa salt from one of our mums' kitchens, confident that, like the kid on the front of the packet, we would catch one if only we managed to put salt on its tail; but they were always too elusive for us.

Under strict adult supervision, we swam in the creek until our teeth chattered and our skin wrinkled. We used blown-up tyre tubes as canoes, as 'bar' for water tiggy. We emerged covered in a fine coating of mud looking like chocolate Paddle Pops.

The creek—always the creek—was our most magical playground.

Kookaburras laughing; koalas grunting. Magpie song.

Snippet of white underwing as a dollar bird flaps across the creek, settling on a high branch, there to watch, hawk-eyed, for dinner on the wing. Dragonfly dinner.

Sharp, twittering bursts of colour as small groups of double-bar finches flit in perfectly synchronised unison from seedy grass clump to wattle blossom to seedy grass clump. Squeaking. Whistling. A sudden burst of reflected sunlight from a hundred glossy backs—then invisible in an instant.

Brilliant flash of blue-green kingfisher, darting; hunting. Splash.

A flock of cockatoos, arriving suddenly, screeching along the water-course, weaving and dodging among the trees, flying off in an hysterical white cloud; leaving behind them, for a short while, a startled silence.

An occasional 'plop' as a yellow-belly breaches and disappears again into brown water, leaving only telltale, silent, evolving rings.

Platypus drifting in the sun on the water's surface disappear with a quick flip of their broad tails as our voices send warning signals; out of sight, out of danger.

A sudden scurrying sound and—splash!—as a water dragon takes fright, panicking that his camouflage is not good enough (but really, it is); then a chain of rings surrounding lizard head zooms across the creek to lap the other side, abandoned in panic as the lizard rushes up the far bank and disappears into the long, yellow grass. A faint pathway of disturbed air and waving grass settles in his wake.

The hollow clank of the windmill provides intermittent background noise as its sails drift their open blades to find the face of the breeze and turn the mill pump, which lifts water from the creek up to the tank near the chooks' yard—garden water.

A light breeze ruffles leaves and blossoms way up high; way, way up in the tops of the giant river gums. Gum blossoms drifting, drifting; gum leaves spinning, gum nuts falling soundless, gliding, onto the elastic surface of the dappled brown water where they float, held up by the surface tension of this faintly wobbling jelly-skin. Blossoms, leaves, nuts, sit like icing on a cake, rising and falling on the tiny, imperceptible wavelets as the gentle breeze scuds along at water level and riffles the surface of the Oakey Creek.

The smells of marsupial, mud, clean brown water, eucalypts and smoke from our little fire spin on the breeze. They drift up from the ground and down from the giant trees above and across the top of the water and weave themselves together into a delicious familiar smell that says 'home' and 'comfort' and 'fun'.

It says 'down at the creek'.

CHAPTER 6

THE LAND

1945 COCKTAIL
Come let's forget life's stern realities,
And build a world of wishful thinking dreams
And tinsel insubstantialities.
Come let's forget that life is what it seems.
                                        —Paddy McCallum

Things could get pretty dry out on the blacksoil plains of plenty. There were 15 years in a row, beginning at the end of the 50s, when the summer rains didn't come, and summer brought only huge, empty blue skies with unbearable heat, dust, flies and desolation. In the worst years a quietness descended on the land, a quietness broken only by the occasional sulky whisper of a desultory breath of wind as some unseen power source turned restlessly on its bed of dry, cracked earth, then lay, still and gasping, under a shimmering haze of heat.

Worn out by foraging fruitlessly, the crows would peck listlessly at flaccid tufts of dry, yellow grass which flopped with a faint 'thunk' seen rather than heard. The air sat like a heavy hand. It pressed down relentlessly, pressing the very life out of things, wringing the last vestiges of moisture from parched, drooping stalks of wheat; it flattened our hair, compressed our faces, rendered our limbs heavy, our hearts heavier.

The heat shimmered with ghostly intensity. The world was alive only with the endless shimmer, shimmer over a tormented land, shimmering away to the far horizon where it dropped over with an imperceptible sigh of defeat.

Sometimes a furtive protest would rise up from the dust in the paddocks, and a vortex-shaped willy-willy would stand upright with the temerity of the utterly desperate and race through the wilted crops to hurl itself at the wall of heat haze—there to die as abrupt a death as its birth was sudden, bold and unexpected.

The smell and texture of dust would begin to permeate our lives. Everything, even our lungs, was coated in the stuff, at first finely and then more copiously as the willy-willy deliveries found their vengeful targets. 'Who are you to think you can tame this land, wrest a living here with your clanking machinery, so out of keeping with the silence of this sleeping old continent?' We bowed our heads in shame. They were right, of course. We knew it.

Dad and Mum, wordless, hopeless, defeated, would sit slumped on the Adirondack chairs on the front verandah. The dying lawn would crackle as Hero, the dog, rolled and wriggled to dislodge the fleas that thrived in such conditions. We kids kept out of the way. We sat, legs spreadeagled on the baked dirt road, trickling dust through our fingers, tormenting any ants silly enough to stray off their ant highways in search of elusive, miniscule dabs of moisture for their thirsty communities.

The smell of the eucalypts Dad had planted in a clump near the house, in defiance of the deadly cracks in the blacksoil plains that tore their roots asunder as they tried to establish themselves, was particularly piquant during drought. They flowered prolifically, driven by their biological urge to continue through their progeny, in the event that they not see the distance till the inevitable rain. Their poignant blossom-smell, the only sweet thing in this awful desolate time, dominated our senses.

The koalas that lived in those trees shifted in the heat, now and then raising a languid arm to grasp a fistful of eucalyptus leaves before hunching patiently back, chewing intermittently, waiting, waiting for the rain. It will rain, they seemed to say. It always does, in the end.

But will it be soon enough?

The silence crept down to the creek where the water, slowly at first, and then with gathering momentum, slipped in silent unseen wisps of vapour into the leaden air. An unfair tax on the living, it paid itself up in dues owed to a thirsting, unforgiving deity.

The leaves on the river gums clung at first to drooping branches as they spread their fingers in the dry air. Then they dropped one by one into shrinking, muddy pools alive with disenfranchised fish, gasping and struggling for survival. The yabbies dug in for the duration. The frogs—those, that was, who managed to find a possie out of the search-and-destroy blaze of the unforgiving sun—simply went into suspended animation.

Rain! The word on every tongue, the desperate wish in every prayer, the dominant waking thought in every mind. Rain.

But still the smell of death hung in the heavy air.

Farming was tough. Very tough.

Dad was born, bred and educated—at the Gatton Ag. College—to it. But Mum wasn't. And no amount of education made it rain on cue.

An only son, he was—as are so many sons of the land—under a tacit obligation to return to the farm.

It was not just obligation, though. Life on the land is like no other. There grows a deeply embedded sense of connection with the lifestyle, and through it, the land. You live daily with solitude, quietness, hard physical work and the unparalleled freedom of open space. You are acutely aware of the weather; the weather dominates your business and your life, and you learn to read it like a book, remembering its patterns over decades.

Your family and your animals are your primary source of companionship. You fiercely love, protect and defend them.

The wider community of similar families thinks and feels the same way.

At the end of the war the Bowenville district was being cut up into soldier-settler blocks, like a similar scheme after the First World War. Farms of 640 to 1000 acres were being allocated through a ballot system to returning servicemen—a new beginning, a thankyou.

The thankyou was a mixed blessing, especially when blocks were allocated to those traumatised ex-servicemen who didn't have experience of the difficulties of wresting a living from the land. Some of the blocks in our district were on-sold fairly rapidly to those with the specialised skills and tenacity needed for this harsh lifestyle.

Our part of the Darling Downs was a flat blacksoil plain. It had always been treeless. The soil—black, deep and rich—is one of the most fertile in the world. It is said that when the first sods were turned the earthworms were so thick that they clogged the plough tines.

The soldier-settlers in the late 1940s turned those first sods, built the first homesteads, under an obligation to make a set value in capital improvements within ten years or relinquish their grant.

Leaving a successful career in the air force—he had reached the rank of wing commander—Dad bought his 1000 acres from his father, who had before him acquired his land from his father. Dad then began his lifetime of backbreaking work.

He ran sheep in the early days, and grew crops. Then the crops dominated, requiring long hours spent ploughing on an open tractor protected to some extent from the harsh sun with a large umbrella, but not at all from the searing heat, dust, flies and noise.

The header that harvested his crops of wheat, barley, sorghum and linseed was towed by the tractor, surrounded as it worked by an itchy brew of chaff dust and husks. There were years when there was no harvest—either because drought had snuffed out the crop along the way, or rain had pelted it into the mud as Dad and his workman waited anxiously to get out and begin the harvest.

In the early days the grain was poured directly from the header into huge hessian bags. My big sisters made their holiday pin money sewing them up. One man manhandled the 60-kilo bags, tossing them onto a bagloader which lifted them onto Dad's old red Dodge truck; the other caught them at the top, and tossed them into neat piles on the truck bed to be conveyed into the railway siding at Malu, 15 kilometres away. There, they were weighed, taken to a giant shed for storage and later removal by train, and the farmers' payments calculated by the wheat and barley boards.

Later came bulk bins and silo storage—too late for ruined young backs, but a welcome innovation as farming methods, irrigation, water storage and larger machinery made the storage of greater yields necessary.

We grew up with our bare feet connected to the blacksoil. The great Australian salute made necessary by the constant need to wave flies away was ours by birthright. We were raised to the great silence, punctuated by sounds like koalas grunting at night down at the creek, birdsong, the unparalleled music of rain on the tin roof. The bleating of sheep, the yapping of dogs, the roaring of loud engines, the creaking of the windmill, the clucking of hens, the occasional banging of a loose shed door were the background noises to our days. Not people; not voices other than our own.

We grew up to the sounds, smells, hopes and fears that are germane to country living. They demand a certain kind of stoicism. Those of us who know it recognise it in each other. It's what R.M. Williams recognised in me many years later.

Nineteen fifty-six, the year of The Flood. As so often happens, it follows several terrible years of drought, and precedes many more.

I am three. The weather is hot and humid, and then the rain comes, and comes, and comes. The yawning cracks in the blacksoil close up, then swell with a voluptuous bounty of moisture. The soil becomes puggy, then claggy, then waterlogged, then totally, utterly impregnable. The bare earth takes up the water. It takes it up, swollen and replete, fecund with the promise of new life, till it can take no more.

And then the water begins to run off.

The rain continues to fall, and the land has nowhere to accommodate it. There is just one place lower than the Downs, and there the water goes. Into the creek.

From the house we watch the creek as it gulps the water thrust upon it in a demented orgy of relief. Barely is there time for the water to soak down to the roots of the frantic old river gums than more water fills the washouts around the tops of their roots where we had played cubbies in drier times. And the water keeps coming, now gushing down the imperceptible downward gradient that ends, ultimately, in Adelaide—Adelaide and the sea waiting at the bottom of the worn, flat continent, thousands of miles away, for a body of water that would arrive months after it had fallen from the sky in Queensland in answer to our prayers.

Already our hearing is saturated by the ceaseless drumming of the rain falling on the corrugated iron roof. A wonderful sound, how it gladdens our hearts every time we hear it! But now the rain has stopped and a new sound comes to us. At first it whispers as from a far distance. It is an assembling army milling around just out of concise earshot, its mutterings, occasional shouts of command and sharp cracks of gunshot intermittent, its soldiers preparing for a final assault. Then it gathers strength and becomes a roar, a gut-wrenching roar that takes our breath away and frightens us to the very core of our beings.

And now it comes. Flood. We kids shut the casement windows on the sun verandah to keep out the terrifying sound.

As the waters rise up the trunks of the trees, the neighbour's geese sail blithely past like white ships on a broiling brown sea. Unlike many other creatures, they are in their element.

Yellow-belly are overcome with a plenitude of oxygen brought about by some phenomenon of physics. They roll onto their sides in a narcotic stupor and bob to the surface, where they swirl gracefully on frothing eddies.

Snakes, goannas, lizards whirl past and grasp onto any handy tree, there to lodge themselves beside soggy birds and small animals taking refuge, in an unspoken amnesty for the duration.

Inert, furry, inanimate clumps drift swiftly past. Buffeted by the current, there is no rhyme or reason to their passage. They are past caring. The drought has left them weak, and the flood now catches them vulnerable and lacking the strength to struggle in another dimension—that of bounty rather than lack.

And the waters continue to rise.

Dad puts a stick at the highest point of the flood so he can measure and time its growth. Then as that stick disappears, another one. Then another. We watch out the sunroom window as the water climbs inexorably past Dad's markers, past old zeniths, past the blue garden gate, into the impregnable garden. Up to saturate the dust under the house. Past the saturated dust and up to the floorboards. Up to lap the verandah of the hut out the back.

The wildlife just goes with the flow. It goes with the flow, rolling with the punches the way the wide brown land has dictated from the beginning of time. Grasping at anything stationary, even if it happens to smell of human; better the lesser of two evils. A snake finds itself washed up at last on a human's verandah—ours. A goanna gratefully rests its weary, waterlogged bones on one of the bearers under our house. The sheep, designed for a different lifestyle, just continue to float past. Too hard, Australia. Way too hard.

The current is pretty slow in our backyard, well up above the creek banks, even though the flood height has exceeded expectations and past records. We wade across to the hut and our playroom, fearfully marvelling at the sudden brown ocean that has replaced the parched world we had grown used to. But the flood has reached its peak.

As suddenly as it came the ocean leaves us. It leaves in its wake the smell of death mixed with the rich, sweet smell of mud. Once again our creek takes on its old familiar form. But there are changes.

A new high-water mark is scoured in the cliff on the outside bend on the other side of the creek just visible from the house. Huge clumps of debris litter the upper branches of the massive river gums, way, way above our heads; there are great logs, thick wads of yellow grass, the odd furry remains or pathetic paw wrapped ignominiously into the whole. And underfoot, everything is washed horizontal, the yellow grass and the roly-polies and the prickle clumps and the broken branches and leaves and blossoms all covered with a thick gravy of sludge that slowly dries into huge chocolate cakes for our childish tea parties. Soon the green of fresh new grass will be the dominant colour on the palate of our small world.

The big kids are chafing at the bit to go down and see what has arrived with the floodwaters, what has gone. And what has changed form forever.

This, then, is flood. It is a fearsome wonder that evinces a primeval fear in the pit of your stomach. It is a quiet, beauteous force. It inexorably ends one sequence in the circle of life on the land, and ushers in another.

CHAPTER 7

SCHOOL AT BOWENVILLE

O lovely, liquid-eyed Jane
She never ever gives me pain
And on the whole her philosophy
Tho' sound, is quite extr'ordin'ry
— John Collins, Teacher, 1958

The hub of the hope that hummed around the farming district of Bowenville in the 1950s was the Bowenville State School. In 1958 there were more than 120 students enrolled there, the most recent being predominantly third and fourth siblings in the large families of the era.

By the end of my fourth year, my three sisters went there, setting off each weekday morning on their bikes to traverse the 2 miles of blacksoil road between our house and our front gate. There the school bus collected them, and all the kids from the farms roundabout, and took them the 9 or 10 miles over the gravel road to school.

The thought of school and all it offered was just too exotic for words. I was dying to go. Kindergarten Hour on the ABC at 11 a.m. was a highlight in my day. Lining up all the dolls on the end of my cane bed on the sun verandah to teach them 'school' was all very well, too, but it just didn't fill those endless hours of solitude until my sisters' bikes appeared out of the afternoon haze while I waited, swinging on the garden gate, for a first glimpse of them.

The clomping of their shoes on the back stairs and the thumps as their hard Globite schoolbags hit the back table and the chatter—about 'Teacher' and Mervyn and Sharpie and Pam—were so resonant with the excitement of the wider world that I couldn't bear to be left out any longer.

So, off I went at the age of four.

My bike was tiny. Its wheels needed at least two revolutions to Sally's one. My little legs, so recently out of nappies, pumped miserably at the pedals but it was no use; I couldn't keep up. The big kids would disappear off into the haze and leave me to pedal on alone, tears making runnels in the dust on my face but fear of being alone in this big empty space my greatest motivator to keep going.

'Wait for me! Wait for meeeee!' The refrain of the fourth child.

Tina's bike was an in-between size; she had graduated from the tiny bike a year ago, so her wheels made more distance for effort than mine but less than Sally and Prue's. She hovered and sympathised and exhorted me to keep going, but Tina lived in her world of dreamy contemplation anyway so the 2-mile journey was full of fairies and pretty princesses and imaginary friends for her; not the spectres that beset me under that huge empty sky.

Eventually we reached the front gate. We leaned our bikes up against the fence next to the grid and tramped the last few yards to the huge mailbox, where we waited in descending order for Stan and his idiosyncratic school bus.

The school bus was a converted horsefloat, painted bright pink, with steps that had to be lowered from the door that opened from the outside. At first the long seats were wedged against the outer walls to minimise their movement; eventually they were nailed down for more security.

Stan was a bachelor, a man of few words. When the noise in the horsefloat rose to a pitch even he could hear through the window into the driver's cabin, he simply stopped the bus. If that wasn't enough, he opened the window. If that wasn't enough, he called out 'Rardo, rardo, youse up the back.' That was extreme.

'Rardo, rardo, youse up the back,' the most we ever heard Stan say (and even that was infrequently), entered our family lexicon as a term of admonishment.

On my first day at school I hugged one of the solid black posts that held up the building, and wept. It was not like I thought it would be. It was the wider world no doubt, but it was alien. There was no Mum. It took several of the big kids and the headmaster's dog to prise my fingers off the post and urge me into the classroom upstairs.

I was not the first new kid to attach herself to the comfort of one of those posts, and I wouldn't be the last.

School offered myriad wonders. It constituted all that I knew in the day-to-day that was outside the isolation of our house on the creek, our farm, my immediate family.

John Collins, more often known as 'Teacher' or 'Pop', was the head-master. He had a dog called Bluey who was actually black and white, which was a bit of a mystery. But that is how it is with blue heelers.

Bluey was born to be a kids' dog. His favourite thing in all the world was leaping into the air to catch rocks thrown to him by kids. This was forbidden, because it didn't do Bluey's teeth any good. Every now and then this rule was enforced, and the kids and Bluey were sad and unfulfilled and frustrated for a while; but eventually good fun won the eternal battle over good sense, someone picked up a large piece of blue metal and threw it into the air above the small lawn in front of the school, and Bluey revived from his sad reverie and leapt into action.

Pop Collins believed in the power of classics over a young mind. Each morning after parade he ranged the whole school around the classroom for a group recitation of 'The Lady of Shalott'. Alfred Lord Tennyson's lyrical words rose and fell in piping voices on the leaden Australian air, pushing aside the dust and defying the inevitable cultural tsunami that sat in the wings of our futures. And Wordsworth, whose 'Ode to a Daffodil' was one of the first things I learned to write down.

Pop Collins taught us the magic of words. He taught us to aspire to beauty of expression. He taught us to seek to discover the subtleties of language, the power of verbal communication, the importance of the history it conveys.

He did this through recitation. Its effect was subliminal, as we were far too young to understand anything except the concept of the mystery. Pop's intellectual gift became firmly embedded in me, me with my pudding-bowl haircut and sticky-up part, huge brown eyes and skinny arms and legs, dressed in my simple blue box-pleated tunic with a short-sleeved white blouse underneath, short brown socks and brown shoes. There was about as much sophistication in me as there was in Bluey the dog, waiting downstairs for the huge handbell to ring and announce the arrival of a bunch of illicit rock-throwers to make his day.

But Pop Collins, Teacher, relegated to the backblocks out there on the Western Line in southern Queensland, offered us all the most precious knowing that he had to give—the power of words.

In those formative years his intellectual influence was immeasurable.

*

Our lives were structured; routine was paramount. Discipline was paramount, and this was clothed in routine. Routine had been the touchstone during the recent war; it was often all the generation who lived it had with which to manage the uncontrollable chaos of their lives. These ideals, hard to set adrift, overlapped into the rebuilding era in which we grew up.

The most overt of these was the morning parade at school. It was nothing if not military.

The heavy handbell was rung and we scrambled off the 'ocean wave'—a huge communal circular swing that was central to our lives, and claimed the finger of Jenny Dolan, and the prototype of which, it was rumoured, similarly accounted for many other childish fingers at Queensland's state schools. We rushed onto the parade ground in front of the school and arranged ourselves with military precision into straight lines according to our rank and file; or perhaps it was our grades.

The subordinate teachers wandered up and down the lines, making sure we were standing properly to attention, isometrically arranged, pleasing to the eye. The bell rang again and we were given a rousing address by the General, aka the principal Mr Collins or his successor, Mr Allen. Then we sang the national anthem, 'God Save The Queen'.

A flag-bearer approached the flagpole behind the ocean wave which still wobbled with the inertia of our hurried departure as it spun and rocked on its axis. As one we did a smart left-turn and watched in some awe as the Australian flag rose solemnly up the pole. Then, led by Mr Collins (or Mr Allen), with our hands over our hearts, our eyes on the flag, we recited, 'I love my Queen, I honour her flag, and I shall cheerfully obey her laws.'

Then we did a smart right-turn to the front and to the strains of the 'Colonel Bogey March' marched with synchronised steps up the stairs and into our classrooms.

We often had marching drill so that these manoeuvres could be performed with precision. And at the annual Quinalow Sports Carnival, where all the schools in the district competed in athletics, the marching display was a highlight.

The eyes are the windows to the soul, and mine in my stick-insect's little face have the intensity of those of a praying mantis under a microscope.

They follow the big kids around the room as they file in and take up their places. Soon it becomes obvious that they are riveted on one face only. My sister Tina's.

The shame and fear of betrayal in those eyes are palpable. Sibling disdain has power in this place, it travels home on Stan's bus with us and overlaps into the realm of safety.

'What's going on?' say Tina's eyes. I shift uncomfortably and look down at the rough wooden classroom floor. Her eyes follow mine.

A puddle is growing beneath my place on the bench seat I share with Mary McLennan. It spreads ignominiously across the floorboards, a silent stain, a disgrace. Then, as we both watch in dismay, it finds a crack and begins to disappear, faithful to the laws of liquid and gravity. Soon angry cries drift up through the rafters from the makeshift classroom below. The sound of desks being hastily moved around confirms the lack of wisdom shown by the powers that be when they placed the Grade 1 classroom directly above anywhere that houses items of value, like heads earnestly bent over copy books, and for that matter, the copy books themselves with their ink so given to blotching, their precious cursive letters so laboriously achieved with scratch pens dipped in inkwells.

There is, of course, collateral damage along the bench, with Mary McLennan's uniform assisting haplessly in the soaking up of the remainder of my unwelcome widdle.

But although Mary McLennan fusses, when the time comes for revenge it is as complete as it is equally unexpected. Wees in the Grade 1 classroom are a penny a dozen; Mary's faux pas is unprecedented at the Bowenville State School.

We sit in class (it is a year or so later), paying attention like good children. The Grade 2 class is ranged along the desks according to the placement of the individuals at the last end-of-term exams—those who came first, second and third are in the front row. The remainder are numbered off according to perceived aptitude, with the real 'dummies', who are left without any doubt whatsoever as to who and what they are, at the back of the classroom. The fact that their 'dumbness' is often the result of a need for spectacles, or a hearing problem, and that therefore their being placed at the back of the room only exacerbates matters, is not part of the philosophy of education in this era.

I am sitting directly in front of Mary McLennan, a mistake I never make again. Mary McLennan is being very quiet, uncharacteristically so. Not even knowing the answer can entice her to lift her arm and shake it violently, calling out 'Please Miss, Please Miss' to attract attention to her brilliance.

Possibly I don't know the answer. At any rate, I am sitting quietly being as good as gold when—suddenly!—Mary McLennan stands up, leans over her desk and vomits with guileless completeness on top of the whorl on my head.

They do not know what to do with me. Indeed, I don't know what to do with myself. There is not a living soul at the Bowenville State School who is equipped to deal with a situation that includes a sobbing child covered head to toe in bile and the inevitable carrots (where do the carrots always come from?) that Mary McLennan has not had for breakfast.

Mary is unctuously assisted to the sick couch downstairs, and showered with sympathy and cool washcloths.

I, meantime, am hazed without ceremony at flapping arms' lengths by gagging individuals, careful not to touch any part of me, into a small, airless storeroom. They ring my mother and instruct her to come without delay to collect me. Mum lives half an hour away along a gravel road. I wait an eternity, my golden crown an ignominy witnessed only by the spiders in the corner of the storeroom, for the comfort of my mother's floured apron in which to sob distractedly with the humiliation and unfairness of it all.

Mum is not overtly demonstrative on this occasion and with good reason. I follow her stiffly to the car (by now Mary McLennan's breakfast has begun to set) where she bundles me into the front seat and whisks me off. She accepts me exactly as I am, vomit and all, and that, I have to say, is one of the more precious gifts of my childhood.

Months later when I am asked what I would like for Christmas, I say—'I'd like to put Mary McLennan into a bag and drown her in the creek.'

I still think that is a reasonable sentiment.

CHAPTER 8

WE PROGRESS

There was a very embarrassing oversight at the entrance to the Bowenville State School from which I knew I had to protect the sensibilities of my mum.

Mum was a city lady, unaccustomed to the rough edges and somewhat ribald wit of country people. There were unexpected mysteries that just jumped out at people like my mum, and one of them was the sign on the school gate.

'Please Shut this Buzacott Gate,' it said.

How rude!

Life was full of words and many were inexplicably out of bounds. Most of those started with the letter 'B' (bugger, bastard, bum, bloody, bally, blanky, blinkin'—even bloomin') and had doubtful connotations. In fact, such was its power that just hurling the letter 'B' with all its possibilities was an effective insult.

And here at the door to the seat of learning was yet another of them in bold black print. How to lobby to have it removed without drawing attention to it at the same time was an eternal conundrum which worked on my political instincts, but which to my everlasting dismay I never resolved.

*

A couple of cataclysmic events intruded on our otherwise insular lives and made waves in the schoolyard, where we brought from home and compared our views of the outside world.

In November 1960, in the way of quite a lot of stars of the era, Johnny Horton was killed in a plane crash. He was Tina's heart-throb, 'North to Alaska' being her favourite song, and Tina and her friend Beth were heartbroken.

In August 1962 Marilyn Monroe died. Going to the drive-in pictures at Dalby was everyone's main form of entertainment outside our farm lives. Film stars lived on celluloid and were supposed to be immortal. We were mystified and grief-stricken.

Elvis Presley lived on though, and we wouldn't have missed a movie.

It may be a measure of my own priorities then, that when I was told on 22 November 1963 that President Kennedy had been shot, I said, 'Who's President Kennedy?' But faithful to society's expectations I do remember exactly where I was, and how shocked we all were because of the gravitas that issued from our wirelesses and our parents.

More pressing concerns were matters like the fact that the school inspectors Mr Busy and Mr Piddle (as Dad called them) or perhaps it was Mr Pizzy and Mr Biddle, were making their annual appearance, and whether we would come up to scratch. It didn't help matters that Teacher, Mr Collins, solicitously moved Mr Busy's (or was it Mr Piddle's?) chair when he stood up to address us, and Mr Biddle (Mr Pizzy?) sat back down unexpectedly to no chair and ended up on the floor.

But the years rolled relentlessly on and ushered in one change after another. Teacher left and was replaced by Mr Allen as headmaster. My sister Nicki was born in October 1962; I had enough of a grasp of the facts of life by then to know that this was cause for some embarrassment, since my parents were so old (Mum was 40) and obviously had done something proactive—presumably only once—to make this travesty occur.

Our family went to Broadbeach for the months leading up to her birth. Tina and I attended the Broadbeach State School. Now that was scary! We lived cheek by jowl with people in houses on either side of us. We caught a town bus to school. And the school was huge, imposing, and populated by kids who were streetwise in a way you just didn't get to be in Bowenville.

I compensated by getting involved in the marbles craze that was sweeping the Gold Coast. All my pocket money was spent on new marbles and tombolas, because at Broadbeach they played for keeps. I invariably lost my marbles every day, while the town kids' marbles bags got bigger and bigger. Then I would stand forlornly, relegated to the role of observer until next pocket-money day.

Back at Bowenville with a new baby sister, life resumed its rural cadence. We learned to dance in Bowenville's tin Memorial Hall. The gypsy tap, the pride of Erin, the barn dance and a good old-fashioned waltz with its one-two-three one-two-three one-two-three taught us rhythm and that boys had sweaty hands and clumsy feet.

We were made to drink the government-sponsored small bottles of warm milk that were delivered in the morning and left out in the hot sun until morning tea break, by which time they were often well on the way to being yoghurt (that as-yet-unknown delight for the future).

The girls were taught to sew; daisy stitch, chain stitch, blanket stitch all blossomed in myriad colours on blue school-issued samplers.

The boys were taught basket-weaving. While their pursuit always looked miles more interesting than ours, I have often wondered just how many of those boys have found a need for the skill of basket-weaving since their days at the Bowenville State School; whereas those hours spent labouring over the samplers, pricking our fingers, losing our thimbles, marvelling at Miss Ewing's capacity to thread a needle despite the rather astonishing length of her fingernails, must surely have borne fruit for most of us girls in terms of useful life skills.

In my case it hasn't gone much further than sewing on buttons and darning socks, a skill which is now obsolete.

While boys still did more interesting stuff, my yearning to actually be a boy decreased in direct proportion to my growing awareness that it was rather nice to chase and kiss them—even if they were insultingly unwilling.

There were times, too, when being a girl was a definite advantage. Such as when Mr Collins or Mr Allen had cause to storm across to the corner of the room where the cane was kept, and snatch it up to deliver a punishment.

The offending boy would be stood in front of the class, a tragic figure with knocking knees, white face and clenched jaw. He would be instructed to hold out his trembling little left hand and down would come this innocuous-looking but cruel instrument with the weight of a grown man behind it.

The child's crime was often no more than having underperformed in the classroom. His punishment was compounded by the shame of receiving it in front of the class.

While we girls wondered how much it really hurt, we never had to find out. But it made you wince to see how the boys shook their hand afterwards and sucked their throbbing fingers and tried hard (sometimes unsuccessfully) not to cry.

Mr Deane minces across to the window and pats the back pocket of his tight, shiny green suede trousers, flicking some chalk off the ends of his fingers as he does so and carefully slapping the white powder from his precious fancy duds.

Those duds are so unlike those our fathers wear, which are grey, with floppy wide legs and deep cuffs, blue countryman's shirts and ties and ample grey felt hats which are an essential part of their accoutrement—the hats removed indoors, doffed on meeting a woman, held over the heart when a funeral procession goes by.

Mr Deane's outfit is most unlikely in Bowenville. The tight, drainpipe trousers leave nothing to the imagination; the hat he puts on when he leaves at the end of the day, or supervises sport during lunch hour, is a natty, sporty little affair, somewhat improbable for the task of protecting his face from the harsh sun but nonetheless (and this is obviously the greater priority) the height of fashion in Mr Deane's faraway world.

A quick glance over his shoulder reassures him that his Grade 4 class is engrossed in the writing task he has set them—completing in cursive handwriting the six or so words he has half-written in white chalk on the blackboard. He pauses a moment and turns again, taking in the tableau. Tongues poke out of the sides of cherry-pink mouths; the lead smell of pencil shavings mixed with the scent of 20 sweaty little bodies permeates the room.

The occasional paper shuffles, the odd chair squeaks and scrapes as those bodies wriggle, impatient at the enforced stillness. The squealing of graphite pencils on slate insinuates itself along with the murmur of Miss Ewing's voice from the Grade 1 classroom through the partition.

A movement at the back of the class, as Barry Murphy leans surreptitiously back on his plank seat to see what pearls of wisdom Gary Wilson has written. Daryl Luscombe, meantime, just stares at the ceiling, seeking inspiration, possibly finding none in an academic sense and possibly, in fact, not seeking inspiration at all; just counting the fly spots.

We girls ostentatiously curl our free arm and our bodies around our work so no one can see to cheat from us. Sink or swim! It's every man for himself when you want to earn the laurels that are bestowed on those who come first, second and third in our term exams.

A blowfly's wings make an urgent whirring sound as they batter against one of the casement windows that fill half of the entire southern wall of the Bowenville State School. The fly escapes into the languid air outside, no doubt seeking the temptations of the school toilets.

The toilets at the Bowenville State School are a dumper affair set some distance away from the school. Some people call them dunnies, some call them thunder boxes, but the polite name is 'toilet'. Whatever they are called, it's the smell that dominates.

Housed in small stumped conjoined wooden rooms, each enclosed casement wooden toilet affair conceals a large tin. That's what you 'go' in. The mystery of where it goes after that, and who removes the tin through the small door that opens from outside at the back, and deals with the contents, does not concern us, so we simply do not wonder about it.

What we do know is that the education-department-issue toilet paper is shiny and rough and only just serves its purpose, and that the sawdust in the large box beside the toilet is for putting on top of our doings once we're finished. And that we have to put the heavy wooden lid down or the blowies will teem in with their horrible blowfly buzzing voices and their bumbling great bodies bouncing off our bottoms when we sit down to go.

When we're finished we wash our hands at a trough with lever-action taps, and either rush back to continue playing, or saunter back to return to class.

Either way, there is no malingering in the actual toilets. The smell sorts that out. It is the tangible sort of smell that etches itself onto your brain, rising unbidden to attach itself to your early memories of the Bowenville State School.

Mr Deane, meantime, pats his green suede trousers pocket again, gaining reassurance from the gesture. He shrugs his narrow shoulders under their matching green suede coat, and surreptitiously loosens his tie and collar. Hot.

He seeks out his reflection in one of the windows and, with another quick glance at his class to make sure no one is watching, whips out a greasy comb and runs it through his magnificent oiled quiff. A quick flick of the wrist is all it takes, the comb-marks like an evenly ploughed paddock which is not flat and endless like those on the farms all around the district but proffer a wonderful exaggerated hillock of a curl, slick and shiny, with a long oily tail pointing at Mr Deane's right eye.

The comb safely restored to its pocket, whence it would be withdrawn at least another half dozen times that day, Mr Deane claps his hands to draw everyone's attention to himself.

'Now, Grade 4, remember what I said: You don't say "inythink"—it's "inythink".'

One small person gleefully observes the whole pantomime. Jane Paull absorbs every mannerism, from the mincing walk to the slicking of the mane to the idiosyncratic pronunciation of the English language.

That night and many others I re-enact it for the edification and amusement of my family.

CHAPTER 9

UNFOLDING

Wrought by brave hands long dead the past has laid
So great a heritage before our feet;
We can with grateful hearts and unafraid
Work on to make the present strong and sweet.
                                        —School hymn,
                        The New England Girls' School, Armidale

As a bud unfolds to admit the morning sun, so the cosy cocoon of my life on the Oakey Creek began to open up by degrees to expose me to the outside world.

For my twelfth birthday I received my first wristwatch, a rite of passage that was a symbol of my imminent adolescence.

In the way of change, each unfolding was irrevocable. My childhood was slowly departing and from each step there was no going back; and strangely, I soon found that I didn't want to anyway.

The home that had been so full of my older sisters now held just me and a baby sister on whom my parents doted. I was gangly and awkward and it was time for me to follow my older sisters into secondary school. But, since I had started school at such a young age, I was too young for the change of curriculum at the interstate boarding school where my ultimate destination was to be for my secondary education.

So for a year, in 1965, I stayed on Stan's now somewhat more modern bus each school day as it stopped off at Bowenville to collect the big kids from the farms on the other school bus routes, and continued a further half hour's drive on to Dalby to the high school.

I put aside my blue box-pleated pinafore and shoved my scrawny little frame into the ugly brown box-pleated tunic that I was obliged to wear at my new school. It completed my anonymity in a sea of brown there.

In my experience, the sensation of being a new girl never gets any easier. I'd been king of the coop at Bowenville, one of only three girls in my class, and now I arrived in an alien town world in what seemed to me a huge place where no one knew, or cared, who I was.

On my first day I met and latched onto two other girls from outlying farms, Kay Davis and Marjorie McMahon. They became my bosom buddies and security for a year which is memorable on only a couple of counts; the other kids, mostly town kids, were breathtakingly bold and savvy. The teachers—who were dedicated to the task of inculcating their charges with a good education—had their hands more than full enough just maintaining law and order with the town kids who seemed to know no fear or favour, except for each other.

At that point I firmly made up my mind not to follow one of the few vocations open to a female, that of teaching. There was no doubt my hide was not thick enough to manage the vicissitudes of teenagers in the 60s.

There was a boy called Vern with whom I fell hopelessly in love from a distance. I never actually spoke to him. My frantic one-way love affair was conducted mainly on the school bus where I waited each afternoon for him to walk past, a man-boy haplessly swinging his schoolbag and quite unaware of my adoration. If I sighted his face, red and ravaged by acne, I went into a dreamlike state that sustained me for most of the tedious hour-long bus trip home.

In a valiant effort to make useful women of the girls in their charge, the school taught us domestic science. This included some tips for life which are now rather startling in the light of the giant leaps forward for women's liberation that were happening in the big city at the same time.

We girls were taught how to organise the days that would inevitably become our lot as the good housewives of the future; to make the beds, prepare balanced meals for our future families, clean our homes, sew our clothes.

We had (girls only) cooking lessons, we had (girls only) sewing lessons. We learned how to do box pleats, knife pleats, darts, facings, hems. We learned to pin and to tack, to cut out patterns, even how to make patterns. The lessons assumed and built on our sewing sampler skills from our primary school days.

I took home apple crumbles on the school bus, Anzac biscuits, Madeira cakes, lemon delicious puddings, shepherd's pies. I made clothes I refused to wear, and have never used a knife pleat for anything since but still—I know how to do it!

And, to ensure that we achieved the greatest goal of all, that of hooking a man in order to fulfil our ordained life cycle and become a wife, we had etiquette and deportment lessons. My family took great delight in the practical aspects of those, since I was known to be a lost cause in the femininity stakes. I regaled them at nights with demonstrations of how to walk in stilettos, toe down first, holding my gloves with fingers outwards. How not to speak at the table with my mouth full; how to stimulate the appetite of my diners with an attractively presented meal; how to wait table on my family correctly.

My greatest learning, though, from the Dalby High School was the surprising fact of my own insignificance. It was humbling. The Dalby kids all knew each other, having been at the Dalby State School together all their school lives and, being town kids, able to meet and play together out of school hours. Those few fellow students from the Bowenville State School who took the giant step into secondary school with me disappeared into the maw of one or other of the many huge buildings distributed over its acres of space and left me utterly alone with my Bowenvilleness; it seemed that Kay and Marjorie were the only two other human beings who noticed my existence during the day.

Each afternoon I returned home on Stan's bus and became visible again. I took off the ugly brown uniform and left my anxiety with my schoolbag on the back table. The muddy waters of the Oakey Creek welcomed me. Our neighbours the Freshneys had rescued a baby koala from its dead mother's pouch and were raising this fluffy bundle of marsupial personality as their own. We visited and held little Pooh, or admired her as she sat on the back of the sofa watching TV, chewing on a bunch of gum leaves with mindless concentration as the Cartwrights went about their business on the Ponderosa Ranch in *Bonanza*. Our neighbours the Hirsts, just a hop, skip and jump over the bumpy creek crossing, visited us on a regular basis. We occasionally went to the drive-in at Dalby, where the novelty of fish and chips for dinner was the main attraction. It was fantastic watching a movie in the comfort of the family car, snuggled up with a pillow and a blanket and sucking on Maltesers, even if the window did have to be somewhat open to allow the speaker to be pulled inside the car and its cord slung across Mum and hung over the steering wheel. We still went to tennis parties at the weekends at other people's homes on farms within a 40-kilometre radius.

All was as it should be once I was home again.

But the next step in my education loomed larger still. Boarding school. It seemed impossible that I would leave the comfort of home and actually live at school for months at a time. But my sisters had each done it and soon enough I went, too.

The New England Girls' School (NEGS) in 1966 was a last bastion of Victorian mores. Situated in Armidale, in the New England district of New South Wales, it espoused English virtues and Victorian dogma rigidly administered by a staff of all-female teachers.

This seemed perfectly natural for a girl who had never seen a black person or an Asian, who heard only British BBC accents on the wireless (including that of our prime minister 'Ming', or Bob Menzies), whose personal history led only back to Protestant Mother England and who had no imagination of any other way of living.

Many stories abound of the manner of children's depositing at their various boarding schools—of parents who, unable to bear the moment of parting, pretended they were just nipping off to speak to a teacher and then disappeared altogether, leaving their distraught child to manage the separation as best he or she could.

For my part, there was no ceremony. I was duly kitted out in the formal school uniform, a virginal white shift (known as a 'sack'), with a belt tied in a bow around the waist and white crosses embroidered on the front; brown seamed stockings held up with suspenders; white gloves; freshly shined brown shoes; a straw hat, a blue blazer and a brown handbag. I had two suitcases containing exactly the right quantity of our day-to-day uniform consisting of named bloomers, linings, tasselled girdles, plain blue tunics and white under-blouses, a voluminous red-lined cape for rainy days, and with no more than the prescribed allocation of 'civilian' clothes including one pair of jodhpurs and one pair of black court shoes (no slingbacks allowed); as well as a 'rug bundle' held together with a leather strap, which contained my eiderdown and the rug on which I could sit demurely on Sundays in the expansive grounds as long as I did not remove my court shoes.

All this and I were deposited on a Greyhound bus in Toowoomba along with another 40 or so NEGS girls in January 1966, and we set off on a five-hour journey into what was, for me, the unknown.

I had been blooded already by my Dalby High School experience. Strangeness was no stranger to me. I had already vanquished it. And girls—well, I knew girls; I was, after all, one of five daughters. Here on the bus was a gaggle of other country girls from properties as far afield as Charleville and Charters Towers. Children still, they all exuded a worldliness that somehow resonated with me. They spoke a language I understood, in a lexicon that was unique in many ways to our school and became a hallmark of mutual recognition.

My older sisters each made their mark at NEGS in different ways. Sally was known to have been clever and witty and mischievous and a born leader. Prue was an athlete, a champion swimmer and gymnast. Tina was a good all-rounder and had a circle of close friends who adored her.

The bud which was my life opened up and transplanted itself into the fertile field of Armidale and a closed boarding-only community of several hundred young women who were shut up together 24 hours a day, for three school terms a year. We were released into the outside world for one mid-term weekend and a maximum of three exeats (day leaves) each term.

We wrote home once a week. There were no phone calls; the

occasional telegram celebrated a birthday or special event. Our incoming letters were thrown one by one into a heaving sea of eager blue tunics by a prefect at morning fruit break. Standing on an upturned box with her back to the huge brick wall of the dining room, and facing the large courtyard where we congregated expectantly, she held the basket of letters over her arm. Calling out the name of each recipient, she then threw the letter in her general direction. The excited owner of the letter scrabbled among the bloomers and shiny brown shoes until she found the trampled missive and scooted off to sit with her legs in the sun and read news of home, or clumsy words of love from an Armidale School or Kings School boy smitten with her maidenly charms.

Our main concerns were boys, our looks, whether we had good legs (faithful to the era, we showed off as much leg as possible at all times), whether we were fat, whether we had lots of friends, what end-of-term parties we were invited to.

The school's main concerns were our education, our virginal purity, our religious wellbeing, our development as ladies, and our adherence to a set of draconian and inexplicable school rules, such as: no speaking in the bathroom; no washing your hair at any time or place other than on Saturdays in the allocated hair-washing basins near the main courtyard; no taking of food into dormitories; no speaking after lights out; no bare feet at any time; no shouting; no running except on the sporting field.

At mealtimes, which we attended en masse in answer to a gong, we sang grace, in Latin in two parts, before and after meals. We had white linen table napkins and napkin rings, and the captain who sat at the head of each table of 12 girls served our stodgy meals from huge ceramic platters and supervised our table manners—whether we were passing the salt to our neighbours, whether we were talking with our mouths full, whether we were using the butter knife, or whether we were observing the meal in silence if we had been allocated this frequent punishment.

We were expected to, and did, own up to crimes and misdemeanours and fulfil any punishment that resulted. We attended the beautiful, brass-roofed chapel every morning and twice on Sundays. We sang hymns and psalms in Latin and English, embellished by the descants, altos and sopranos sung by the school choir sitting in the chapel's nave. We had prayers and a hymn at assembly every night.

We slept in large dormitories with rows of iron beds with coconut fibre mattresses. There was no heating or cooling. We were required to make our beds every morning, and turn the mattresses once a week when we put clean sheets on our beds. Our sleeping space was inspected every day, as were our shoes for evidence of the polishing we were required to do daily. We had to wear slippers and dressing gowns to the bathroom. We had to wear large blue bloomers over our undies ('linings') to avoid the possibility of—what? The mind boggles.

Such an atmosphere did not encourage free thought. Our lack of awareness of the outside world was quite breathtaking. So obsessed were we about the concerns of our small world, most of those concerns being vapid social matters like boys and end-of-term parties and dances and clothes and how good we did or did not look, that we must have appeared to those who tried so hard to inculcate us with knowledge to be empty-headed young creatures.

It was a great place to be as a teenager, incarcerated with a huge peer group in extraordinarily insular circumstances. We joked that it was a nunnery—a Protestant one—but, in fact, that is exactly what it was.

Thirty years later, reading in Li Cunxin's book *Mao's Last Dancer* how he and his brothers scratched in the surrounding fields to find a

Peter Paull, DFC and Kathleen Mylne, my parents, on their wedding day at St John's Cathedral, Brisbane, on 28 January 1946.

Cousins at Lota House in Manly, Queensland, in 1956. (From L to R): Clare Galwey, Sally Paull, Camilla Galwey, Prue, Tina and me.

Me at Bowenville State School, 1961, wearing the blue pinafore with the white blouse underneath, the state school uniform. School photos were a dreaded annual event.

My sister Tina (left) and me
on the swing at Yarrabin,
Queensland. The swing was
Tina's domain, she spent
hours on it swinging and
singing happily to herself.

Lota House, overlooking Moreton Bay at Manly, Queensland, a watercolour
painting by my grandmother, Kit Mylne. Kit was taught to paint with
watercolours, and play the bagpipes and violin, at her finishing school in
Edinburgh.

Great Aunt Paddy McCallum. Dad's maiden aunt was a well-known character whose knowledge of Queensland genealogy was encyclopaedic. Her love of the Australian bush and its people influenced me greatly.

Lifelong friends at NEGS, Armidale, 1969. Back row (L to R): Susie Shaw, Humpy Taylor, Rob Chandler, Peta Atwill and Bina White.
Front row: Minnie Fulloon, Susie Payne, me and Jenny Campbell.

Dinner camp at White Falls, Toomba, Queensland, with R.M. Williams' Santa Fe boots, 1971. I had removed my boots to paddle in the creek, but had struck a patch of quicksand. My cousin Edgar snapped this photo as I emerged, much relieved.

Hippie Hitchhiker Jane, New Zealand, 1972. Being cold was a constant in New Zealand, despite the thick jumper, which was knitted from the wool of a local sheep by a friend's grandmother.

Me in Glacier National Park, Canada, 1975, underdressed for the weather as usual. We stopped to give our little Vee Dub a rest and to survey the magnificent sculptured towers around us.

On the Winton to Longreach
endurance ride, 1980. Every
part of me ached by this stage,
but none more than my feet.
They required some attention
before I remounted and
re-entered the fray.

Riding Rockybar Somali, R.M. Williams' rangy purebred Arabian gelding,
with halter in the Tom Quilty 100 Mile Endurance Ride, 1979.

I offer an improvised emergency drink to Dusky on the 250-kilometre Winton to Longreach endurance ride in 1980. Note Dusky's bridle— hand-made, double-stitched with gaucho knots—created under R.M.'s tutelage.

single turnip to share between the whole family for dinner, during those same years in the late 60s while our concerns were about whether or not we were fat, was a rude awakening for me. Not that that information was available at the time. All the same, our lives did not run to the details of the discomfort of others; such is the self-absorption of teenagers.

The friends I made from my four years at NEGS formed the core friendships of my life. Over the 40 years since that time, we have shared births, deaths, marriages and divorces, our lives weaving in and out of each others' like the giant family of sisters we became.

It's snowing. Evening prep is interrupted because of the excitement this occasions. Defiant of the school rules which would usually have us stay indoors, we run outside to enjoy the miracle.

Twirling our red-lined capes like ballerinas we spin and run and laugh, holding out gloved hands to catch the snowflakes that are beginning to settle on the rosemary hedge that defines the boundary of College Garden.

We lift up our faces and close our eyes, wondering if it's true that every snowflake is unique. Then we run again, to where the snow has started to build up in the lee of the hedge, and, shrieking, scoop up enough to make snowballs that we throw at each other.

I spin around and—suddenly!—in the flickering light that struggles down from the windows above I spy a solitary figure standing, statue-like, on the pathway that separates the garden from the brown brick classroom block. She is small—tiny—and erect. Her grey hair, flecked with snowflakes, is pulled back into a severe bun behind round spectacles that are perched on an elfin face. Her sensible tweed skirt almost covers thick brown stockings which in turn disappear into shining, old-lady lace-up brown shoes.

Her arms are folded across a grey twinset buttoned up to the neck over a white, lacy blouse fastened with a pearl brooch at her throat and there is no doubt about it—it is me that Youngie is watching.

Trouble.

My attention captured, her small gloved hand removes itself from the weft of her folded arms and beckons to me. I crunch across the snow towards her, heart pounding, inexorably drawn like a mouse fraught within the morbid gaze of a hungry cat.

'Yes, Miss Young?' I say to our revered Senior Mistress, old as Methuselah, the bastion of NEGS since the days before my mother was a student there, from whom a simple look is as severe a reprimand as a tirade of fiery words from anyone else.

'Jane Paull,' she says (this is the first time she has addressed me outside the hallowed confines of her Latin class). She knows who I am! I try not to tremble as I await my chastisement.

'Jane,' she says again, a soft expression crossing her lined old face, her eyes looking at me in their intent way as if to capture some of my fleeting youth. 'Did you know that when I was a wee gel I used to play ice hockey on the loch at Clunie with your grandmother? We made sticks from branches we found in the woods, and used a turnip for a puck.'

Youngie. Wee Ruthie, the vicar's daughter from the kirk at Clunie in Perthshire, Scotland, childhood playmate of my grandmother Mimi, who, just months after this encounter, would die at the age of 82.

CHAPTER 10

WHEN THE GATES SWING WIDE

Jane is not cooperative and is not tidy in her dormitory.
—Miss Graves, Housemistress,
The New England Girls' School, 1967

Give of our best! So when the gates swing wide,
And through the larger world our way we choose
Of life's high enterprise, which we descried,
Never can we the vision wholly lose.
—School hymn,
The New England Girls' School

While it was something of a point of honour among the young ladies of NEGS to be seen to be 'naughty', the dedicated staff of teachers did manage to impart quite a lot of knowledge to us, some more so than others.

The calibre of person selected by the discerning NEGS board to head the school was, naturally, of the highest order. Not that we recognised it at the time. Miss Loyalty Howard came from England where she'd had a distinguished career with the Secret Service during the war. The details of her war service were so top secret that they did not come to light until after her eventual death in the rose-covered cottage in Kent to which she retired.

We ungrateful little savages, the young ladies of NEGS, saw only a lonely woman whose duty it was to torment us. The nature of her job decreed that she present herself as aloof. The buck stopped with Miss Howard, so when you were called to her office it was because she had to tell you someone had died, or that you were in deep trouble; there was not much in the way of exchange of pleasantries and she never became familiar with us.

Miss Howard maintained her aloofness with the aid of her little red sausage dog, Bronty, who harboured an unseemly disliking for young ladies. Whenever she was seen abroad with the ever-vigilant Bronty, taking the air within the 100-acre school campus (which included a nine-hole golf course) that was her domain, everyone gave the duo a huge swerve. Even so, Bronty inflicted a few war wounds on the unwary.

There were many marvellous teachers at NEGS. They included women who had brought with them a vast array of life experiences with which they added colour to our microscopic view of the world. The war was relatively recent. Our geography teacher, Dr Raadgever, was a highly educated woman who was an émigré from war-torn Holland. Her occasional firsthand accounts of what her country had been through were riveting.

There was one teacher, however, who managed to rise above the fray and penetrate our obligatory teenage disinterest—the indomitable mistress of English, Mrs Barry Hall.

Barry Hall, an erudite and eloquent South African with the bearing of an empress, was a refugee from the politics of apartheid, which she found abhorrent. Every teacher imparts a little of themselves in the course of their work. Mrs Hall's gift to us, apart from her formidable delivery of language and her gift for teaching, was individual acknowledgement. She managed to give each of us the impression that she believed in us, while at the same time she made no secret of the fact that she understood we could strive to do better. She used her erudite, ironic humour to goad us into paying attention as she brought to life the mysteries of language and communication.

And many of the mysteries of life as well.

Her praise was all the more valued for the fact that it was not cheap. We loved and revered her. She possibly never realised the enormous effect she had on many of us, me in particular, in her position as role model and mentor.

Barry Hall forever holds a special place in my heart.

Years after I had left school, when I was a station cook on a remote property in North Queensland, I received news that one of my dearest school friends had graduated from university. I knew that my marks had been better than hers at school and was living to regret decisions I had been forced into making at a too-young age that had had a profound impact on my life's direction. Robbie's graduation brought this into stark relief. I wrote to Barry Hall and bemoaned the choices I had made, my lack of professional qualifications. Her response was immediate and predictable—she told me to stop moaning, not look back, and do the best I could do at whatever I happened to be doing. It was timely advice. I took it to heart and have tried to live by it ever since.

As my life has unfolded, I know without a doubt that the world at large has been my university and that my teachers have lined the way, appearing when I needed them. I have followed many paths in many guises. Life has beaten me up many times, and I have beaten it up at times, too. But the skills and knowledge I have brought with me in the ever-growing snowball of my experience could never have been gained without my being open to them.

Our values at NEGS echoed the values of the times.

While the overarching ethos of my cohort was girls with a bush background, the other students were not all country girls. There were daughters of judges and lawyers, corporate giants and businessmen. Some were very rich but the school strictly monitored a sense of equality so that we all had exactly the same quantity of civvie clothes, the same amount of pocket money. The fact of the uniform disguised any differences in wealth and I was quite unaware that some of my classmates were daughters of scions of the Australian business world. Wealth was not flaunted. It simply was not an issue.

An American Field Scholarship coupled with the generosity of her host family, the Trudes, brought a real American girl, Lisa Haldeman, into our midst. Lisa was an exotic creature who valiantly negotiated the wide chasm that separated our social values, and became an integral part of our scattered network of lifelong friends. In company with a very excited Lisa and 600 million others, we watched 'Mankind's Giant Leap' on 20 July 1969 on a television especially set up in a science lab for the occasion.

Otherwise, television was not part of our lives.

Maths was never my strong point, but I managed five A's and a C (maths!) in the school certificate at the end of fourth year in 1968. I was on course for higher education but this was never going to be possible for me without a Commonwealth scholarship. There was no HECS in those days, nor was there Austudy to help support students whose parents could not make the costs associated with university.

My sister Sally had won a Commonwealth scholarship; whether or not I would have will forever remain a mystery. I never had the chance to sit for one.

Nor, for that matter, was a university education by any means an expected part of a woman's repertoire, especially a country woman. Many girls left school without matriculating, some immediately after junior or school certificate.

As it eventuated, drought intervened. Sending four daughters to boarding school had taken its toll on my parents' resources; the dreadful, heartbreaking 15-year drought leading up to the end of the 60s finished them off. When I sent a complaining letter home towards the end of fifth year, with the all-important sixth year yet to be conquered, my parents responded by pulling me out of school.

It was a shock, but it seemed like an okay idea at the time. Years later Barry Hall told me that, distraught that I was leaving school, she approached the headmistress to see whether anything could be done. When Miss Howard indicated that my parents' decision was final, Mrs Hall invited me live with her and her family in Armidale so that I could complete my leaving certificate at the Armidale High School.

Perhaps my prior experience of high school dampened my enthusiasm about accepting this generous offer. The thought of being closer to home—not to mention a complete lack of career guidance—outweighed more sensible considerations about my future. I would soon marry and be kept. That was the unspoken expectation.

At the age of 16 I opted to leave school and, living with my Mylne cousins in Toowoomba, have a go at the Queensland senior certificate through the Toowoomba Coaching College.

The culture shock was enormous. From living in an insular, regulated environment at NEGS with more on-tap friends than I could possibly manage, and staff whose job it was to pay attention to what

I was doing and monitor my progress, I found myself suddenly and quite unceremoniously thrown out into an uncaring world.

The staff at the coaching college gave me a book list, and showed me the spot near the window of their dank and dusty premises up a set of dingy stairs in Margaret Street where I would teach myself all I needed to know to pass the senior certificate. There was nothing familiar about the Queensland curriculum, no one came near me or offered counsel or support, and I stuck at it for a month.

Seeing that the people who were learning secretarial skills across the room at least received the benefit of teaching support, I begged to be allowed to switch to the secretarial course. Which I did, and gained the core skills of my future profession as an administrator.

The 70s were a time of change. The upheaval of the 60s flowed over into the new decade and took with it a set of beliefs that I found very exciting. It was uncool to stay in one place for long; it was groovy to travel. It was uncool to opt for early marriage; it was cool to break rules. Only 'pills' were conservative; it was groovy to be open to new ideas and to express them, even if you didn't (as I didn't) fully understand what they meant!

In the psychedelic 60s, Mary Quant promoted thick black eyeliner and heavy mascara highlighting huge eyes; Twiggy was thin and boyish and wore miniskirts that got shorter and shorter, so that air hostesses had to take lessons in bending down rather than over. Witches' britches peeped suggestively out from miniscule skirts. Step-ins fiercely corseted recalcitrant flesh under wildly colourful empire-line dresses. Skirts were slung on hips with huge, wide belts. Hot pink and lime green were in. Being overweight was definitely out.

Cliff Richard had his 'Summer Holiday' overland across Europe, and The Beatles sang of fresh young love.

But in the 70s the cutesy images developed a more sultry bent. The Beatles took up drugs and transcendental meditation, and their songs lost their innocent flavour. James Michener's *The Drifters* (Random, 1971) took the travel ideal from a bunch of fresh-faced pals singing innocent songs on a converted London bus to the politics of super-cool draft-dodgers, bespeaking romance and freedom and magnificent adventure. Dustin Hoffman in *The Graduate* ended up far from innocent. Bob Dylan and Cat Stevens and Carole King sang about 'rebellion' and parents who didn't understand.

The Youth Culture was in full swing. Our 'oldies' knew nothing. It was time to get out into the world and do our own thing, which did not involve our parents either as partakers or supervisors.

Germaine Greer was rising up and, along with her cohort of fellow intellectuals, was saying the unsayable—Women! Be bold! Make your own life! You don't need marriage to define you!

Rebellion was in the air. It was fun, as long as you didn't bring it home.

I was caught between a conservative background and the exciting notions of revolt being bandied around through the music we played constantly on our transistor radios or, for the supremely 'with-it', cassette recorders.

I decided to gather life experiences. But first and foremost, I had to earn a living.

Each step I took inexorably drew to me the unique combination of skills and experience that I brought with me to the establishment of the first office of the Australian Stockman's Hall of Fame in 1979. In the eight years that I moved from job to job, place to place, gathering knowledge and experience, I didn't stay in one place long enough to qualify for annual leave.

My first job, which I started in October 1970 at the age of 17, was as office girl at a small Ford dealership in Toowoomba.

I was given the job in part because I assured them I was on the verge of getting a driver's licence and could therefore run errands. I eventually got the licence, but steadfastly refused to drive in town.

I acquired my driver's licence from the local cop in the one-horse town of Jondaryan. Somehow I managed to pass the cursory verbal skills test; somehow I managed not to stall when I did the mandatory hill-start on the one available hill in flat Jondaryan—the railway crossing.

Actually driving once I was equipped with the licence, on the other hand, was not an option. Owning a car was as far removed from my means as owning a spaceship.

From time to time Jack Guy, my boss at Elvery's, in between puffs on the ubiquitous cigarettes that generated a semipermanent haze of smoke emanating from his office, tried to insist that I fulfil the qualification that had clinched the job for me from the many contenders—and drive. My fear of Toowoomba's traffic was, however, greater than my fear of Mr Guy and I ran all his errands on foot.

I earned $23.40 per week after tax for a 40-hour week which included Saturday mornings. I thought I was in clover.

'Have you wiped down the leaves of the rubber plant today, Jane?'

'I don't have to polish the leaves of the rubber plant, Lindsay! Give up, you drip! You're pulling my leg.'

'Yes, you do! It's part of your job description! It is. It is!'

I huff and puff my way back into the small office of the Ford dealership. I note that once again the stamp sponge has dried out completely while I was out for lunch. Dry as chips; amazing!

'Hey!' I call over to the spare parts section. 'The stamp sponge is dry AGAIN! I can't believe the evaporation in here!'

Sympathetic noises issue from spare parts. The muffled guffaws which follow them are, I assume, part of another conversation.

Brian, the office manager, looks wide-eyed and innocent as he always does. A clean-living and handsome bachelor, he is beyond help; at the ancient age of 35 he still lives at home with his mum and dad, rides a pushbike to work and wears a grey cardigan. He clips garters onto the outside of his trousers before he sets off for home each day on his bike.

The most overt symptom of his irretrievable drippiness, however, is the fact that he does not, never has, and will not, smoke. Or drink.

The phone rings. It's an internal line, one of four. Lindsay Bergan from spare parts gives me the number he needs me to ring for him, 21711, and adds, 'It's urgent. If they're busy, please keep trying. I really need to speak to them.'

The number is strangely familiar. I dial it, waiting for a response so I can pull down the switch for the spare parts extension and put them through. The line is busy.

'It's busy,' I call across to Lindsay.

'Keep trying, please,' says Lindsay. 'I need to speak to them urgently.'

I try the number again and again. The little shutter on the top row of the telephone switchboard winks its silver eyelid down at me, complicit in a joke that is slowly revealing itself to me.

I check the number. The guffaws from spare parts burst out from behind the rows of aluminium shelving that house box after box of esoteric objects. The light dawns; I have been ringing myself.

It won't happen again. But the leaves of the poor rubber tree go unwashed for the whole of my tenure, except for one day when I make the mechanic Rob put the whole potplant out in the rain.

And I finally find out that it is a daily task for one of the boys from spare parts to dash across and squeeze the stamp sponge dry as soon as I go out for lunch. The fact that they sometimes forget adds to the mystery. My *daily report as to the status of the stamp sponge, delivered loudly and with an air of wonder each afternoon exactly on cue when it comes time to wet the stamps to put onto the day's letters, no doubt adds colour to a job which might otherwise be somewhat humdrum.*

When I am eventually told, I note wryly that there is every possibility that I might have avoided the embarrassment of getting chewing gum stuck to a stamp in the course of licking it when the stamp sponge was dry. But no matter. I'm paid a fortune and I'm in clover.

CHAPTER 11

THE SCHOOL OF HARD KNOCKS

I'm sick of these town bugs.
—Jane Paull, 1971

Faithful to the heritage of my forefathers, the romantic notion of the bush and the north lured me away from the security of a regular job with regular wages. I began the period of my life which included gathering experiences in what was frequently the time-worn 'school of hard knocks'. The freshness of youth and pure ignorance were more often than not my greatest allies.

While I financed myself entirely by scrimping and saving when I was 'in the money', I was very fortunate in that, after each foray into the world, I had a home and a loving family to retreat to on the Oakey Creek.

Halfway through 1971, after just seven months at my first town job, I decided I was sick of town. I cast my fate to the wind and began my wandering life. My paternal grandfather's birthplace was to be my starting point.

My cousin Edgar Bassingthwaighte, like me a descendant of both William White of Lota House and Graham Mylne the elder, piloted his family's aircraft. At the end of May he flew me to Toomba, their family property at Charters Towers. To say 'at Charters Towers' is to use the term loosely. Toomba is 100 kilometres from Charters Towers, its nearest town.

Edgar's trip on this occasion was to bring up Warwick vet Syd Miller and some extra musterers for the mandatory tuberculosis (TB) and brucellosis testing that were part of the massive eradication scheme of the early 1970s.

Toomba, or 'Place of Many Waters', had been the horse paddock on the huge station Bluff Downs, established several generations before by my great-grandmother Helena's brother Ernest. Toomba's claim to fame, apart from its extraordinary beauty, was that it never ran out of crystal-pure surface water, because of its fabulous wealth of underground springs on part of the run. This could not be said of the open savannah country in the rest of the district.

In 1971 Toomba Station sprawled across 286 square miles. Some of its vast area took in part of the massive basalt 'Wall' that flowed from Hughenden to the Burdekin River. The Wall is one of the wonders of nature. A relatively recent geological feature, it was a superficial lava flow that cooled quickly, creating gigantic bubbles. At nights when camping close to The Wall you could hear the occasional explosion as one of these bubbles gave way somewhere across the vast expanse of impenetrable basalt. Some of the holes thus made were so enormous that from the air it could be seen that gigantic trees that had taken root in them had still to reach the height of the rim.

The Wall incorporated pockets of verdant land, some accessible, some not. In contrast to the tough savannah country that made up the bulk of the station, the pastures in the pockets were like an Irish field. Crystal-clear water, held up by the basalt not far below, ran in a constant stream from pocket to pocket. The ground was springy beneath our horses' shod hooves.

Over the years a lush tropical rainforest had grown up among the jumble of black rocks. Bird life abounded—ducks, swans, geese, brolgas, jabirus, parrots of every description. Huge kangaroos basked in the sun, so secure in their birthright that they barely moved when disturbed.

The shorthorn cattle were fat and contented. Except for the ticks. Ticks and, until the eradication scheme put an end to it, TB.

In his Beechcraft Bonanza, Edgar delivered us after 5½ hours' flying to the Toomba airstrip where we were met with the news that Edgar's brother Ernest, the station manager, had broken his leg in a fall while mustering that morning. Ernest and his wife Robbie had gone to town in the ambulance and it seemed that I was 'mother' for the duration.

It was my first experience of the real outback. I was captivated.

Toomba was still run to a large degree in the old way of outback stations. Horseback was the only method of mustering. The horses were shod by their riders, each of whom had a string of half a dozen or so. Toomba was and still is famous for its bloodstock: Australian stockhorses descended from thoroughbreds.

A modern concession to time constraints meant that the horses to be used for a muster were taken out to the furthest yards and left there, while the musterers (or ringers) returned home to their quarters at the homestead each night in the Toyota driven by Ernest at a batting pace through the scrub. Each morning, after an exhilarating and somewhat hair-raising drive out to the yards just before first light, the horses were caught and saddled and the day's muster began.

The Barcoo poley saddles were equipped with a leather saddlebag on one side and a leather pouch holding a tin quart pot on the other.

Each morning in the huge station kitchen a sandwich lunch was made from last night's roast between thick slabs of high-top white bread with a generous dollop of chutney. This together with a couple of the station cook's homemade biscuits and a large piece of fruitcake was wrapped in as interesting a piece of newspaper as promised to provide some lunchtime occupation under a gum tree at midday.

An orange was tucked into the saddlebag; and to complete the day's supplies, a neat little envelope was deftly fashioned from a small piece of newspaper to hold exactly the right amount of tea leaves and sugar to pour in one swift motion into a boiling quart pot to make a perfect pot of tea. And, believe me, there is no cup of tea that is the equal of that brewed in a quart pot beside a small open fire made of sticks.

The cattle mustering completed, and the cattle yarded ready for dipping and reading the TB results, we had lunch and a siesta while the sun did its worst with North Queensland's unforgiving midday heat.

The unrelenting sun necessitated the wearing of long shirtsleeves and a neck scarf which doubled as a face mask in the dust of the yards. Leggings to protect our legs from the spear grass—which had put paid to the early settlers' attempts at establishing sheep in the north and was a torment to the unwary—were also essential. The outfit was capped off with a tall light-coloured Akubra felt hat—tall to create a protective pocket of air to insulate the wearer's head, of a light colour to minimise its attraction to heat, and shaped with steam to fit the owner's distinctive 'bash' which was a matter of intense pride.

While to me, inculcated with television's *The Cisco Kid* and *Bonanza*, a black hat meant baddies, in the north it meant a new chum—someone who thought it fitted the tough outback image, but was in fact ignorant of one of nature's basic rules.

I had been brought up with the regular killing of a sheep for our table. Offal was no mystery to me, and nor was fresh meat cut up from the corpse of a skinned sheep left hanging overnight in the yards. But my first experience of the killing of a beast to feed the dozen or so people on the station was something else altogether. There was a vast amount of meat! It had to be butchered expertly into the right cuts, rolled into roasts, with the brisket and silverside salted in coarse salt for a week or so in the meathouse.

John the 'cowboy', or gardener, grew vegetables, milked the house cow, and ran in the work horses in the morning on the recalcitrant and unwilling night horse. We were woken by the muted sound of his curses and the cracking of his whip through the morning mist that rose off the creek as, splashing through the creek and ignoring his colourful language, the horses did their utmost to circle back around him and avoid capture.

Everything in the north was big, starting with the personalities of the individuals who were relentless in their teasing of the southerner who actually thought that mutton was meat and who, it soon became obvious, lacked a great deal of other knowledge as well.

The station cook at Toomba, bless her heart, was a tiny, red-faced woman. Much to my mortification, since she didn't make much effort to make herself lovable, she shared my surname—though with the lack of a second 'l'. Mrs Paul ruled through our stomachs with a rod of iron. She had seen off three husbands and had no intention of finding a fourth; her pet galah, Peter, a bedraggled-looking creature, was her constant companion.

Peter was the only soul who was allowed to call her by her first name. He called out 'What're yuh doin' Lil?' all day long as she went about her business in the hot kitchen. 'Cookin',' she would reply, but 'What're yuh doin' Lil?' was Peter's only acknowledgement.

My first experience of the outback, Toomba has always held particularly special memories for me. After my two-month stay, I returned a couple of years later to work as a stockman for a year. First, though, I grew my CV with a stint as a station cook myself.

The Clarkes and Nimmos needed a cook at Fanning River Station, at Mingela in goldmine country between Charters Towers and Townsville. I managed to camouflage the fact that my experience in the kitchen was limited to mopping the floor when coerced, coupled with foggy memories of the valiant efforts of the domestic science teacher at the Dalby High School.

Somehow the intricacies around the science of boiling water had managed to elude me as well. This fact soon came to light when the men started to complain about the tea I made. It was weak and the tea leaves always floated; how was that?

Tea being the staple drink of the bushman—some of whom were known to put the tea leaves directly into their mug and pour the boiling water on top, chewing the tea leaves afterwards—this serious omission could have caused a revolt in the ranks. Chrissie Marsh, my friend and the governess of the four Nimmo children, quickly took matters in hand.

Chrissie had discreetly noted that cooking wasn't exactly my forte, either. I was mistress of a huge tin kitchen with a concrete floor and a gigantic table in the middle. There were several fridges and a giant stove. The expansive pantry held all manner of possible ingredients waiting only for someone with expertise to turn them into edible foodstuffs. It quickly became obvious that someone was not me.

I credit Chrissie with my somewhat fundamental, but substantial, cooking skills. While I consider myself now to be the best gravy-maker west of the Divide, I know that it is only due to Chrissie's tutelage.

She taught me how to cure the eggs with Kwik Kurit, how to make a boiled fruit cake, how to make a white sauce, and how to deal with the enormous rolled roasts that resulted from kill days when the whole kitchen table groaned under the weight of meat.

Killing the turkey for Christmas dinner was a team effort that took on a life of its own. Once again my inexperience got the better of the situation. I held the poor creature by its legs and looked the other way while Chrissie chopped. The head came off, but the wings started to flap so that the turkey and I took off in a shower of blood, me holding on for grim death like Mary Poppins to her umbrella.

Above all, Chrissie taught me how to prepare and deliver meals cooked almost to perfection, and simultaneously, to a hungry family of seven upstairs, and a hungry cohort of three or four stockmen in their separate dining room adjacent to my kitchen.

On one day—Tuesday 12 October 1971, a day that boasted a temperature of close to 100 degrees Fahrenheit in the non-air-conditioned kitchen—I baked two pumpkin cakes, a boiled fruit cake, a brownie, a chocolate slice and a batch of biscuits.

As well, in addition to a breakfast of steak and eggs for everyone, I cooked a stew and all the accoutrements including rice pudding and custard for a dozen people, and produced a lunch of cold meat and salad.

What's more, I made two enormous pots of very tasty tea for both morning and afternoon tea which I served with a selection of brownies and biscuits.

Not to mention that I did all the washing up from all these activities by hand.

My wage was $32 per week for a six-day working week.

*

Fanning River Station, east of the Burdekin, lay in the path of a new marauder. The cane toad. The progenitors of today's pests were twice the size that they are now, and possibly twice as repulsive. They often took refuge in the relative coolness of my kitchen—much to my horror.

The geological bedrock that secreted the gold that had caused the mad rush of my great-grandfather's time, and brought fabulous wealth to Charters Towers, also created fantastic limestone caves at Fanning River. If it wasn't for my claustrophobia I would have appreciated more the unexpected beauty of the underground formations that Chrissie showed to me on one of our days off.

We drove across a heat-seared landscape of anthills and prickly scrub. The ground was stony and dry, the ambient temperature well over a hundred. The landscape had a beauty of its own but it was certainly not inviting.

We reached a small rocky hillock covered with tussocky grass and parked the Toyota under the shade of a tree. Then Chrissie lit a lantern and we crawled on our bellies through a seemingly endless, pitch-dark aperture in the rock. I contained my growing panic only barely, especially when Chrissie fumbled with the lantern and it went out, leaving us in a close, dark underbelly. Thoughts of Tom Sawyer roiled in my head.

Eventually (the lantern relit) we could stand up and make our way into a cavern of limestone wonders. I chose to hear Chrissie's verbal description of the static 'waterfall' that could be accessed only by squeezing through a tight passage; and I was relieved to feel the heat and see the sunlight again when we wriggled our way out after an hour or so in the earth's belly.

We had a fantastic social life in the north. Tennis parties, picnic race meetings, horse sales, weekend house parties at neighbouring stations, flights in station planes to Dunk Island and the crocodile-infested Bowen River rodeo and campdraft, gatherings of the young at the ancient and favoured Excelsior Hotel in Charters Towers. I was under the drinking age of 21 but have no recollection of that making much difference to my presence among the throng in the pub.

By Christmas I returned to the south and some solid tractor-driving for Dad to bankroll my next expedition—a six-month stint in New Zealand.

I lie face-down on the expansive pine dining table at the Toomba homestead.

The right leg of my jeans has been pulled up to the knee, exposing an expanse of white calf from which protrudes just the very tip of a small, sharp object—the bottom end of a spear grass seed.

The barbed seed has entered my leg through my trousers during the day's muster, and viciously worked its way deep into my flesh. Contrary to the unwritten law of the north, I was not wearing leather leggings over my elastic-sided R.M. Williams Santa Fe riding boots.

I have taken some convincing but at last I have been made to realise, despite my disbelief and earnest protestations, that my options are limited. It seems there is only one way to save myself the pain and misery of a festering sore (and possibly, adds Edgar with a wicked gleam in his eye, the loss of my leg—although this is not a part of the story that I believe). The seed must be removed as soon as possible.

My efforts with the needle have been fruitless. What they say about the barbs of this horrid, tenacious little seed pointing backwards like a native spear must be true. The only way it can, and undoubtedly will, travel through my flesh is forwards and deeper into my leg.

The noises of the mellow tropical night provide a small, but only a small, distraction from my current predicament. I hear the rustle of flying foxes in the huge mango trees outside the open door. Mickey birds squawk and the leaves rattle as the bats disturb their rest. The cows in the distant yards are still settling down, the bossy ones scuffling for position in their endless pursuit of domination, those pushed aside calling their calves to follow them.

Cicadas call and frogs croak down in the reeds at the creek. A duck suddenly splashes in a panic, spooked by some predator. The night horse sneezes in the small paddock next to the house; Mrs Possum scuttles down out of her home in the ceiling of the storeroom to begin her night's hunting. It seems that the darkness is alive with activity as a multitude of animals settles for their night's rest, or leave their homes for a night's business, depending on their bent.

Close at hand is a more pressing concern. Pete Gardner has found the sharpening steel and is making an ostentatious show of noisily sharpening the carving knife in full view of my horrified gaze. His eyes twinkle behind his thick black glasses. 'Got to do this right,' he says, his hearty, distinctive laugh so contagious that I am caught between a desire to laugh with him and a need to object loudly to what is being planned for my leg.

He stops sharpening for a moment, and whisks a bottle of rum onto the table beside my face. 'This is your anaesthetic,' he says gleefully. 'Do you want it in the bottle, or out of it?'

Already smarting from the secret ignominy of having saddle sores on my backside from the long day's mustering, I indicate that the 'out of the bottle' option is my preference. Perhaps it will take the sting out of my bum. I lift my head and take a long swig straight from the bottle.

Pete excels in the role of lead distractor. Mike Wragge is operating assistant, taking a firm grip on my flailing leg. Syd Miller holds a vial of antiseptic. With several quick motions, cursed lavishly by me every step of the way, Edgar digs the seed out with the tip of his pocket knife. 'Swab, swab!' he calls as I howl in protest.

It's over. The seed is out. I won't ride out again without leggings.

CHAPTER 12

TRAVELLING LIGHT

Got a griffin in my closet and I let him out for tea
At half past five on every other Thursday.
He's not very big only nine foot four
But he's good at keeping down the weeds
And blocking up the doors.
My parents think him just another riddle
Like country ways
And quiet days
Inside tall forests to gypsy fiddles.

—Robin McGovern, Glenhope,
New Zealand, 1972

I set off for New Zealand in February 1972 for an indefinite period. I had the princely sum of $100 in traveller's cheques and $45.88 in my bank account. This was supplemented by the sweet ignorance of youth, the belief that everything would work out just fine, and the understanding that all that I needed would appear at the right time.

At least someone had pointed out to me that it was a good idea to buy a return airfare. The airfare had cost me $200 return. My sleeping bag, in contrast, had cost me $9.90. These days those costs are just as likely to be the same as each other.

I was met at the Auckland airport by my good friend and cousin Bina White (also descended from great-great-grandparents William and Jane) and our friend Sue Alexander. A sophisticated pair of young women, the difference in our approach to travel and indeed to life was immediately evident in our attire; Sue had a very glamorous white full-length kangaroo-fur coat for the New Zealand cold. She never appeared on any morning, despite the vicissitudes of our travelling conditions, looking less than having stepped out of the proverbial band box.

Bina was exactly the same, without the fur coat.

I, on the other hand, wore a felt scarlet-coloured hippie hat with a band of beads over a carefully cultivated Afro hairstyle which was created from my dead-straight black hair with the help of a hair-dresser's potent chemicals.

Alternatively, I wore a brow band à la Bob Dylan, though mine was a rolled scarf.

My main outfit consisted of purple hipster flared jeans, a cheese-cloth shirt and a leather thonging macramé and bead necklace that had been given to me by a pot-smoking hippie called Trevor on Magnetic Island.

I was far from home and trying out a different persona.

But despite the differences in our philosophical approach to image, Bina, Sue and I were old friends from similar backgrounds and worked well together as travelling companions.

Bina and Sue had already been in New Zealand for a month. They knew the ropes. They had acquired an ancient green Morris Minor which they had aptly named Windybottom. The car salesman who had sealed the deal on this particular purchase must have been still rubbing his hands with glee.

Windybottom had a few idiosyncrasies that are worth mentioning by virtue of the absolute skulduggery of the salesman who unloaded her on this hapless pair; it was undoubtedly his ilk that brought about a tightening of laws in the matter of roadworthiness certificates (no such thing in 1972, apparently). Her brakes worked only intermittently; she had a dodgy petrol pump; the starter motor was dicky but no matter, there were two of us to push-start her; and the ignition worked only with Sue's nail file (owing to the simple matter of the loss of her key).

This more than justified Sue's perfect fingernails. During the course of our travels she taught me how to use the file on my own nails, an improvement on nail-biting.

Thinking back on how we all happily loaded ourselves into the coffin on wheels called Windybottom, merrily push-starting her from Auckland to the Bay of Islands and back again, slowing down with the gears and stopping by pointing her up the nearest hill and applying the handbrake, makes me wonder at the miracle that we survived.

More than once she simply stalled in the middle of the highway. My diary records 'had flat tyre and steering wheel fell off' as if such an occurrence was nothing out of the ordinary. And nor was it, with respect to Windybottom.

The brakes failed, with me driving, at the top of the range going down to Rotorua. Not to worry; with Bina delivering a rapid-fire report on the status of the cars careening towards us from the left, Sue keeping a fraught vigil to the right and shouting out instructions, and me desperately working the gears, we managed to slip through the traffic at the T-junction without getting wiped off the map.

After Windybottom's timely demise we moved on to a different set of dangers—hitchhiking. We had to get around somehow and until friends lent us a car for a tour of the South Island, by thumb was how we travelled from Rotorua to Wellington. Sue's fur coat must have been an incongruous sight beside the road. My two attractive and glamorous companions no doubt accounted for many of our lifts.

It goes without saying that New Zealand is a magnificent country. In 1972, provided one stuck by certain golden rules, hitchhiking was quite an acceptable way to travel. It was a great way to meet people, and they were in the main hospitable, generous and kind.

Our travels coincided with Germaine Greer's historic trip to New Zealand on a wave of controversy and fuss. She had just published *The Female Eunuch* to a mixed response. Strenuous efforts had been made to stop her from travelling to New Zealand and spreading the message of female equality that threatened the very comfortable status quo of 50 per cent of the population of the Western world. Naturally, all the publicity about the controversy resulted in young people attending her lectures in droves.

We went, of course, since we were in Wellington on 9 March when she addressed a wildly enthusiastic throng at the university. We followed the demonstration of uni students that surged down the main street to the police station calling out 'fuck' and 'bullshit' in protest against Dr Greer's prosecution for using bad language.

As we stood somewhat nervously, awed by the audacity of the natives—who by this stage had run out of steam (someone had spied a potplant in the window of the police station and everyone started calling out rather foolishly 'The fuzz are growing marijuana')—a window opened in an office building way above the crowd and a bucketful of water was thrown out.

I, an interested if not totally innocent bystander, who hadn't said 'fuck' once and had no intention of doing so for fear of being arrested on the spot, took the full pail on my Afro.

It dampened my enthusiasm and my cheesecloth shirt. But the experience of being (sort of) part of the demonstration and seeing Germaine Greer in person was exhilarating.

Friends lent us a car to travel around the South Island. This mode of transport was much more reliable than either our thumbs or our poor deceased Morris Minor friend. We floated around the magnificent countryside, absolutely agog at the glaciers, ice and snow and man-made embellishments from one end of the island to the other.

Some of the costings I recorded at the time make an interesting contrast with today's figures, not only in their relationship to today's figures but in their relationship to each other. A new muffler for the car cost us $6.50. A new tyre was $17.50. It cost $2.50 for the three of us to stay at a motor camp in Queenstown for two nights, while it was $3 each for membership of the Youth Hostels Association, but 60 cents per night to stay once a member.

My wages when I started a job, after Bina and Sue returned home, were $25 per week in addition to my full board and keep.

I discovered that there is no better way to get to know a country than working and living with a family. It was easy to suspend my hippie identity for two months and become nanny, housemaid, stud record keeper and farm worker for Gavin and Wendy Falloon and their young family on their Angus cattle stud at Taumaru, Masterton in the Wairarapa region.

While it was vastly different from the Australian bush, it was anything but tame. Climate and landscape play as big a part in New Zealand's rural life as they do in Australia, but from a different perspective.

Where heat, dryness and distance were issues in North Queensland, being adequately dressed to combat the effects of freezing rain and snow were matters of more than mild concern to me in rural New Zealand. Horses were not necessarily shod, but riding involved scaling such vertiginous landforms on the Falloons' coastal property, Pukunui, where we occasionally went to muster, that it was necessary to climb off our horses and scramble along hanging onto their tails just to gain some of the heights.

Gavin had a team of six sheepdogs—huntaways and collies—without which mustering would have been impossible in this wild country. He managed each dog with its own particular set of whistling, from one hilltop to another. It was absolutely magic to watch them respond to him. The sheep would burst out of impenetrable scrub on some distant hilltop, tiny figures; the only sound above the wailing of the wind and the crashing of the nearby ocean was Gavin's whistling and the distant barking of the dogs hot on their tails. His dog team could have been the prototype for Murray Ball's endearing 'Dog' in *Footrot Flats*.

My childhood friend Virginia (Rosie) Reynolds joined me in New Zealand and we embarked on possibly the most foolhardy of the adventures that were gradually adding layer upon layer to my learning in the School of Life.

It was winter, it was New Zealand, we were ill-equipped, short on funds and low on adequate warm clothing, but we decided it would be a good idea to hitchhike around the South Island—about as close to the South Pole as you can get and still be on land. I had recently turned 19 and while, naturally (it was after all the 70s), I believed in the goodness of the world in a land of Peace and Love, 'wet behind the ears' would probably have been a more apt description of me.

We discovered that it's not just in strangers' cars that hitch-hiking poses dangers. It is when and where they drop you off. When we found ourselves benighted on a remote mountain road in a tiny settlement with no youth hostel and plummeting temperatures, we were lucky that the local vicar let us sleep out of the weather in the church hall.

We pressed on the next day and were dropped off at the entrance to a mountain pass where we sat for two hours in the snow, freezing, waiting for a lift, nary a human soul or habitation within cooee.

We ice-skated, one of a growing list of 'firsts', on the frozen mountain lake, Lake Idah. Our enthusiasm for skating was tempered when a nearby skater disappeared with a small shriek of dismay through a patch of thin ice, emerging soaked, bedraggled and semi-frozen.

Even when we arrived eventually at Mt Cook a couple of weeks later, bedraggled and semifrozen ourselves as well as broke and hungry, we still had no notion of the thin ice on which we so blithely skated daily.

It had taken four rides to make the distance up the snow-lined gravel road that led to the Mt Cook settlement. Once there and ensconced at the youth hostel we lived off milk that had been left outside the back door of the general store, and which had frozen during the night. Usually the crows had risen before us and pecked away the cream that had burst the silver tops off the bottles as they froze; but no matter, we were happy to share.

This milk, its price kept down by the New Zealand government's subsidy of the dairy industry, would otherwise have been thrown away. At 4 cents per glass bottle it was still beyond our means until we found a job. Once we mixed it with a packet of dried mashed potato we fortuitously found in Rosie's backpack and heated it on the stove at the youth hostel. It was good to have 'solids' for a change when the alternative was nothing.

Even the water in the toilet bowls at the youth hostel froze. Whether or not it was an unusual winter in 1972, we certainly learned about life at another extreme. And self-sufficiency. Undeterred by mere physical considerations, our hunger satisfied with milk and reconstituted mashed potato, our priorities ran to perfecting our skills at playing pool at the youth hostel where we worked out how to fiddle with the trigger to release the spent balls so we didn't have to pay.

Eventually, and not without an indecorous amount of grovelling to the manager, which involved actually getting down on our knees and begging, we managed to get jobs as housemaids at the Hermitage Resort. In that role, to our amusement and horror, we had to dress up as hybrid Swiss maids in a uniform consisting of a gathered tartan skirt, a white frilly blouse and a frilled white apron.

Rolling mosses gather no stone. As we travelled around, staying in youth hostels and on the floors of people we met, we were occasionally offered a joint of the ubiquitous pot. Everyone fiercely believed that pot itself was innocuous and harmless; it was only the fact of the company it brought you into, we were told, which led you onto heavier drugs like LSD. As well, those money-grabbing people in the government, whose duty it was to spoil anything that looked like fun, banned it because it was easily grown at home, thus dudding them out of their cut in the way of duties.

I have since learned quite differently on all those counts. I now understand just how dangerous a drug is the marijuana grown hydroponically today—so much more so than that on which I had the odd puff in 1972.

At any rate, I decided not to incorporate it permanently into my lifestyle.

The six months I spent in New Zealand added a great deal of grist to the mill of my experience.

Hitchhiker's Guide to New Zealand 1972

There are a few golden rules associated with hitchhiking.

To start with, only do it in New Zealand, where your parents don't know what you are up to.

Next, if you are a girl, only do it in pairs. More than two of you causes problems with attracting a car that has room for three; only one of you causes problems attracting a car driven by the wrong kind of person.

Third—even if there are three of you, don't get into a car with more than two people in it, and one of those must be a woman; and never, ever accept a lift with people you meet in a pub.

We are about to break most of these rules, and live to regret it.

It's a wet and windy New Zealand day: 6 March 1972, if you want to be precise. The three of us and our suitcases take up our position together in the morning, on the road leading out of Mount Maunganui. Thumbs aloft, we are armed with ignorance, faith, and high hopes of getting all the way to Napier by nightfall.

We get four lifts to Gisborne—that's a good run in the world of hitch-hiking. But at Gisborne, it starts to rain. So we go to a pub.

There we meet three blokes. They seem nice, respectable sort of fellows; they're fun, too. They offer us a lift across the lonely mountain road to Napier. 'Yeah!' we say. 'Yeah, great!' And into their car we cram, three on the bench seat in the front, and three in the back. No silly new-fangled notions like seatbelts in 1972.

It's a great trip; great scenery. Everybody is laughing. At the top of the pass, miles from anywhere, it begins to drizzle. Then, for some reason we can't quite fathom right away, our driver pulls into a layby.

'Right, girls. You know the drill.'

'No, we don't know the drill. What drill?' we reply as one.

'Fork it, or walk it.'

Very quickly the atmosphere in the car moves from fun to fraught. It could be described as more than mildly hysterical. One of us jumps shrieking out of the car and runs in the drizzling rain around to the back door and gets in. The person closest to the other door in the back seat has no choice but to get out and move into the front. This goes on for quite some time, a sort of grisly 'then they all rolled over and one fell out' routine accompanied by our tearful objections and protestations.

The blokes seem to realise that they have misjudged the situation, but they can't backpedal without losing face. Nor, it seems, do they want to force the issue. Lucky for us. Well, sort of lucky. They refuse to start the car until there is some kind of compromise.

Suddenly we hear the sound of a car coming along the lonely road. It's like music to our ears—it's the first car that has been along the road since we reached the impasse on the mountain pass. We run to the edge of the highway and flag down a little fat middle-aged bloke who has been until this moment happily motoring along in an MG, whistling a jaunty tune. With a mixture of gabbled words, sniffles and tears we convey our sad predicament. Our three captors look on sullenly.

'What—do you want me to fight them?' says little chubby chappie anxiously, eyeing off our three lusty young Lotharios with more than a modicum of dismay.

'No, no,' we reply. 'Just get us OUT OF HERE!'

His happy day ruined, our unwilling knight in shining armour takes down the roof of his MG. He has to; it's the only way we can possibly fit in. Our would-be rapists gallantly help him to stack our baggage in every available square inch of space. We three girls hop in, sobbing. One of us is ensconced in the passenger seat, nursing a suitcase. The other two sit up on the boot, our baggage under our feet.

We are driven like beauty queens in a parade all the way back to Gisborne. The next day, rattled by our experience, we take a safer option and jump the guard's van of a goods train. We get to Napier in four hours.

CHAPTER 13

DRAW THE CHILDREN HOME

AN EVENING PRAYER
Abide in this, Thy home, the very centre
Of all that Love can give, tho' far they roam;
Shed forth Thy light on all who here would enter,
And draw the children Home.

—Kit Mylne, 1934

Even though I was now a Woman of the World, once back in the somewhat bemused arms of my family on the Oakey Creek, chameleon-like, I put my hippie beads in a trunk and resumed the persona that fitted in with country mores.

There was no point in rocking a boat that was already showing signs of taking on water. Mum and Dad were obviously wearying of the struggle on the land. In the way life has, there had been no time for their war wounds to properly heal before they were thrust into the new responsibilities that go with parenthood and wresting a living from farming.

This coupled with years of drought left Dad, war hero, feeling much less like the hero he might have been if a string of bad years on the farm had not taken such a toll on his spirit. And his strength.

Meantime, while most of Mum's chicks were off in the world, and her 'baby' was ten and still very much a child requiring her attention, Mum had had enough of country life and was starting to unravel.

For me, home wasn't the same as it had been; I wasn't the same as I had been. My childhood home echoed with the absence of my missing sisters and the emptiness of the workman's cottage where my playmates Johnny and Jenny and Greg, their baby sister Lou and their parents Doug and Mary McIntosh used to live.

It must have been emptier still for Mum and Dad, with no son to take over the farm. What was the point? They were, no doubt, wondering where the busyness of their lives had gone to. Where, in fact, their lives had got to at the ages of 50 and 55. It's a common theme. In those days the cure was 'stiff upper lip'. It didn't always work.

Dad realised that it was time to sell up and started to take the necessary steps.

When I came back from New Zealand I added house-painting to my CV. As was our wont in those days, wanting to be fashionably brown-skinned and knowing full well that we would never become old to regret our foolish disregard for the care of our skin, my sister Prue and I stood on the scaffolding in our underwear in the hot sun and painted the exterior of the home she and her husband JJ had built on their sheep property at Deepwater in New South Wales.

We ended up brown, the house ended up white, and all parties involved thought that was quite a satisfactory result.

Now, of course, when my skin specialist clucks his tongue over the ruined skin on my back and shoulders, I rue the days spent frying on beaches and lawns, on horseback and on top of the science block at school, when I lay in the sun until my skin blistered, peeled off, blistered again and peeled again. All in pursuit of a particular idea of beauty.

In much the same way we thought that nature was an infinite resource, that the roadsides would accommodate and hide the rubbish we habitually and thoughtlessly tossed out our car windows, and the oceans and skies would swallow up our effluent.

My final job for that year was for a couple of months at Moorlands Hereford Stud at Kulpi, north of Oakey and not far from home. There, more painting was called for, along with other jobs, in preparation for their annual bull sale.

Laurette Reynolds at Moorlands was a woman of tremendous energy and vitality. Keeping up with her marathon work ethic was almost beyond me, even though I was 19 and she was over 50. Her prize-winning garden was, I discovered, the result not simply of the subtropical climate and fabulously fertile volcanic soil at Kulpi.

It was maintained and continually expanded with a mammoth amount of effort and planning. Mrs Reynolds was aware of every portion of the great plan of her wonderful garden—what needed watering, what needed weeding, what annuals needed planting, what needed pruning, what required fertilising with barrowloads of manure from the bull sheds.

The stud's jackeroos helped and while I was there for a couple of months I helped, too. But Mrs Reynolds bested me for sheer energy and determination. Once her day's work was done outside, she kept the accounts and stud books inside.

A teacher does not have to set up a classroom and enforce the discipline of pedant. Just observing the outcome of cause and effect, effort and result, underpinned by the never-say-die attitude of a woman who never seemed to let a complaint even form in her head, let alone leave her lips, taught me a salient lesson about life.

Laurette Reynolds's attitudes had been forged in the bush (she was a Drysdale from Augathella), were typical of her ilk, and continue to serve her well in her old age.

Moorlands was run to a large extent with a staff of jackeroos from all over the world. They created a small Commonwealth of Nations at Kulpi and it was there that I came into contact with the archetypal Pommy jackeroo.

He was probably an honourable or a lord, and I don't remember his name, but he was an Eton lad with a very toffee Pommy voice. He developed an incongruous friendship with another of the jackeroos, a typical Aussie local yokel, rough as guts and with a refreshingly colonial disregard for class distinction.

They became known around the ridges as Eton and Drinkin'.

One evening at one of our marathon parties at the jackeroos' quarters, someone started a fight with Drinkin', who was more than somewhat under the weather and unable to defend himself because of the unfortunate circumstance of having a broken leg. Eton went beetroot red in the face and, drawing on his bellicose ancestry that doubtless went right back to William the Conquerer, took the miscreant by the scruff of the neck and the seat of his pants and threw him down the stairs.

As he stood in the doorway, backlit by the bare lightbulb in the sparse kitchen, dusting the last unsavoury molecules of the wrong-doer's clothing from his elegant hands, he called out in his exceedingly upper-class English voice, 'Now, you fucking get out of here and fucking stay out. And don't fucking come back.'

We were more than mildly surprised.

*

Around that time there was a spate of farming accidents involving young men in our wider group of friends, illustrating just what a dangerous lifestyle they led.

One friend, Rodney, almost lost his foot in a cotton harvester. Another, my neighbour Angus, came horribly to grief with a grain auger and spent a long time in hospital with stomach injuries.

Steve did a serious injury to his arm but the worst of all was Will, who suffered the trauma of having a tractor overturn and pin him down for hours until he was discovered and rescued with horrific injuries to his torso.

In the same decade Fraser lost his right arm altogether in a hay-baling machine.

They say that once you have crossed north over the Tropic of Capricorn you are always drawn back. The north beckoned again and I was asked to ply my cooking skills, as well as my mustering skills, on another North Queensland station. This time at Fig Tree Station in the Collinsville district.

Fig Tree was a pioneer cattle property managed by a tough man called Rhett Webb. When Rhett was a child of seven, his father had taken him out on a long muster one day and deliberately 'lost' him in some thick scrub miles from home.

With his father, unbeknown to Rhett, keeping a watchful eye on him, Rhett had to find the nerve and skill to navigate his way home on his pony. It was much like throwing a child in the deep end of a waterhole, which was quite an acceptable way to teach a child to swim in those days. It certainly gave Rhett a crash course in some fundamental bush lore.

Thus there was no sympathy to be had for me when on a scorching December's day I lost a beast during a muster. I was mad with thirst, having gone without a drink of water for six hours and ridden about 30 miles over rough country behind a mob of cattle. One old cow must have left a calf behind because she kept trying to double around behind me. Eventually I let her go in some thick scrub as I figured I would lose them all if I chased off after her.

As I waded dramatically into a dam and fell fully-clothed into its muddy waters like the explorers Burke and Wills, thirst-crazed and gulping the water recklessly on my arrival at the meeting point with my contribution to the mob, Rhett wanted to know why I was one cow short!

As a woman it was expected that I would work all day in the saddle, and cook for five (relaxing!) men once we got home. Which I did. The rewards were manifold as the weekends were once again taken up with race meetings and visits to far-off destinations in station planes. So commonplace was light-aircraft travel as a mode of transport that one young manager rolled out of bed the morning after a dinner party and flew his guests (including me) back home to Fig Tree in his Cessna 182 while wearing his pyjamas.

There was only ever one possible place to be at Christmas and that was home with my family. I was duly transported back to the south by Scotchy Walker in his Cessna just one week short of Christmas.

My family celebrated in the usual desultory 104 degrees Fahrenheit, without the comfort of air conditioners which simply had not become domestic appliances. Mum slaved over a hot turkey with all the trimmings in the midday heat.

Christmas always meant a special gathering of the Protestants of the district at the tiny Anglican Church in Bowenville. When we were young, the service was able to commence only after the Paulls arrived and Prue dashed inside to remove the green frogs from the church organ.

Our neighbour Michael Hirst was famous for his booming voice and enthusiasm for singing, Christmas carols being a particular favourite of his. I am sure the whole of the small town of Bowenville braced itself for the onset of his dulcet Yorkshireman's tones as he sang his own esoteric words to the well-known tunes. 'Hero my dog has fleas' was one of his favourites, which he sang at the expense of the dignity of the Paull family dog who did, indeed, often have fleas, much to our chagrin. Then once the vicar decided we'd had enough of being Nearer my God to Thee, and the service took off along more traditional Christmas lines, we learned that contrary to popular myth the shepherds had actually washed their socks by night, all seated round a tub, when (no doubt to their immense surprise) a bar of Sunlight soap came down and they began to rub.

It was all good fun in the spirit of Christmas.

Our wider family always gathered on Boxing Day at either the Mylnes' house in Toowoomba or at Yarrabin. Each year our grandmother Norn lined up the nine grandchildren on top of the garden fence and took a photo. Then, when the garden fence could no longer take the strain of our growing bodies, we congregated on the front steps.

Afterwards, we played Twister, hookey, quoits and ping-pong in the heat.

They were memorable times.

As we bid adieu to 1972 change was in the air. In the new year my parents sold Yarrabin to a young couple starting out in life, Berry and Di Freshney, and moved to Toowoomba. I stayed at Yarrabin for what would prove to be my last few weeks at my childhood home.

I stand at the blue back gate, next to the Norfolk Island hibiscus with its lovely pink flowers and horrible brown spiders. I ignore them now, because I am surveying my childhood domain.

Tears blur my vision. Soon, as the memories come up with the feelings that belong to each sacred place, they will course down my cheeks. I have just learned that Mum and Dad intend to sell Yarrabin. This then, is goodbye; the grand farewell. I am leaving tomorrow.

I turn my back to the creek, which is timeless. Rather, it is the man-made things that draw me to them to pay my last respects. They resonate with long-gone voices; reek of sweat and toil, hope and heartbreak. They teem with the shrieks and laughter of children, gone now. Mine, my sisters' and cousins'; the McIntosh kids'.

The gate squeals, then bangs shut behind me with a click as I set out for one last stroll around my erstwhile kingdom.

Here is the chicken hutch where we created the headquarters for our club, the Three Jays—John, Jenny and Jane; it sits askance now, dilapidated, disused. How quickly nature claims its own! The club is long forgotten; John, Jenny and Jane have grown up and gone their various ways.

And now the machinery shed with its workshop attached. The workshop was a holy place, a place forbidden to children with their prying little fingers and tendency to 'borrow' tools and forget to bring them back. It was a man's domain; here, Dad and Doug worked together with their heads bent over vices and greasy workbenches, doing mysterious things with tractor parts and oily bits of metal and all the while talking, talking.

'Your father will never die as long as my husband lives,' says Doug's wife Mary to me many, many years later.

Teary-eyed, Doug, keeper of the war stories that we were denied as daughters, looks on. 'Did you know this?' he says, sharing a trinket from the treasure chest of knowledge about my father that he keeps close to this heart.

'No,' I reply. 'No, I did not know that. He never told us those things.'

Ah, the loss!

I turn my gaze from the silent workshop and wander through the cool darkness of the huge machinery shed. The giant doors strain against their tethers in the breeze, their faint clang filling the empty silence in this once-busy space. The header stands idly, waiting for a harvest that may or may not come; such is life on the land. The old red truck, with its mechanical hand still intact and in current use even though it has been superseded by a modern invention, the indicator, sits patiently. Thus has it sat many, many times in the queue at the railway siding at Malu—in the early days weighed down with bag upon bag of wheat and then in later years with its bulk bin filled to the brim with golden grain awaiting testing for quality and moisture, then decanting into the amorphous well of bounty being augered relentlessly under the receiving grill in the weigh station, lifting the rich offerings of the Darling Downs up into towering silos awaiting in their turn, decanting into trains on the western line, heading east to the mills and ports.

The silence rings in my ears now. I sniff the air and remember the seasons when the noise of mice in this shed was so deafening it defied all other sounds; the smell of them still lingers. Plague mice. They teemed everywhere—underfoot, up and down the tin walls which reverberated under their myriad feet, their impetus launching them upside down across the underside of the cavernous roof as they ran in their millions, the shed a giant treadmill ringing to the tumult of their endless energy.

I remember the excitement in the pit of my stomach and clutching my ears with the sudden deafening bellow of the header roaring into action, Doug pumping the accelerator, raising and lowering the giant comb to test its readiness for work.

Outside now, and here is, still, the diesel tank sitting on its long legs. I chuckle wryly as I remember how Lambie, a particularly bumptious pet, used to bail up us kids on the tank's ladder. And across a patch of gravel road, the spot where the Bomb stood—Dad's old original 1929 Chev ute, abandoned and become a favourite plaything in spite of the spiders it harboured.

And here right beside where the Bomb once stood mouldering are some 44-gallon drums of petrol. What fantastic playthings they became once they were empty, huge unicycles on which our bare feet ran and ran as we raced each other up and down the dirt road. This homeward stretch of road, where we once set off on expeditions on our ponies—slow on the outward journey, bolting home on the inward—where we used to sit down and watch the ants plying their trade routes. Where Johnny and I regularly set up our galah trap, a wooden box propped up with a stick and some grain scattered in a trail leading into and under it, a long piece of string attached and us sitting at the other end, trying to be very still and quiet, not realising that any galah with half a brain would get its grain from one of the ubiquitous piles out in the safety of the open.

On this stretch of black dirt road I fell off my bike while doing my first no-hands, and took all the skin off my cheek so that I had to stay home for a week. There was an upside. I, a huge sticky bandage glued to my cheek, got to see Princess Alexandra arrive on the plane in Oakey while all my sisters were at school.

Across this road the occasional koala would amble with its ungainly gait, warily changing trees.

In the Wet the whole 3-kilometre length of this road turned into a bog. We either stayed at home then, or, if we had been out and had to get home, Dad braved its stickiness and gunned the old Ford Customline NEJ336 for all she was worth. When she was overcome, after slipping and sliding and roaring, going further and further down into the muck, making a rutted mess of the road, till she stuck fast in the mud, then we little girls got out and pushed. Afterwards, mud-spattered, resplendent in itchy wheat-bag raincoats, we trudged home in the rain while Princess Mum waited in the car for Dad to bring the tractor to collect her.

Today, though, it's dry. And hot. I wander around my former fiefdom scuffing at the dirt, stooping to pick up a clod of Darling Downs soil and smell its goodness. The sounds and memories of the past run like a newsreel through my head. Today they will all be carefully packed away, consigned forever to that part of my memory which is what constitutes being me. All safe in my heart to take out and inspect at will.

It's sad, this saying goodbye. But all the same, the memories are a living thing.

Never again will I live on the blacksoil plains.

CHAPTER 14

WIDE BROWN LAND

In early January 1973, two months short of my 20th birthday, I set off for the last time from the sanctity of the Oakey Creek for another adventure.

This time I went with two mates, Rosie Reynolds and Jenny Waddell, affectionately known as 'Jenny Wren'. We crammed all we needed, and much that we didn't, into Rosie's little Toyota Corolla (named 'Titalota' or 'Titty' for short, by Rosie's brother-in-law Quentin McLean) and sallied forth to discover our own wide brown land.

It was to be a working camping trip to wherever we got, with Perth the ultimate destination. We weren't particularly familiar with the intricacies of camping so each of us contributed according to our personal priorities towards the comfort of the trip.

Rosie's contribution was the car, without which we would have been very much stuck at home; as well, Rosie packed a plastic blow-up canoe and a paddle (well, why not?). Jenny Wren had a blue two-man tent, without a fly, for a little privacy and to protect us from the weather. Not that, as we discovered, a tent without a fly does much in rain. But the southern regions of Australia where we were headed had a Mediterranean climate, which meant winter rain, so we didn't have too much misadventure on that score.

I brought a blow-up lilo, which was actually meant to be a mattress for me but which, in the absence of pillows for any of us, served us as a three-person pillow. The remainder of our bodies just had to put up with the comfort of Mother Earth—with the plastic floor of the tent beneath us, the roof of the tent between us and the weather.

We soon found that dressing in the tent was awkward, as was negotiating our way into 'bed' each night. But youth is indomitable. The three of us scrambled into our two-man tent each night like puppies, lying either on or in our sleeping bags, our three heads on my lilo just inside the door. The stars were our night-light, and sleep overtook each of us in mid-sentence as we chattered and giggled our way to meet our rest.

Many was the night when one or other of us discovered, too late, that a small stone had been overlooked in our careful sweeping of the site before we pitched the tent.

It would be an interesting experiment to try to fit the three of us into the same two-man tent now, 40 years later!

Rosie had answered an ad for factory workers in Berri, South Australia. They were expecting us in mid February and we were off to make our fortunes in the Riverina.

We were hopelessly inadequate to the task of pitching our tent at Yamba, on the New South Wales north coast, on the first night of our expedition—so many little strings and pegs and half-posts that required putting in the right place, with coordinated pulling and banging. We couldn't make head or tail of it, and got in a terrible tangle. The two blokes who came to our rescue, and then witnessed the three of us climbing into something not much bigger than a dog kennel, must have been somewhat sceptical about our chances of making the distance—whatever that was.

We had set off in tandem with another carload of friends—Susie

Shaw, Rob Chandler and Chris Selby. They were doing a smaller version of our grand tour in Susie's red Torana. Getting six of us organised and pointed in the same direction each morning proved to be something of a logistical nightmare. Our car spent a lot of time waiting for theirs so when they headed inland for the nation's capital, and as we were heading for Melbourne anyway, we decided to stick with the coast route.

After one last chat across the lanes in a Sydney traffic jam, we set off on our separate ways—the other three heading west and us hugging the great ocean road like erstwhile beach bums set on ruining our skins a bit more under the Australian sun.

To this end my lilo proved useful on another count—floating lazily on the sea under the blazing sun.

It is amazing to consider that all our travelling was done without the link to home so easily provided nowadays by mobile phone. Our parents never knew exactly where we were, and our news from them was intermittent according to which major town we planned to eventually pass through. Their letters were addressed 'post restante' to post offices or friends and relations we anticipated visiting along the way. Our postcards and long, descriptive letters with news already a week old were their only reassurance that we were still safely on the road.

We had a ball. Footloose and fancy-free, it was much like a smaller version of Cliff Richard's 'Summer Holiday'. We travelled from beach to beach, our direction set by whim and the wind. Occasionally we dropped in on Rosie's ubiquitous relatives and cadged a meal or a bed for the night. We were young, everything was fresh and new. And exciting.

Eventually we arrived in Melbourne.

For the first time since leaving Elvery's my office skills were called upon when I got a temping job as a clerk with Sportswear Distributors in Melbourne city. Pre-computer, using a dinosaur of a calculator, my work consisted of multiplying accounts and adding the results over and over all day, as well as a little typing. I was being paid for what would be done these days by computer in nanoseconds. All the same, I was a person in work. And my fundamental understanding of the workings of things administrative was growing with the application of such menial tasks.

The extremes of our cultural life in Melbourne included seeing the celebrated new movies, *The Adventures of Barry Mackenzie*, *Portnoy's Complaint* and *The Godfather*. We were given free tickets to see Kahmal's first-ever theatre appearance on 2 February. Then moving up the intellectual scale somewhat, I found it worthy of note that David Frost interviewed the Prime Minister's wife, the indomitable Mrs Margaret Whitlam, on TV on Monday 5 February 1973.

I met the manager of the Spanish dancers performing at the Princess Theatre, who invited me to see the show from backstage; when he followed up his invitation with the rather startling admission that he loved my 'beautiful tits' I decided that backstage with a hot-blooded Spaniard might not be the best place from which to watch the spectacle. I gave that one a miss.

My temp job ended with the offer of another temping job for Sportswear Distributors at Adelaide, and a permanent job in the Sydney warehouse of their new business, Witchery clothing, starting in May. So I had a plan for the distant future, and in the meantime our short careers as fruit workers were about to begin.

Mildura and picking grapes at a vineyard was our first stop. The living quarters we were shown to were filthy and forlorn. It wasn't an auspicious start.

Grape-picking looked so easy! We started work at 7.30 a.m. and already in the rows of vines there were hordes of women on their knees snipping off the bunches of grapes and whipping them into small aluminium baskets. The boss told us the 'average' person picked 120 such baskets a day, for the reward of 6 cents per basket. We did our sums; $7.20 each per day. A fortune! The three of us got down on our knees and started to pick. And pick. And pick.

The experienced women had already chosen the rows with the fattest, heaviest bunches. They chased us away if we looked like moving in on their territory. As they whisked off the grapes like the stoic automatons they undoubtedly were, their piles of baskets between the rows got bigger and bigger, while ours remained a pathetic contribution.

Our knees ached. Our backs ached. It was stinking hot. We started to get tetchy—first in general, then with each other. After a day's backbreaking work we earned a combined $13 and had filled 220 baskets between the three of us.

We definitely were not 'average'!

We stumbled back to the so-called 'living quarters', dispirited, exhausted and with hardly enough strength left to be able to bat away the cockroaches that infested our domain. When we were prodded awake next morning for another round of this awful undertaking, our eyes met across the filthy breakfast table and no words needed to be said.

By 10 a.m. we left Mildura and crossed the River Murray. By mid-afternoon we were at the beautiful little town of Berri in South Australia. We reported in to the Riverlands canning factory and were issued with hairnets, caps and rubber gloves. We were given keys to rooms at their hostel, and told to report for work at six the next morning for a nine-hour day. The hostel was basic, but an improvement on the vineyard's shameful offering.

We persevered with this job. While we didn't exactly get annual leave, we did manage the distance of ten days and left $60 richer each. The funds went directly into 'kitty', with which we paid all our communal costs—food, and the cost of running the car, including petrol when we remembered to put it in.

Running out of petrol seems to have been a problem that raised its head more than once. The problem was, service stations sold such nice ice-creams, hot chips and other delicacies that when one loomed into sight it often didn't occur to anyone to look at the fuel gauge. Consequently it was not unknown for us to zoom into a service station, buy an ice-cream each and a packet of chips, and zoom happily off into the wild blue yonder only to run out of petrol a few kilometres down the road.

Before we could take off across the Nullarbor (which at that time sported a challenging 270-plus miles of dirt road) our zigzag route took us back up into Victoria for a number of bull sales at famous Hereford studs.

We went via Lorne, as you do—it was a very short distance on the map. Anyway, I wanted to see the place to which my grandfather and his family used to travel by coach halfway across Australia from Charters Towers to Townsville, steamship from Townsville to Geelong, then the Cobb & Co coach from Geelong to Lorne for their summer holidays at the turn of the century. Having arrived at Lorne, they then lounged around dressed up to the nines in suits and bow ties and boater hats, presumably until it was time to do the whole marathon trip back the other way. We liked Lorne but I wasn't sure that I would have made the trip from Charters Towers especially.

March is stud sale time in Victoria. With Rosie's mum Laurette Reynolds making up a fourth person in 'Titalota' we went to the South Boorook, Yarram Park, Midgeon, Merindoc and Glenden sales. It was quite an experience, a sort of catching of breath in the last outposts of civilisation before setting off into the real unknown—destination Perth.

One memorable day in our travels west we arrived in a small town of unknown name too late to find the caravan park. So, encouraged by signs of habitation not too far and not too close, we pitched our tent in the darkness, hopped into our pyjamas, wriggled into the tent with our heads on my lilo and slept soundly.

We were woken late in the morning by traffic noises and on sticking our heads over the top of the lilo discovered that we had established our camping site on a traffic island in the middle of town. There were some tricky manoeuvrings and dashes to the car before we were clothed and westward bound again.

We empathised with Edward John Eyre as we crossed the Nullarbor, especially when (as was our wont) we called in at the service station at Ceduna to get ice-creams—and forgot about the petrol. Fortunately we didn't get too far out of town before Titty began to cough and we managed to crawl back and redeem ourselves.

We tackled the Nullarbor with a great deal of bravado. Over 270 miles of dirt punctuated by sharp stones on a completely isolated road is no small matter, especially in a Toyota Corolla loaded to the hilt in high summer and before the days of air conditioning. Luckily again we were fortified by ignorance of the dangers and made it across without mishap. In a spurt of industry we drove 600 miles and were rewarded with our first sighting of the Indian Ocean and the strange vista of the sun setting over the sea.

We were lured by the luxury of beds into hiring a caravan at the Sorrento caravan park for a week or so. Then our final foray into casual work landed us a job as car-washers at Lynford's Ford dealership in Perth.

Once again it was obvious to us that our fortunes were finally just around the corner. We were to be paid the princely sum of $4.50 for every car we cleaned. The place seemed to be full of cars that needed cleaning—we couldn't believe our luck!

There was a catch. The cars they wanted us to clean were the ones that had followed us across the vast dusty expanse of the Nullarbor Plain on the backs of huge semitrailers. In preparation for the journey they had been covered completely in a thick coating of wax. As we soon discovered, it was the devil's own job to get it off. The cars had to be spotless. And we were expected to clean the engine as well.

Day One, Tuesday 20 March, with three of us hard at work, netted four cars cleaned: $18 in total. Day Two was harder, for some reason. We took home $13.50. The next day we landed two station wagons which took all day to clean: $9. We were obviously not improving our skills. That day we decided that spending our days on the beach, going to Rottnest Island with a boating person we had met, and exploring Perth were, if not more profitable, certainly more enjoyable pursuits.

We were getting very experienced at quitting. We collected our meagre pay and spent the next day on the beach.

Perth is magnificent. Every Australian should visit it at least once—I was to visit a couple more times with the Stockman's Hall of Fame board within the next ten years. In fact, every Australian should probably cross the Nullarbor just to show solidarity with our cousins in the west, and to gain an understanding of the vast distances and arid landscape that define our national character.

The cliffscapes of the Great Australian Bight as evidenced at Eucla are to be seen to be believed. You can see the great Southern Ocean eating inexorably into our land, its heaving seas clawing at astounding landforms that bare their geological wonders in brave defiance of the inevitable. Bit by bit, rock by rock, surmounted by a landscape of such arid beauty that its cruelty can be easily forgiven, our land at its southern extreme is slowly crumbling into the sea.

We returned east in our valiant little car. I took up my station at a calculator as a trainee for Witchery in Adelaide. The others kept going and I followed them to Melbourne on a Greyhound bus a week later.

I am standing in my place in the Riverlands canning factory at Berri. It's a cavernous building. Huge. A combination of sickly sweet smells roils around me. Noisy, full of clanking and movement and wraith-like people going about their jobs; everything, machines and conveyor belts and people busy busy busy.

Everyone is wearing hairnets and funny little caps and rubber gloves. Including us; me and Rosie and Jenny Wren.

To my right are what seem like acres of conveyor belts loaded with pieces of fruit. To my left is a place I haven't been, the business end of what happens here—where the cans go after we have filled them up with their fruit and they get sealed up and cooked in the huge steaming vats. It looks like a forest of stainless steel machinery over that side. That's the men's domain. We women are doing the boring stuff over with the fruit.

The women ranged along the sides of the belts are sorting, sorting, their eyes only on the moving pieces of fruit in front of them, under the watchful eyes of the supervisors who stand on walkways that criss-cross above us.

I am on fruit salad, which is one of the better jobs. Actually I'm thinking about anything but my present task of plonking a small measure of processed (and somewhat colourless) cherries into each open can of fruit salad that goes past me.

I tasted a cherry yesterday when the supervisor wasn't looking. It tasted like cardboard. I spat it out (not in a can of fruit salad, of course). That's how awful it was. I usually love cherries.

Doing cherries is an important job. I like to think I have been elevated to this job because of my obvious talent for canned fruit salad, the final product. The truth of the matter is that sorting peach pieces on the peach conveyor belt yesterday afternoon gave me motion sickness. They couldn't afford the likelihood of my contaminating the fruit salad with carrots—and the rest of the contents of my stomach—so they moved me on to pineapple pieces, thence to the pinnacle of doler-out of cherries.

On our first day—the day before yesterday—I was tasked with taking bruises out of peaches. The peaches bobbed along in a river of moving water at waist level and I was going okay until the woman next to me cracked up.

I had been thinking that she seemed such a decent, simple woman— she had a rather vacant look about her—and that perhaps that was why she seemed to be okay with this sort of boring job. Then suddenly she started screaming, 'Enough, I've had enough,' and sobbing. The supervisor had to escort her out of the peach section and put her on something else.

That shook me.

It's pretty difficult standing all day; nine hours on wet cement, with half an hour off for lunch! I ask you! Anyway, I asked the supervisor if I could find a high stool and sit down—honestly, what difference would it make?— but no, definitely not, no sitting down.

Yesterday Rosie and I were together on pineapple pieces but they separated us because we were laughing so much. 'No fun' either, it seems.

My thoughts roam to last night in the communal bathroom in the women's hostel. I saw my first condom and it was—phew—it was eeeenormous! Someone had filled it up with water and hung it from the ceiling, so it was a huge misshapen thing that looked like a balloon but wasn't, with a funny pointy bit at the bottom. It hung almost to the floor.

At first Rosie and Jenny Wren didn't know what it was, either, but one of the other women said it was a condom. She thought we were trying to be smart, saying we didn't know what it was. Once we convinced her that we really didn't know, it was worse because then she thought we were a bunch of dills.

They're a pretty tough lot, the other women at the canning factory hostel. We realised straight away when we got there that it's best to keep a low profile.

It's absolutely stinking hot in the South Australian February heat so today I wore my yellow halter-neck top, the one I made, to work in the morning, without a bra naturally. It was lovely and cool and much more comfortable.

I still can't believe that the supervisor came stomping up to me mid-morning and frog-marched me back to the women's hostel to change into a proper shirt. She said the men were 'distracted from their work by my inappropriate attire'.

What?

So now here I am sweating away in a proper shirt and a bra, legs aching, plonking cherries into each can as it goes past on the conveyor belt. One can, another can, another can, another can. It never ends. Nine hours! And you know what our pay was yesterday for a day's work? $8.95!

I'm not sure how long we're going to last at this job.

CHAPTER 15

Maria Theresa

The Cracked Pot

The pot is cracked and though man tries in vain
To mend the cracks, the contents seep away—
Despite man's dire dismay. There still remain
The Potter, and the Water, and the Clay.

                                          —Paddy McCallum

The teacher who was put my way in 1973 came in an unexpected form. Marie Redman was the antithesis of everything and everyone I had known closely in my life until I started working as her office assistant in Sydney.

In contrast to my country background, she was city to the core. Contrary to my white Anglo-Saxon Protestantism, she was devoutly Catholic. Whereas my familiarity lay with horseback and the earth, the silence of wild places and the sounds of nature, hers was with trains, buses and concrete paths, the tall buildings of Sydney city with its endless discordant noise, and the hustle and bustle of city life with people, people and more people.

Marie was the great age of 27 to my 20 years. She was profoundly capable at her job. Whereas I, on the other hand, had basic office skills and not much else at all.

It would seem that when the manager Mrs Dehan had offered me the job when I temped for them in Melbourne, she had seen potential in me. The Clay was there; the Potter was yet to work her magic.

Witchery had only recently made its move into New South Wales from its origins in Melbourne. Offering a range of budget women's fashions that have since moved from strength to strength, it had begun its interstate march into the suburban shopping centres that were beginning to emerge in the new age of commerce.

While I was with Witchery they opened shops at Blacktown, then Roselands, then Merrylands and Liverpool. By the end of my 11 months with them there were 12 retail stores. Our job, Marie's and mine, was to record and reconcile the cash takings for each store.

My pay was $70 per week. A fortune.

Witchery's Sydney warehouse and office were in Kent Street, Sydney city, behind the Sydney Town Hall. The possie Marie and I shared looking out over the rest of the warehouse with its racks of clothes, where storeman Frank and clothing manager Maureen plied their trades, also looked out over St Andrew's Cathedral School. The street below was a favourite haunt for homeless men sunning themselves with their backs to the brick wall as they swigged the contents of bottles secreted in amorphous brown paper bags.

'White Lady,' said Marie. 'Metho and water.'

Now and then they stood up to have a pee in the laneway.

We sort of envied them at times as we sat at our desks, working our fingers to the bone.

*

I watched Marie with awe, knowing in my heart that I could never reach the pinnacle of her competence at office administration. There was nothing—nothing—that fazed her. There was nothing she did not handle in the way of office management with pert good humour and aplomb. Really, it took my breath away; in fact, it terrified me, to observe through watching Marie just how competent a juggler one had to be to keep the intricate cogs of a business turning smoothly.

As we worked, as Marie taught me everything I needed to know (and much more, if only she knew it!), we chatted and smoked Marlboros endlessly. I heard the story of her background and her life, so completely different from mine. She could have come from Mars as far as I was concerned. I was fascinated.

Marie was a convent girl, the first product of this remarkable female-power source that I had ever got to know closely. The nuns—who called her Maria Theresa—had goaded her when she misbehaved with the dreadful insult, 'You're the type who would marry a Protestant!' I found this quite startling as a form of insult, being a Protestant myself. 'And you know, I did!' said Marie, laughing, and although she was devoted to her husband Gary I think the taunt still stung.

But before her marriage, in the mid 60s when she was 21, Marie and her girlfriends—who came in to city jobs each day from the western suburbs on the train—used to go to Whiskey A-Go-Go in Kings Cross on Friday and Saturday nights. There they met American soldiers on R&R from Vietnam.

With pockets full of money and a determination to have a good time, the soldiers were an irresistible source of fun for the local girls. Every week or two there would be a new lot, fresh faces having a break from the trauma of war and splashing their leave pay on the girls who came to meet them.

Marie was a good Catholic girl. 'Make no mistake; there was no funny business. We just wanted to have fun,' she told me. 'And we did.'

Her stories resonated with me, so similar to my mother's tales of the American boys who took them dancing in Brisbane during the Second World War. I was fascinated that history had repeated itself 30 years later.

Marie and I both kept up with the fashions of the times. My get-up consisted of floppy-legged trousers and huge wedge clogs that raised my height by many inches, chunky jewellery, frizzed hair, brown lipstick and nail polish, and lashings of black Mary Quant eyeliner.

Marie, despite having a healthy head of hair, always wore a wig. I never saw her real hair. She always wore false eyelashes, false finger-nails, long skirts and huge wedge heels. I never saw her legs, either.

As we plied the tasks that have long since been handed into the care of computers, balancing the daily cash sales (no such thing as credit cards) of each store, adding up the ticket stubs from the sold items, then adding them up again using the company code which camouflaged their wholesale price, we yakked and yakked, and smoked and smoked.

Marie's fingers danced over the keys of her electric calculator as, in the haze of cigarette smoke, she told me about her amazing life. Our calculators sang their clumsy song all day—click, clack, whirr—our fingers a blur of movement. Our eyes never left the paperwork as we turned each stub over and entered our long lists of calculations.

'Gary and I have a steak, frozen chips and a cob of frozen corn every night for tea,' said Marie as her calculator struggled to keep up with her fingers. 'I go out and buy them at lunchtime and take them home on the train.'

'You can get corn fresh, you know,' I told her once, remembering sadly Dad's faraway vegetable patch and the sweetness of the corn he brought in and left on the kitchen bench for Mum to cook. 'It's delicious,' I said as I finished the Blacktown figures and neatly wrapped the stubs up with a fresh rubber band.

Marie was amazed. So, at lunchtime I bought her two fresh cobs of corn from the fruit barrow on George Street.

'We didn't like it,' she informed me next day, returning to her desk after lunch hour with more frozen cobs. 'Thanks all the same.'

For my part, I was so out of my depth in the city that I couldn't bring myself to step off the kerb to hail a bus, for fear of drawing attention to myself. Some mornings I walked all the way from Woollahra to the city along New South Head Road, if there was no one else at a bus stop who wanted to hail the same bus as me.

When I first moved to Sydney to take up my job, I lived alone in Aunty Peg Galwey's flat on Edgecliff Road, drowning in loneliness and fear of my alien surroundings. Then I moved into a hippy commune of sorts in a dilapidated old mansion called Hawthornden, at Woollahra.

Hawthornden had in its halcyon days been the residence for the managing director of P&O. Those days had passed, however, and a community of at least a dozen people now lived there, as well as a couple of goats, some geese and a very large Old English sheepdog.

The grounds were extensive, with a fabulous view over Sydney Harbour, and a grass tennis court. The only room in that fabulous place, now restored to its former glory, that was not taken up as sleeping quarters was the magnificent ballroom with its parquet floor. The current incumbents had each painted their rooms with whichever colour took their fancy; and none was dull. There was lime green and gold painted in the elaborate entrance and grand staircase. One girl had painted her room plum, with gold trimmings.

The room I took, which suffered rather horribly with damp and had once been a scullery, had been painted bright blue. On workdays I entered and left via the ground-floor window of my bedroom, since the fact of my job and the conservative clothing I wore to it attracted somewhat negative attention from the rest of the inhabitants.

My Hawthornden time was the beginning of the final vale to my hippie manifestations. I lived a double life. Each weekday I set out for work dressed in the garb of office clerk for a fashion distributor, and at weekends I flung this image aside and fitted in with the eclectic mob who were my housemates.

One of these was Steve, who was exempt from paying rent because he was a genuine hippie with tattered khaki trousers and a long beard. Steve lived on a wooden bench in the greenhouse, despite its lack of much of its glass. There, he spent much of the day sitting cross-legged, playing a Jew's harp. And, presumably, smoking pot. There's not actually much you can do in the way of music with a Jew's harp, but nonetheless I thought Steve was absolutely wonderful. And indeed he was a great guy. I often wondered what became of him. His girlfriend was a titled girl from England, called The Honourable Selina Something-or-Other.

One day a young, unmarried pregnant woman moved in. She was taking refuge from her Italian family in Adelaide who were insisting that she either have an abortion or give up her child for adoption. Neither option was acceptable to this brave young woman and, alone with the shame and derision of her family, unsupported by the father of her child, she fled to Sydney.

Antoinette had steadfastly refused to name the father of her child to her angry father, no doubt knowing that he would either kill him or force him to marry her. Nor did she divulge his name to us—or, for that matter, the fact of his impending fatherhood to him—until well after her child was born.

There was no form of social security support for unmarried mothers and I have no idea what she lived on. But I remember clearly the day her waters broke when we were playing tennis. Much to the bemusement of the staff at the Mothers' Hospital at Paddington, half of this huge and loving household went up there with Antoinette when she gave birth to her son. She brought her baby home to her extended family at Hawthornden.

That baby would be almost 40 by now.

My year in Sydney was a time of gathering knowledge and experience. While those served me well later, and I found a niche that strongly suited my skills in terms of my business career, I found city life intolerable.

There was a bloke, a lovely young man with a life firmly bound to the city, who wanted me to stay and make a life there with him. I couldn't do it.

I yearned for the earth under my feet, for quiet and nature.

I longed for the river gums with their untold tales of what they have seen while standing sentinel over the years, riveted in one spot as generations of creatures pass by them in a never-ending parade of endeavour.

I was hungry for the smells of horseflesh and dust and sunshine, the slow drawl and laconic humour of the country people with whom I was at my most comfortable.

Mum and Dad had moved into their new home in Campbell Street, Toowoomba. Mum was ill. Dad was at his wits' end. I was exhausted and heartsick. I needed to get away to a place where I could reconstruct my life.

I still hadn't had a job long enough to get annual holidays, but I'd had enough. Handing in my notice at Witchery (it wasn't so easy this time; they were very disappointed), breaking the heart of a young man who did not deserve such treatment, I packed my bags and caught an overnight bus to Toowoomba. I wept with a mixture of sadness and relief all the way to Quirindi.

I am sitting at my desk at the Witchery warehouse in Kent Street, Sydney.

A ribbon of sunlight streams across the top of the shadow that falls across my window. It noses its way down into the street below, where an ageless drunk sits on the pavement with his back to the brick wall of the school. His beatific expression as he lifts his face to the sun belies his desperate status of homelessness. Apparently without a care in the world, he takes the occasional swig from a bottle secreted in a brown paper bag between his outstretched legs.

He can't see me up above in the window across the street and nor would it matter to him, no doubt, if he could. With some effort he finds his way to his feet and weaves his way to the dubious privacy of the alleyway behind him. Fumbling, he undoes the string on his shaggy old pants and shapes up to the wall to have a pee.

A sound behind me as Marie returns to her desk. She has just been to the loo herself. The contrast between the two lifestyles, those of our pet drunk across the street with his alleyway dunny and ours in the comfortable surroundings of our workplace, is brought into stark relief. My imagination is working overtime.

Clearing her throat, Marie reaches for another package of shop dockets and prepares herself to do the figures for the Liverpool branch. She arranges the papers around her workplace—summary sheet, cash register roll held down with a bulldog clip, swing-tag stubs released from the constraints of their rubber band, fresh roll in the calculator. She reaches for a Marlboro, lights up, takes a puff, sits the fag in her ashtray.

Then in a calm, friendly voice she says, 'Hey, Jane, don't you just hate people who don't put a fresh roll on the toilet paper holder when they use up the last roll?'

No rancour. Puffing away with a little smile on her face, whizzing through a huge bunch of sales tickets on her adding machine, no more is said.

I have nothing to say in reply. It's a rhetorical question anyway. We both know I was the last person in there.

CHAPTER 16

THE BUSH AGAIN

Wind bloweth where it listeth
Our windows keep it out.
But when hard hail persisteth
It knocks the windows out.
Our blessings, while we've got them,
Are easy to forget
But when we haven't got them
And everything is wet,
We think of our redressings
While we bewail their lack,
And mean to count our blessings
If we ever get them back.
—Paddy McCallum

You can take the woman out of the bush, but you can't take the bush out of the woman. It was becoming something of a recurring theme. I had checked in at our new family home in Toowoomba over Christmas and now I returned like the proverbial bad penny to soothe my soul in the bosom of what remained of my family at home.

My older sisters Sally and Prue had married and moved inter-
state. Sally's new home was Wongwibinda, the focus of the climax of
Judith Wright's book about her family, the Wrights of New England.
Generations of Men had been one of our set reading books at The New
England Girls' School (NEGS).

Sally and her husband Edward Wright eventually moved into
the house with the heart-shaped garden which Edward's great-great
grandfather Albert had promised to his bride, May, in 1886. It was
her prize for uprooting from Goulburn and starting afresh in the
wild and then virtually unexplored New England district of northern
New South Wales.

Prue and her husband Jonathan Graham lived also in the New
England, on their sheep property, Oakhurst, at Deepwater.

Tina was a nurse, living in Sydney.

Nicola was still a child at school, living with her elderly parents
and ailing mother in Toowoomba. In that era of a social expectation
that mothers were young, Nicola suffered the indignities which have
since been visited many times on my own children—that of having
people comment with complete innocence how kind was her 'grandfather' to come and watch her perform in the school play or on the
sporting field, and give her money for an ice-cream.

The grandfather was, of course, poor old Dad, in his late 50s so very
much older than the prototype father figure of the times but devoted
nonetheless to his youngest daughter and relishing the involvement
in her life which town living and the proximity of her day school
brought into their lives.

The rest of his daughters had spent those years far away at boarding
school.

Mum, meantime, never a great adaptor to change, took some time
to adjust to the shock of attaining the town life she had so yearned

for. I hovered, but wasn't much use in the counselling stakes. Eventually time and tide, good friends and loving family washed her heart and started her living again. But 1974, the year I attained my majority and could legally go to the pub, and vote, was a difficult year for our family.

I hankered for the bush again. The gentler countryside of the New England was my first rural destination after my year of city dwelling. I eased myself back into the saddle with a stint at being a station-hand for a season of AI (artificial insemination) of the cattle at Wongwibinda, overseen by the graves of old May and Albert Wright on a distant hill. The New England is a beautiful part of the world, it was a good season, and there is no better time to be there than when the grass is green and the crystal-clear little streams are flowing.

While there, though, I acquired my first permanent mark of a horseman's 'blooding' when a mare I was saddling objected to my over-enthusiasm with the girth (which I was doing up too tightly, as her saddle had a tendency to slip) and grabbed my upper arm in her mouth.

She lifted me off the ground and held me aloft with her teeth, shaking me for good measure until I managed to wrench my arm roughly out of her locked jaw. My arm was frozen black and blue for weeks, and the permanent lump in the muscle of my left bicep still, all these years later, causes masseurs to stop in alarm, thinking they have discovered something I should know about.

My respect for horses heightened considerably, I moved on to North Queensland and back to a world where horses were the dominant feature of life and livelihood. I went back on the payroll at Toomba. While I lived in the homestead with Ernest and Robbie Bassingth-waighte and their two little boys Edward and Thomas, I was on a stockman's wage and worked, in the lexicon of the north, as a ringer.

Not much happens at Toomba during the summer's Wet season of January to March; it's a time of tremendous rain, averaging 20 inches over the Wet. During those months domesticity is enforced on those left in charge of the station. Equipment is pulled out for repairs, greenhide hobbles and ropes are made, and saddles and bridles are greased and counterlined as the rain drums down and down, restoring the waterholes and bringing vitality to the land. There's not much coming and going over wide flooded sandy creeks and rivers. Reduced to invisible underground trickles and quicksand during the Dry, during the Wet they turn into wild, frothing torrents that fill the broad banks to overflowing.

Once the summer rains ended and the land began to dry out enough to get about, it was urgent to get to the cattle and begin the round of dipping for the ticks that caused the lethal redwater disease. Toomba had a shorthorn stud at that time and steadfastly held to the retention of this British breed, which in terms of colour, temperament and beef production was a wonderfully productive animal; however, because of its susceptibility to the growing problem of ticks, it was losing its suitability for the north.

Bos indicus breeds, including Santa Gertrudis, Brahman and the Australian droughtmaster, were beginning to make inroads as the breeds of the future because of their tick resistance and their general ability to adapt to the tough conditions of the north. However, in the dying days of the British breeds, it was shorthorns for Toomba and their attendant regular mustering and dipping.

At the start of the new year's mustering the bloodstock was brought into the horse yards after their prolonged spell over the Wet season. Australian stockhorses were the working stock of Toomba, bred from the station stallion, the thoroughbred Snip, whose grandsire Hallmark was a winner of the Melbourne Cup. Everyone hung over the steel rails to see how they looked, vying for a chance to select the best horses for their personal team. Not much of an expert in those stakes and not knowing their history, I took what I was allocated, and hoped they weren't buckjumpers or bolters; I was not altogether immune on that score, but for the most part the handful of horses who were 'mine', with their individual idiosyncrasies and personalities, became my most important friends and companions.

A cattle station far from town is a small, complete community whose symbiosis is a must. Each person plays an integral part in the team, each equally important in the function of the whole. The community at Toomba in 1974–75 when I was there consisted of Ernest, the boss, whose back atop the lead horse was my view each morning as we set off on a muster, his pistol in a pouch on his saddle and his blue heeler Blue following close behind; Jim, Ray and Daryl were the three other stockmen, born to the lifestyle, shaped by its mores and expertise and steeped in its stoicism. Not to mention ruthless towards me with my southern heritage, femaleness and inability to sit a bucking horse; well, not once it got its head down between its front legs, anyway.

John was the cowboy gardener, who tended the vegetables, milked the cow, and ran in the horses on the old night horse, Tonking, with his impossibly hard mouth and determination to beat the horses into the yards each day, as John swore loudly and hauled at the reins—old Tonking's only excitement in an existence he obviously considered demeaning, and a far cry from his glory days as a race-horse and stallion.

On the home front was the cook, Mrs Paul, a lonely figure who with dogged determination wielded her power over us through her domination of the victuals. And Ernest's wife Robbie, a brilliant artist although her time was fully occupied keeping house and their two little boys Edward and Thomas.

The stockmen, the cowboy and the cook lived in cottages set on high stilts above the flood peaks. I slotted in between, living with Ernest and Robbie and the kids in the main homestead among mango trees that abounded with life both nocturnal and diurnal, and Biddy the retired cattle dog who lived solitarily on the back verandah.

Dick the Dogger, who to my knowledge had no last name and seemed to have no need for one, arrived in his idiosyncratic Austin Gypsy four-wheel drive while I was there. He camped by himself near the homestead and quietly went about setting his dingo traps with a lifetime's skill. He disappeared as silently as he had arrived, his job done for that year, his return arranged for the next.

The workers' lives revolved around the routine of the station and the relationships that were entwined involuntarily, bound by mutual dependence and an overriding love for what we were doing. From time to time, for a race meeting or a campdraft or a rodeo, a stockman would go to town, a visit which often resulted in a 'bender' and either a sore head on Monday morning or the temporary absence of the reveller, perhaps for a week or so. But as this only happened a couple of times a year, and a blowout was acknowledged as a therapeutic necessity, the recalcitrant was welcomed back to the fold with a wry nod and not much said.

Our days were regulated by the unremitting North Queensland sun. Winter or summer, it was extreme. Musters were organised around its heat, with early-morning starts and the midday siesta (albeit under a gum tree 20 kilometres from home) a must for the sake of the cattle as much as their human masters.

Toomba was a place of unsurpassed beauty. The basalt wall adjacent to the homestead created its own world with its pockets of verdant pasture and crystal springs, surmounted by tropical rainforest and filled with more than 200 species of birds. This was perfectly counterbalanced by the magnificence of Toomba's open savannah country at the other extreme.

A man-made canal diverted spring water from the pockets across to the sandy Lolworth Creek with its massive paperbarks and Carbeen trees. A permanent set of falls below the canal, known as White Falls for the chalky nature of their bedrock, was a picturesque picnic place and swimming hole and an ideal lunchtime camp with cattle.

Toomba Lake had filled to the brim during the extra-huge 1974 Wet season. The swampy country was green, dotted with fat red cattle, shaded by ancient white gums and Moreton Bay ashes. Lotus lilies had been introduced to the swamps, their huge pink cup blossoms blending into the countryside as if they had been created to match the galahs.

The drier country further out had a beauty all of its own. Its scrub was stockier, but the bounty of flowers none the less for that. The trees, germane to the north, yellow jacks, sandalwood and Burdekin plums, and many another whose names have escaped remembrance, were prolific. Wildflowers abounded. It was lovely.

One day on a claypan on the way out to a muster we came across a mob of feral pigs. Loathed and detested for their destruction of the natural habitat, no mercy is shown to these savage predators. Everyone marked a pig and chased it until it bailed up and turned for the attack; then Ernest's pistol came into its own as he cantered around despatching them all. But on this occasion a mother with a litter of piglets was with them. I leapt off my horse, grabbed a tiny, multicoloured piglet and didn't have the heart to relinquish it for the executioner's bullet. So I decided to keep him, squealing with ear-piercing shrieks for his mother.

The problem was, it was morning. We had a day's muster in front of us. There was no sympathy for my maternal instincts and no leave pass to return to the homestead with my new baby; so I had to work out how to deal with him for the day.

He struggled too much when I shoved him into my breast pocket. There was nothing for it but to strap him into my saddlebag and carry my lunch in every available pocket instead. With a squalling little pink nose sticking out the front, and a curly black tail sticking out the back, emitting a bad attack of scours from his traumatic experience, we made quite a sight (not to mention smell) as we brought the mob home that night.

I christened my pig Sylvester. Little Edward, who at two years old was my shadow when I was at home, had a rather empty-headed dog called Rattle. The four of us became a team, going for evening walks to the little creek near the house. Rattle and Sylvester scampered and played, barking and squealing, chasing each other and knocking Edward down in their enthusiasm, Edward bouncing right up again and rushing off to embrace the nearest one of them that he could catch. Then we watched them wallow together in the creek while we discussed with philosophical intensity the wonders of the world as seen through the eyes of this most delightful bush babe.

Arms akimbo, eyes agog, I listen with amazement as Ernest assures me that part of being a stockman is shoeing my team of horses.

What? Who? Me? But I'm only a . . . well, you can't have it both ways. Either you are a stockman, or you are not, occurs to me before I open my mouth and betray my foolish thoughts.

I avert my eyes from Ernest's laughing gaze and swing my arms with what I hope is a jaunty gesture. Sure! Right! Bring it on.

I am handed a set of shoeing tools and a leather apron like the others, who are already sweating and grunting and cursing as they bend to their task of shoeing their horses. Then I survey with some alarm the huge flank held up by the dainty hoof that is awaiting my ministrations.

It seems like an awful lot of horse for such a small attachment as that bare hoof.

Ray is fully engrossed in shaping up a ragged hoof to make a flat surface for the shoe. Ernest resumes his place at the anvil, tapping a fore shoe with a hammer and inspecting it carefully after each slight adjustment, holding it at arm's length and looking at it this way and that with one eye closed to make sure it's perfectly aligned.

Daryl has selected a set of horseshoes from a nail on the wall, and is holding his horse's hind hoof out at a seemingly impossible angle, placing the shoe against it, taking it off again and having a good think; he changes his mind, straightens his back and selects a smaller set of shoes for this horse.

They each go about their task with seemingly consummate ease.

I look on aghast as Ernest saunters over to his horse and takes up a position under its near shoulder. He lifts the foreleg, sets down the top of the hoof gently on his bent knees, and, with spare nails held between his lips, begins to hammer the perfectly shaped shoe into place.

One, two, three taps, then a few in quick succession and the nail is through, a murderous length of sharp nail precariously perched on Ernest's leather apron. But with a fluid motion he twitches off most of the lethal protruding end with his shoeing tongs and quickly drives another nail through the opposite side, which holds the shoe firmly on the hoof.

His horse, Whistler, starts to pull away and Ernest growls a warning through teeth clenched around the remaining horseshoe nails. Whistler's ears twitch; is that a mischievous grin on his hirsute lips?

Another three nails deftly driven in and twitched off and Ernest turns the hoof over. Carefully placing the underside of the hoof on his bent thigh, he rasps a small ridge below each nail end then taps the points over so they clench the shoe snugly in place.

A quick rasp over each turned nail and he runs his hand over the smooth cup of the hoof with an air of satisfaction, sets the foot down, stands up and stretches with a grin. 'See?' he says. 'Easy!'

Easy? I can't even drive a nail straight into a wall. With a sigh I don the apron and gingerly bend myself to the task.

CHAPTER 17

TOOMBA

Christmas always meant a visit home and a gathering of the greater clan; there were firsts, and lasts, as a new generation started to come into being and the old ones started to drop off the conveyor belt of life. Nineteen seventy-four was our last with my grandfather Garg; he and Norn dandled their new great-grandson Joshua Mylne with delight and pride.

There were Mylnes, Wrights, Grahams, Paulls and, as always, our great-aunt Paddy McCallum, puffing away on the constant stream of Craven A cigarettes that gave her voice a particular gravelly resonance—and no doubt lifted her indomitable spirits.

Paddy had an egalitarian approach to the matter of Christmas gifts. Considering them a necessary token, their content was irrelevant to her. So it was that no matter how hard you searched to find something that might please her, while she was undoubtedly grateful for the gesture, she inevitably stored them away to re-give at the next Christmas gathering.

That year my sister Sally spent a lot of time trying to break the code for Aunty Paddy. She searched for what she considered to be the perfect present that was sure to be received with delight and found to be a truly useful gift. She handed it over (it was soap), and noted somewhat smugly that the oohs and aahs on its opening indicated that it would surely be kept and used. But just then someone unexpected walked in. Old Paddy quickly rewrapped Sally's gift and presented it to the newcomer with a kiss and gravelly Christmas wishes. Sal was furious—but the gift recipient was delighted!

I had done my Christmas shopping in a rush, having arrived in Toowoomba on the bus from North Queensland only a day or two before Christmas. I managed to complete my list but at the last moment realised that I had forgotten Aunty Margaret. I rushed into the nearest newsagent and found a book that looked absolutely perfect for her—'If Your Aunty had Bowls . . .'

Aunty had taken up bowls in her old age so it seemed to fill the bill in every respect. The day after Christmas we hosted the traditional Boxing Day family party, the kids eager to get into the above-ground pool and tables spread with too much food as usual. Aunty, who did not lack a sense of humour but was most definitely as prudish as anyone of her generation, was looking at me strangely. Uncle Sandy took me aside. 'The book you gave Aunty,' he said. 'Did you happen to look inside?'

I hadn't. The next page read '. . . she'd be your Uncle' and the book was full of filthy bowls jokes.

Ernest noticed on my return to Toomba after the Wet that I was somewhat unfit when the horses were brought in for shoeing. But no one took pity on me, and I had to forge away at the agonising job until it was done, some of the shoes a little skewed but no permanent damage to my horses' feet.

Shoeing is a skill I have never used since Toomba and one to which I have never admitted; I firmly believe that, much like knowing how to milk a cow or darn a sock, you never let on that you can do it or else you will land the job.

My outback experiences were compounded when I returned to Toomba as 'one of the stockmen'. But there was always that difference, in the fact that I actually lived in the big house, and that I was female. I was the butt of endless chicanery.

One morning I realised that the other stockmen, Ray and Daryl, had dropped behind me on the way out to a day's work, as Ernest plied his lonesome journey in the boss's place in the lead.

'Hey, Jane, would you like a sandwich?' Ray called.

Before I had time to say no, I found that I was actually the jam in the sandwich, and Ray and Daryl were the two pieces of bread practising their hazing skills on me, trying to lift me and my horse off the ground as they urged their mounts to lean into me from either side, rodeo pickup style.

On another occasion I was going through a tie-dying phase at weekends. I had tie-dyed my workshirt to make it more interesting, without realising that I had created a three-ring target right in the middle of my back. It was irresistible to those two scallywags, who, once we got out into the spear grass country, couldn't resist using me for target practice as with Red Indian whoops and calls, they galloped round and round me lobbing 'arrows' at my back. My shirt (and under my shirt, my back) was soon hung with spear grass stems.

For moments of sheer terror in my life, my Toomba year boasts a couple of the more memorable ones. One was of riding into a quicksand bog in the Swamp Paddock. I had been instructed to follow the cattle, as they knew where to go in the waist-deep water and would not lead me off the path. However, there were no cattle to follow when I had to broach the swamp, and my horse strayed into the bog. My second instruction had been that, in the unlikely event that my horse strayed into the bog and I got into trouble, I was to leap off and hold his tail, and his sense of self-preservation would pull us both out.

I wasn't leaping off and holding anyone's tail, thanks. Not behind the flailing legs of a panicking horse. I decided to go down with the ship, and stayed the plunging horse as if my life depended on it, as indeed it did. The drama was probably only two or three minutes long, but it was the longest two or three minutes of my life.

Another terror episode which has etched itself forever on my memory was around the small matter of getting lost in the bush. It was such a landlubberly thing to do, and one which was considered more a misdemeanour than an unfortunate happenstance; so I never really mentioned to anyone my terror at finding myself on one occasion all alone in the world, the sun above and the earth below and mile upon mile of empty space all around.

There must be millions of people in the world who have never had the experience of knowing they are the only living soul for miles around. It can be a very special sensation; but when it is compounded by the fact that there is no sign of mankind's endeavour, not even a fencepost, and that you think that perhaps this is where your clean-picked bones will be found one day many years hence by a passing stockman, it loses its romance altogether.

Thus it was that such thoughts coursed through my head when I was given the job of driving the Toyota back to the homestead from the far-flung Pony Pocket, where the rest of the stockmen had gone for a week's camping and mustering.

They had taken the packhorses and crossed the basalt 'Wall' by a circuitous route. I had ridden with them for that part of the journey; it was magnificent. We picked our way east through the beautiful pockets of green grass tucked into the jumble of basalt rocks that make up the Wall, and eventually came out onto wild savannah land on the neighbouring property, Southwick.

There we met Ernest with the Toyota and extra supplies, and turned tail to make the long journey up the other side of the basalt to Pony Pocket some 10 kilometres to the west. As the Wall was quite impenetrable by vehicle, Ernest's trip to meet us had meant driving east from the homestead to the highway, then north, then west again through wild country to our meeting point, a journey of about 140 kilometres.

I was to take the vehicle home—there was no place for a woman on a week-long mustering camp. Ernest gave me directions. 'Just follow the tracks I made coming up here,' he said, as if it was a bulldozer he had driven up and not a mere motor vehicle.

I set off alone in the Toyota for the long drive through the wilderness, my heart in my mouth. In no time I discovered that grass is nothing if not indestructible; the grass flattened by the Toyota had bounced back into place with alarming alacrity. Path? There was no path! I was wild with terror. I stopped every couple of hundred yards and climbed up onto the bonnet of the vehicle to see if I could spot any tracks; there was the merest suggestion of displaced grass, but was it a cow or kangaroo pad, or was it a wheel track? And where was the other one? The boys wouldn't be coming back for a week; was I to spend a week wandering around the neighbour's 100 square-mile paddock in ever-diminishing circles until someone found me, mad with fear?

Standing on the bonnet, I called out to the heavens for divine guidance. Someone answered. Bit by bit I managed to spot bent pieces of grass and somehow, God knows (God probably does know), I eventually found the main road and was able to make the long journey home.

I learned the true meaning of the expression 'shit scared'; I lost quite a bit of weight that day.

The first six months of 1975 took place in a happy domestic setting—someone else's—with a backdrop of the music of Kris Kristofferson and Rita Coolidge; my hobbies were redolent of the times—tie-dying, macramé, reading, making things. But as the year wore on I began to have interests in town and to seek out the company of my peers at weekends. There was a major adventure I was yet to have before I 'settled down' (whatever that was) and it was not in Charters Towers; I was growing restless.

The Cliff Richard movie *Summer Holiday*, about a group of young people travelling across Europe on a red London bus, had made a huge impression on me. I wanted to see all those places, to be footloose and fancy-free like the characters in James Michener's *The Drifters*. I wanted to see The Streets of London that Ralph McTell sang about.

I talked about it to my friends in The Towers. One of them, Mike, was an Englishman who had travelled overland through Europe, Afghanistan, the Khyber Pass, India and Indonesia with a group of young men a few years before.

While his tales of his travels included a life-threatening bout of amoebic dysentery in Afghanistan, which meant that he had to be repatriated and to join his mates again after a stint in a British hospital, the idea of adventure was enough to set me dreaming. But I knew I would never do it alone. Mike was planning a trip to the UK later in the year, via the USA. Would I like to come with him?

Would I?! So my sights were set on saving up for the trip, and we began to plan what was for me the adventure of a lifetime . . . a road trip across the United States of America, and then, once in England, who knows?

Another day begins in Paradise as we head for the yards to saddle up for the day.

In the horse paddock the mist is still rising along the line of the creek. The bougainvillea bushes at the front gate are a blaze of brilliant colour; the North Queensland sky is crisp and clean, cloudless. The air has a freshness and clarity as crystal-clear as rainwater.

It's good to be alive.

Our breath turns to fog and mingles with the small misty clouds the horses exhale as they shuffle and plunge, turning their backs to us as we move through the mob in the roundyard with our bridles slung over our arms, each of us intent on selecting our mount for the day.

Their sides and necks are still wet from their group plunge through the creek an hour before when John the cowboy rounded them up, whip cracking to wheel them. John's bellowed curses, the sound of breaking water, the occasional rush of wings and cry of a startled bird are our wake-up call over and above the usual morning sounds of the bush coming to life with the advent of piccaninny dawn; those and the cacophony downstairs as Mrs Paul bangs and clangs the pans in the kitchen as she prepares our morning's repast of steak and eggs fried in a deep pan of lard.

We ringers all wear our usual bush garb; blue jeans, long-sleeved workmen's shirts in an array of bright colours, Cuban-heeled R.M. Williams riding boots, leggings, broad-brimmed Akubra hats. There is a jangle of spurs from the others but I won't be needing spurs today—the neat little bay gelding Dusty is my mount for the day and I know from past experience that my main concern will be holding him back, not urging him on.

Dusty is a bolter. I am nervous when I set off on him and he knows it. He snorts and jigs and tosses his head, as the boys goad me and do their level best to set him off by rushing up behind me and clicking their tongues to encourage him to disobedience. Ever their target, I sit him determinedly and hold his head.

As usual, I field unsolicited advice from the boys. 'Hold him! Don't let him run away with you! Sit down in the saddle! Relax—he knows you're nervous.' They know full well that their shenanigans are not helping matters one whit. But anything for a bit of excitement.

Ernest rides doggedly on out in front, ignoring our carryings on; the sight of his back is my usual workday's morning view. The magnificent chestnut hindquarter of his mount Whistler sets a strapping pace as we head off for another day on the never-ending round of mustering cows and calves for dipping.

Through the first gate and heading across the claypan Dusty has settled down somewhat but I can still feel his impatience; he is an explosion waiting to happen and I know that at this stage he still might do anything. He does. A mob of pigs breaks from the centre of the claypan and makes a mad dash for cover. With a series of whoops each of the boys marks a pig and takes up the chase. Dusty stands stock still, takes a stance, humps his back and puts his head down between his forelegs. Then like a dancer answering an internal call to rhythm he begins to spin and plunge, spin and plunge, snorting soundlessly and grunting with the unwonted effort as the dust begins to frame our little drama.

I'm a goner.

The boys look back and see what's happening. They all stop the chase and form a ring around me, shouting excited advice which I have no hope of following. 'Don't let him get his head down!' (Dusty's head is so far down I'm wondering if he actually has a head—or a neck, for that matter.) 'Sit back—sit BACK—ride 'im, ride 'im—don't lean forward—don't look down—sit BAAAAACK!!'

The five or six seconds it takes for me to land on my head on the claypan feels like an eternity. I sit up, seeing the first of the stars that will dance before my eyes for several days. Noting that I am gingerly prodding my torso and stretching my limbs one by one to see that everything still works, the boys register that I'm 'okay' and take off in a pall of dust, chasing a fast-retreating Dusty who is relishing his freedom and galloping for home, reins flailing, stirrups asunder and pounding his pumping flanks.

Soon they return with my recalcitrant mount. Ray, the rough rider, with something of a tendency to youthful bragging, climbs aboard and puts him through his paces. 'See? Ya sit back! Ya don't let 'im get 'is head down! See?' as Dusty plunges and snorts; but despite his expertise, and much to every-one's delight, Ray gets dumped on the claypan, too—not with my 'posthole digger' method of undignified dismounting, but rather Ray rolls like the pro he is and leaps to his feet in one fluid motion, still holding the reins.

Enraged, he leaps back onto Dusty's quivering back and flogs him round the flat. But Dusty knows he's beaten. He will behave now—which is lucky, because although no one inquires as to how I'm feeling, and the boys are obviously disgusted with my poor performance as a rough rider, I'm actually not feeling great and don't for several days. But sympathy is not an easy bush offering, especially when there are no overt signs of damage—or even when there are.

As we ride quietly off to start our day, Phillip the jackeroo is heard to say in an exaggeratedly loud sotto voce, 'Lucky Ray had his mouth shut when that happened; otherwise we might have lost the horse, the saddle, the lot.'

CHAPTER 18

WANDERLUST

Here is a blank, white page, O day unborn,
Offered to you;
What will you spill thereon
Of sweetness or of rue?
Will it be just a day in one December,
Or one marked out forever to remember,
Or black with some dire, sudden, rushing Storm?
—Kit Mylne

There was much of North America that we did not see—but there was a great deal that we did.

In the four months from our arrival in San Francisco on 1 August 1975, Mike and I travelled 15 639 miles. This we did in a VW beetle we bought on the first day for US$850 from a car yard in downtown San Francisco. We sold the car on the east coast four months later for US$600.

Our welcome at the Honolulu airport was not as warm as the weather. In fact, we were struck by the unfriendliness of the 'natives' after our few days in Fiji en route for Hawaii.

Departing Australia in a Qantas plane called 'City of Toowoomba' seemed very fitting. And Fiji with its pristine waters and happy, friendly inhabitants stole our hearts. But the US of A was a reality check at the height of their bicentennial celebrations and no doubt their consciousness of possible disruptions from aliens who were not as happy about them as they were about themselves.

As we disembarked at Honolulu and walked across the tarmac to the terminal, our way was lined with grim-faced armed guards.

All the same, it was a stroke of luck that we chanced to visit the States during their bicentennial year. Their patriotic solidarity was in full swing, stars and stripes every which way we looked. We were privy to spectacular parades that no one does quite like Uncle Sam, with bands and marching girls all set about with stars and stripes, fireworks and excitement.

The first such parade we saw was in Honolulu. There were miles of marching girls all decked out in spangles and long boots, with one lot even joined up to electric wires with neon lights flashing up and down their sleeves and trousers as they marched. I had never seen anything like it.

Then, after the parade, there was a fireworks display. The bangs from the fireworks ricocheted from skyscraper to skyscraper so that it must have sounded like the battle of Pearl Harbor all over again. What an introduction to the States! You could say we were initiated with a bang.

It was a bang of another kind when we flew to the island of Hawaii, the youngest island of the Hawaiian group and very much still growing. I watched with primeval awe as lava spewed steadily into the sea with a savagery of hissing. We nervously peered into the crumbling crater of Mauna Loa as it bubbled and spat like a massive pot of chocolate fudge.

There was 'chocolate fudge' across some of the roads in ridges 6 metres high that had roiled their inexorable way across the landscape during a major eruption the previous year. And yet, Mike photographed a beautiful, lonely flower growing stolidly on the edge of a fissure, in an expanse of rock that had first seen the light of day only a year previously. That lovely little succulent plant epitomised the endless juggle between biology and geology, while the roads blocked by lava were a reminder of man's ultimate powerlessness in that much larger struggle.

We were nervous after our dubious welcome at Honolulu airport; I had never seen gun-toting uniformed guards before. I had expected the US to be another Australia on the other side of the Pacific, but the small cultural differences gradually stacked up.

Many of the things I mentioned in my copious letters home as being newsworthy would barely raise an eyebrow now, since so much that is American has become mainstream in Australian society in the meantime, and we Australians have become more overt in expressing our needs and thoughts. But when a passenger on the airport bus in San Francisco laid into the driver with a tirade of verbal abuse for, as he insisted, driving carelessly on the freeway, with a loud and public altercation ensuing, all of us on the bus being exhorted to take sides and sign a piece of paper confirming the complainer's point of view, my Australian reserve was seriously challenged.

I was so far out of my comfort zone that I was almost under the seat.

Much to Mike's delight, far from signing the complainer's piece of paper, everyone on the bus yelled at him to 'go catch a horse' and clapped with glee as the driver pulled over and deposited him at the side of the highway. It was all too much for me. Such a thing would never happen in Charters Towers!

I thought that Americans seemed to live on chewing gum, TV dinners, Coca-Cola, hot dawgs and hamboigers. I had never seen frozen meals and was amazed at the offerings in the supermarkets. I was amazed at the supermarkets, for that matter. I described all these extraordinary manifestations of advanced civilisation in my letters home as if I had landed on Mars . . . the upside, and the downside.

After the silence of the North Queensland bush, San Francisco was to me a constant cacophony—of sirens, police, fire and ambulance; of traffic; of people; of colour; of noise. The highways left our humble Australian roads for dead; we got onto them, and then watched help-lessly while the exits whizzed by as, sandwiched in a never-ending stream of traffic six, seven and eight lanes wide, we flew along in a motorised cavalcade that seemed to have plugged us into a living thing beyond our control.

The setting of San Francisco was magnificent. The Golden Gate rose 700 feet into the morning fog, 200 feet above the lovely harbour. While we were there, someone jumped off. 'Splat' was how I described this tragic event in a letter to Dad. One is so very blithe at the age of 22.

Our travels took us up the west coast of California from 'Frisco and into a world that was a natural landscape beyond my wildest imaginings. We decided that the Yanks were justified in their ravings about their beautiful land. The redwood forests, once just the words of a song to me, came to life as we pitched our tent below them.

And like the song, from the redwood forest to the gulf stream waters, we drove across it all in a giant zigzag.

Walt Disney's animals came to life for us one by one. The wood-peckers, chipmunks and squirrels were captivating with their cheeky pertness. Wary of being touched, the chipmunks nonetheless were savvy enough about the potential of humans as a food source to run up our legs and sit in our hands when offered peanuts. There, they filled their little cheek pouches to bursting and then scampered off to empty them into their winter stores, only to return for a refill almost at once. I could have stayed forever sitting on a log in the forest except that the many stories of bear attacks had put the wind fairly up me, somewhat blighting the pleasure of camping out.

Nonetheless, over four months we staked a claim to many a chunk of United States soil, camping everywhere we went, rain, hail and shine. We fished—or Mike fished—for trout and salmon, and picked wild blackberries; we spent days being burned by the sun; we froze as we washed and bathed in melted snow waters. We cooked our meals over campfires, read by torchlight and watched out for marauding bears in the evenings.

Through Oregon and Washington state we went, heading north to Canada, and all the way met people who were amazed that we spoke English quite well even though we were from Australia—'Now then, what language do they speak there, exactly? Do what? Uh-huh, uh-huh,' nodding in disbelief as we assured them that English was our first language and, no, New Zealand was not joined to Australia via the Sydney Harbour Bridge.

We drove through the mountains on logging roads until we were above the tree line in lovely little towns where the houses could have been in *Anne of Green Gables*, with huge oaks and maples and conker trees. Someone had to explain to us that the 3-metre high poles beside the roads were to show the snow diggers where the road was in winter time.

We ran the gauntlet of deer that leapt unexpectedly out in front of the car in much the same way as kangaroos do in Australia. And all the while to our left was the great expanse of the Pacific Ocean below rolling cliffs, massive fields of kelp roiling in the waves, fat, spotted sea lions wallowing in the cold waters.

Mum's cousins lived in Summerland on Lake Okanagan in British Columbia. They welcomed us with open arms and feasted us on moose steaks and pumpkin pie, then took us up to their log cabin in the mountains. A beaver dam was causing them grief; to us it was a miracle. It was all so everyday to them, the fabulous minutiae of their lives, and so amazing and exotic to us.

When Mum was two years old in 1924 her mother took her and her siblings to Summerland to stay with her grandmother and the Canadian cousins the Agurs. Many years later—the year of writing this book—Mum, an old lady of 90 with the onset of dementia, broke her leg. As I sat with her in the hospital after an operation to pin the leg, she said, 'Just now I thought I was in a boat on Lake Okanagan; I could see it all so clearly, the boatman, Grandmum's house, the trees on the edge of the lake.' A little pocket of memory had bubbled up 88 years later, and we were able to share memories of a place we had both seen on the other side of the world, 50 years apart, and 36 years after my visit.

The Canadian Rockies were next on our path. Our little Vee Dub gamely took on the dramatic heights of the Glacier National Park, sailing up vertiginous highways over which loomed the most majestic of nature's landforms. In Jasper National Park our place as mere mortals, insects on the face of the earth, was underscored and bolded as we gaped in awe at the towering, sculpted mountains. Glaciers hung from them and dropped down into blue-white lakes in scoured valleys below.

In Yoho National Park we stopped to watch a mama bear with a cub by the roadside; mama bear waddled over to the car looking for all the world like Theodore Roosevelt's cute Teddy Bear, then stood up and put her massive paws on my window. I was given a shocking close-up view of the underside of those great feet which could have taken off my head with one savage swipe; it was a sight that pervaded my dreams as we camped in our meagre tent for the next few months.

We went on a bus tour of the massive Athabasca Glacier, hoping a crevasse would not open up in the 300-metre-thick ice and swallow us; but the pinnacle of our mountain adventures was finding a shower block at Banff and having a bath for the first time in a week. Such practical concerns seem small in comparison to the magnificence of the scenery, but the banality of our personal needs seemed to reassure us that we were significant after all, despite the majesty of our surroundings.

Our tent was encrusted with ice when we awoke in Banff next morning; that was manageable. But when a neighbouring camper arrived with a fistful of pamphlets at breakfast time and announced that he had found something meaningful in his life and wanted to share it with us good folks, we decided the mountain air had sated our capacity for soul-searching, and departed hurriedly for the plains of Calgary.

Once on the plains I felt at home among the farms. We camped under a stand of athol pines like the one on our front lawn at Yarrabin.

Moving southward, we passed through the mountains of Montana and into another series of wonders—semi-arid sweeping treeless ranges, the foothills of the Rockies.

Everything we saw seemed to be the biggest or the longest. The open-cut Berkeley copper mine at Butte was 4000 feet deep and 1½ miles across. That was impressive but, once again, the smell of a dead skunk we accidentally ran over followed us for several days, permeating our car so thoroughly that we had to park it downwind for a few nights, reminding us that large the world might be, but what was happening on your own scale had an equally dramatic effect on your immediate concerns.

The smell of skunk is visceral, and cannot be exaggerated. It adheres to everything that comes within its ambit, and is absolutely dreadful. We experienced it several times. If there is an antidote, we didn't find out about it.

Wonder upon wonder is North America. As if the Pacific coast had not been wonder enough, followed by the Rockies, now we descended into the miracles of Wyoming and Arizona. More of nature's extremes met our astonished eyes as our little car plied mile upon mile of changing countryside. Geysers and steam vents, boiling mud pools and steaming streams mixed with the smell of sulphur as we made our way to the centre of Yellowstone National Park past herds of bison and moose, determined to see the famous Old Faithful geyser and determined not to come face to face with Yogi Bear.

No sooner did we leave Yellowstone than the desert began and with it more colour and sculptured forms of biblical proportions. Many mesas and small canyons—Glen, Fairyland, Marble—prepared us for the ultimate in spectacles, the Grand Canyon. Two hundred miles long, a mile deep, and up to 18 miles wide, the snow-fed Colorado River snakes along its bottom in its victorious march of millennia.

By now we were saturated with wonder. We turned our sights to outsized man-made drama and arrived at Las Vegas ready to lose money at the pokies and indulge in the comfort of civilisation and showbiz, US style, for a few nights.

From the heights to the lows in the space of a month—we camped at the bottom of Death Valley, in a place aptly named Bad Water, 280 feet below sea level. Even our car needed a rest after the marathon effort of negotiating the extreme heat of the desert, so next day at a town with the romantic name of Stovepipe Wells we rested in the oppressive midday heat before tackling the drive to Yosemite. But by now we were so inured to fantastic landscapes that we flitted past the granite cliffs of Yosemite with nary a sideways glance.

The smog of Los Angeles met us long before we got there. At that time children in school were made to sit quietly at their desks at midday to keep their breathing of the toxic brew to a minimum. But for us the many excitements LA offered more than made up for our temporary intake of the leaden air.

We looked at the movie stars' footprints on Hollywood Boulevard, drove around Beverly Hills ogling their homes. We watched practice laps for the Long Beach 5000 with Mario Andretti and Jackie Oliver driving—very loud and very fast. We saw the *Queen Mary*, newly obtained as a tourist attraction and docked at Long Beach; visited Disneyland and Knott's Berry Farm and Universal Studios. And we stayed with my grandmother's cousin Chrissy Agur at Seal Beach, and discovered much to my delight that her brother Joe Inman Kane, who had died recently, had been a movie director and 'discovered' none other than my childhood hero Roy Rogers.

Even though I never got to meet him, the vicarious connection was a huge thrill, especially when I learned he also directed some of the *Bonanza* series.

Our little Volkswagon plies its bold way past a lone coyote to the Yellowstone National Park camping ground. Unlike other, simpler camping grounds we have stayed at in the past few weeks, this one is like a large suburb. Bitumen roads are set out in a grid pattern among the towering pine trees; campsites are numbered off in neat squares, each with a picnic table and benches.

We pay our camping fee and take possession of our allocated space. By now our routine is down pat; out comes the round tent, and in a trice it is set up like home with sleeping bags inside and our clothes neatly stowed on either side of our beds.

We set up the cooking stove and pull out the esky ready to prepare our evening meal. Then we wander across to the ablutions block and take a welcome shower. Back at our campsite, we treat ourselves to a can of Budweiser each (Mike has aptly christened American beer, somewhat weaker than we are accustomed to, 'Gnat's Piss') and prepare to relax as we take stock of our surroundings.

We notice that ours is the only tent. In a makeshift city of campers, we are surrounded by caravans and mobile homes. Wimps, we think. Wusses.

A park ranger's car roams by, a loudspeaker arrangement on the roof. He starts to broadcast a pressing message to the hundreds of campers who are in various stages of setting up for the night.

'Don't feed the bears,' he says. 'Bears are dangerous critters. Do not feed them. Do not leave any food outside. Do not roam around the campground after dark. I repeat, bears are dangerous. Do. Not. Feed. The. Bears.'

Up and down the rows of campers he drives, broadcasting his message of doom as the darkness falls. The clicks of closing caravan doors fill the night, lights go on in windows all around us, and muted cooking smells begin to emerge from the security of a hundred caravan vents.

We sit at our table, eyes bulging out of our heads, heads turning this way and that with anxious anticipation as we gulp our meal, watching over each other's and our own shoulders, our ears straining for bear sounds. Darkness arrives and a terrible silence descends. A silence that is, for me, filled with the footfalls of hungry bears looking for one lonely tent in a sea of impenetrable metal; one lonely tent to rip apart, two lonely campers the only people outside in the open air eating their dinner, their brazen defiance reduced, somehow, to nothing more than utter foolishness.

Only last year, we have been told, a girl was eaten alive by a bear here. Yes, eaten alive! Everyone in the camping ground could hear her screams! Yes, they could! They trembled in their vans as she called out graphic descriptions of what was happening to her; she was torn limb from limb—yes, she was!

Suddenly our tent home seems very flimsy. Suddenly Yellowstone National Park is no fun anymore. Suddenly I want to go home.

CHAPTER 19

LAND OF OUR FATHERS

All along the southern Californian coast there were prehistoric 'monsters' in the form of oilwells pecking, pecking, even out to sea, as they lifted the wealth of oil from below, adding to the fortunes of many a millionaire. Here again was a major difference to Australia—the mineral wealth belonged to the landowner, while our Australian laws see what's below the ground differently—giving rise to a great deal of conflict and angst between the two major primary industries of food production and mineral exploitation.

A map is a very deceptive piece of paper; Mexico was so temptingly close. We thought a quick trip down to Baja California seemed feasible; it meant crossing another desert in the oppressive heat, in a car whose air conditioning consisted of open windows, but we were so close—so close. Or were we? We decided to go anyway. Discretion was the better part of valour in this instance, and rather than run the gauntlet of driving, we left the car in a carpark in Nogales on the US side of the border, and made an excruciating fifteen-hour trip by train to Mazatlan, on the Baja California in Mexico.

On the train a little boy called Riccardo was exhorted by his doting grandmother to sing; he did sing, and sing, and sing, screaming at the top of his voice with more enthusiasm than harmony. It was the

Spanish style, something we were not used to, but the concert was very much appreciated by the locals.

At every stop brown faces appeared in the windows offering 'tacos, tacos'. Conscious of our delicate Western tummies and Mike's weakness for amoebic dysentery, we stuck to coconuts and bananas.

The clattering of thousands of enormous cockroaches scuttling out of our way on the floor of the bathroom in the motel room we shared with an American friend is indelibly etched in the horror portion of my memory. Many of them had leapt out of our beds as we threw back the sheets to see what might lie within.

Mazatlan was beautiful and the locals were friendly (if raucous), but their overt poverty was all around us. We could not help but be shocked at the difference in culture and living conditions so close to one of the most affluent civilisations in the world.

Back in the States we left the magic of California, but not before we had completed the superb coastal trip from LA to San Francisco, on the way visiting Hearst Castle with its eclectic assortment of fabulous antiquities, fishing from the San Simeon pier, watching surfers gamely ply 15-foot waves. Suddenly aware of encroaching winter in the states we planned to visit, we farewelled Mike's Californian aunt and uncle in Petaluma and hurried across to Nevada. There, the same day we left the warmth of San Francisco, we met the first winter snowstorm at Lake Tahoe. It gave us something of a hurry-up.

The states rolled by as we headed to the south-east, the country-side never ceasing to provide a feast of splendour. As we reached the southern states another major cultural difference for the times became evident; it had been less than ten years since the last lynching of a Negro, and feelings were still strong and divided along racial lines. And we reached the bible belt; you couldn't buy an alcoholic drink in some towns, and you had to be careful what you said.

In Colorado we had been wined and dined by a contact, a sophisticated and debonair businessman. We had a lovely evening; then I mentioned James Michener's book *Centennial*, and expressed wonder at his vivid description of the dinosaurs at the beginning, whose bones were found in this vicinity. Our host fell silent. Then suddenly and with a spurt of vehement passion he roared, 'Ah don't know about you, but ah was born from Adam's rib and ah don't have no truck with these dinosaur stories.' We were stunned. It was 1975.

Wyoming, Colorado, Oklahoma, Arkansas, Tennessee spun by in a wash of autumn glory. We stopped at the seat of power, Washington DC, took the obligatory photo of the White House, visited the Smithsonian Institution, ogled the Hope Diamond, paid our respects to President Kennedy and his ilk at Arlington Cemetery, and watched a rowdy session of Congress in the Capitol. Then it was New York and a terrifying initiation into some real city driving, and on the wrong side of the road at that.

My postcard home mentions that from the top of the Empire State Building we could see a new, taller building—the World Trade Center was 100 feet higher at 1350 feet.

At the home of another of Mike's aunts, in Bangor, Maine, we farewelled our faithful little car; we caught a bus back to New York as the bitter November weather descended in earnest. No one shared our ferry crossing to the Statue of Liberty, and after climbing the 300 cold and echoing steel steps up into the tip of Liberty's torch, we braved the cold wind to have coffee outside in the dappled sunshine alone, among rattling autumn leaves.

New York was cold, but Iceland, en route to England, was colder. In fact, it snowed a blizzard during our 4½-hour bus trip around the geysers and hot springs there, but still it was captivating.

*

On 25 November we reached the quaint little village of Kimpton in Hertfordshire, where I lived with Mike's family for four months, catching the train up to London to work at the Copyright Society every day.

Thirty years after my time in this delightful little village, consisting of ramshackle old brick semidetached houses set around a central village green where the locals gathered and played football and cricket at the weekends, I went back to find it, but sadly it seemed to have been swallowed up by an ugly amorphous encroaching suburbia.

Village life in England was very different from what I was used to in Australia. We lived in each other's pockets in a way that the bungalow lifestyle at home simply didn't facilitate. Our lives in Kimpton were inextricably interwoven with our neighbours'. In the evenings everyone arrived home on the train from their workplaces in London and ate their supper; then there was a general exodus to the tiny pub on the corner, where everyone played darts and chatted and shared the details of their lives as a huge extended family. Absences were noted and the absentee was checked upon to make sure all was well with them. It was certainly a different approach to community.

The Copyright Society introduced me to the British public-service work ethic of the times. To begin with, I had never seen a dictaphone, a small omission I did not think worthy of mention when I applied for the job as an audio-typist. It was an awkward-looking appliance, but I did my best, wearing the headset upside down for some days before someone inquired if we did everything upside down in Australia.

Then a complaint was lodged with the management that I worked too fast in the typing pool and showed the others up. An elderly public servant gent in a three-piece suit instructed me discreetly in the mores of taking my time—coffee breaks, reading the newspaper, general chatting around the office, until one or two documents found their casual way into my inbox for attention at my leisure. The concept never really caught on with me; I felt I could have been doing other things with 'spare' time than loitering and idling, and at the slower pace found it hard to work up the incentive to get back to work again.

December brought the promise of snow and a white January to compensate a homesick Australian girl for being away from her family at Christmas for the first time in her life. The north wind soon brought, too, my old school friend Rob Chandler who shared the first of many life experiences with me, building a snowman on Kimpton Common, ice-skating on Verulamium Lake at St Albans, and exploring the local pubs.

Other school friends wove their way in and out of my life, each doing their London thing or, in Susie Shaw's case, back and forth as a Qantas air hostess. We had met up with her in Canada as well, and the list of conjoined experiences slowly accumulated at the beginning of a lifetime's friendship.

Rob and I went to Cardiff to watch another friend from school days, Greg Cornelsen, play with the Wallabies against the Barbarians. Rugged up to the nines against the cold, we relished the reflected glory of actually knowing one of the distant specks on the playing field, and basked in the magnificent singing of the Welsh crowd at Cardiff Arms Park.

Relations, friends, friends of friends—the land of my father brought me in touch with my past and my forebears, although I fear I was too gauche and too ill-informed to appreciate all the familial connections.

Feeling like a recalcitrant 14-year-old I coyly visited my former headmistress, Miss Howard, in her rose-covered cottage in Kent to which she had retreated for her old age and eventual demise among familiar things, with a new sausage dog for company. After her death I discovered that she had been a code-breaker for the secret service during the war, skills she doubtless found useful at NEGS to break the code of the many teenage girls in her charge.

I went to Austria with Rob on a skiing expedition. Two things about it stand out in my memory, and neither of them is the skiing. One was visiting the setting for *The Sound of Music*, and Mozart's birthplace, at nearby Salzburg, with much attendant excitement. The other was taking part in a three-legged pub race at St Johann, attached to a young Englishman; we chose schnapps as the quickest drink to skol in our successful bid to win the prize—but unfortunately I don't remember what the prize was, since the schnapps was pretty virulent, albeit quick to drink.

The bomb threats in London at the time got the better of my courage. I decided to go to Edinburgh with Mike when he got a job on Sedco 703, an oil rig in the North Sea. Standing in the chapel of Holyrood Palace, looking out over Arthur's Seat, and reading the inscription left there by my forebear Robert Mylne in 1671 was a serious goosebump moment. It was both moving and strange to stand in the selfsame spot where someone who shared my DNA in direct lineage had stood 400 years beforehand.

Other Mylne graves in Greyfriars Kirkyard provided me with a tangible place to pay homage to the family who lost so much in their initial foray into the Antipodes when the *Dunbar* sank off Sydney Heads in 1857. Here were their roots as master masons of Scotland for many generations.

Forebears aside, but maybe because of them and in deference to my own grandmother, I was enchanted with the Scots people, even if I couldn't understand much that they said. I often thought people were speaking German in the street, until I realised it was sometimes actually Gaelic, sometimes just the broader of the Scots accents.

I got a job with the Scottish Society for the Prevention of Vivisection (SSPV). Luckily, I didn't have to answer the phone, with that veritable tongue-twister of a name; they have since changed their name to 'Advocates for Animals', a much more user-friendly title. Either way, the principle of protecting animals was close to my heart, even if the stories they used to get their point across were more than a little harrowing.

It was a small workplace, and a fantastic little cross-section of Scottish people. We got on very well; our senses of humour coincided and lightened our days.

There was Mr Clive Hollands, the director, who wore a different embroidered silk waistcoat to work each day and had pretensions, in the nicest possible way. He was aiming for a knighthood and made no secret of the fact.

There was Doris Taylor, an elegant woman with her hair in a chignon and a wonderful sense of humour.

There was Dave, a young Scotsman being groomed to take over from Mr Hollands once he got his knighthood and retired. There was a problem with Dave—he spoke with an incoherent Scottish accent; so Mr Hollands had arranged for his protégé to have elocution lessons, to straighten him out. Dave used to regale us with the results of his 'electrocution' lessons, which happened every Tuesday evening, and then relapse into Braw Scots gibberish while Mr Hollands wasn't around, which left us all in hysterics. He never did acquire the pretensions that were essential to the job.

Middle-aged Miss Flockhart, the other typist at the SSPV, was a stout Scottish lady who wore sensible shoes, thick stockings and a tweed skirt with a laced blouse buttoned to the neck. She spoke with a gentle Scots brogue, always showing us how loose her waistband was since her diet started, and sneaking chocolates from her top drawer when she thought no one was looking.

Miss Flockhart was delightfully innocent in the ways of the world. One morning Mr Hollands received a letter written in French. I offered to take it home to my French flatmates for a translation. As Miss Flockhart left to catch the early bus at the end of that day, she paused in the doorway and ahem'd loudly to catch my attention; everyone stopped working and looked at her. Then she said in a loud voice, 'Now then, Jane, don't you forget your French letter!' and swept out of the office, leaving me with a red face and everyone looking at me in astonishment.

The cost of living in comparison with wages was the greatest eye-opener about the value of my homeland that I had ever encountered. I became vegetarian by necessity; except for haggis, which I loved, meat was absolutely out of my budget range. Most of the Scots I met didn't have driver's licences, since owning a car was never a like-lihood. If I learned one thing in all my time away, it was how fortunate we are in the standard of living we enjoy in Australia.

The struggle to get on top of the financial situation bested me in the end; it proved impossible on my meagre wages, even though I also worked a waitressing job at nights to save enough money for the European travelling I had longed to do. One by one my friends departed for Europe and the Mediterranean, fresh from Australia and still flush with funds. I had exhausted my reserves in the States.

Scotland was beautiful, and I travelled around the places of my grandmother's childhood in Perthshire. But a soul raised under a bril-liant sun begins to wither under constantly bleak skies. A year away was long enough. I returned home.

*

I'm sitting on the floor of the back office at the Scottish Society for the Prevention of Vivisection, just off Princes Street in Edinburgh. My legs are spreadeagled on the carpet. There is a pile of dusty papers between my knees—and a growing pile of rubbish in a bin behind me.

I've been in trouble again with my Australian work ethic—they can't keep up the flow of tasks at the SSPV office. I keep on getting things done and it makes everyone uneasy.

But what tasks! Last week I typed addresses onto letters that were sent to all sorts of famous people—Malcolm Muggeridge, Spike Milligan, Cliff Richard, Senator Edward Kennedy, J.B. Priestley, David Frost . . . I think every bishop in England has received a copy of the letters I have been typing, and the brochure with all the horrible pictures of animals being mutilated in the name of science.

Let's hope they all respond! At this rate Mr Hollands will get his knighthood in no time.

Anyway, Mr Hollands comes in a few days ago and says, 'Right, Jane, I'll fix you. This cupboard in the back office needs a good clean-out and tidy-up—that should keep you busy for a good few days.'

It certainly has! What a lot of accumulated junk. I had to find a ladder to get to the top, and bring everything out and spread it all over the floor to sort out what's to keep, what's to throw out, what's to be packaged up in brown paper and string to store in case anyone ever wants to look it up.

So here I am in a cloud of dust and Mr Hollands comes in to see how I'm getting along. He stands at the door for a while surveying the scene. He's wearing his purple embroidered waistcoat with his suit today, with a gold fob chain, his black shoes polished to a glossy sheen and his hair looking as if it's been stuck down with glue, it's so perfect; he looks terribly dapper.

I can see he's busy thinking, so I keep quiet and wait to see what he comes out with. It doesn't take long.

'Goodness me, Jane! That IS a dirty job I've given you!' he says. 'I bet you feel like having a bath every day when you get home!'

He sees the look on my face.

'Oh, you Australians! Always bathing!' he snorts in disgust, and leaves the room before I can say anything.

CHAPTER 20

ANCIENT LAND

Green grass is springing after rain
On a tawny sanded bank.
The summer day is on the wane;
To the creek where cows this morning drank
In the shade of a river gum,
Out to catch yabbies with bits of meat
The homestead children come
On bare brown hurrying feet.

—Paddy McCallum

Sunshine! Sky! More sky! And so blue! Surely I must chain myself to the ground or I will float away into the vast, cloudless expanse.

It was amazing to be home. The incomparable smell of Brisbane—warm air despite midwinter; fig trees spreading lascivious, leaf-laden limbs in an extravagant riot of rich green against blue sky, the golden orb of the sun blinding my starved eyes with an orgy of warmth and colour.

The slow brown river rolling seawards as it always has; unhurried traffic making its way along Kingsford Smith Drive to destinations unknown.

Then gum trees, brown creeks with deeply scoured blacksoil banks, waving tall yellow grass, bougainvillea flowers along the sides of the highway, market gardens being watered by giant lengths of irrigation pipes until, at last, driving up the range to Toowoomba I knew that on my own doorstep was a beauty that was the equal of every marvellous landscape I had seen during the past year.

Never again would I take it for granted! The sound of bellbirds floated through the open window of Mum and Dad's Fairlane as we broached the final steep ascent to Toowoomba. I breathed in crisp, clean Darling Downs winter air and my heart sang.

It was so good to be home!

But sitting around in my parents' home was not going to refill the empty coffers of my bank account. Mike rang from Adelaide, where he had returned on the strength of a job he had taken with Esso as a mineral exploration field officer, and offered me a job as a cook in a mining camp at Oenpelli in Arnhem Land in the Northern Territory. It was a restricted zone, Indigenous territory, and Esso had an exploration licence.

It was too good an opportunity to resist. I caught a bus to Adelaide where I met up with Mike and, after a few weeks' preparation, flew to Darwin.

The drive to Oenpelli from Darwin was across 250 miles of barely inhabited tropical paradise and crocodile-infested rivers. In the casual land of the Never-Never, the best of well-laid plans are apt to waft off into the wild blue yonder. Mike's chief field assistant, Murray, didn't turn up for the drive to Oenpelli, apparently having discovered something better to do; the field workers were all found to be enjoying the hospitality of the Border Store with its endless supply of alcohol, more attractive to them than the idea of work.

Our campsite was in the middle of nowhere, surrounded by sparse scrubland on a base of red sandy soil. It consisted of a cluster of tents around a central cooking caravan and it was hot—very hot—in October.

The nearby swamps were full of uranium, as evidenced by the frantic ticking of the Geiger counter that went crazy as we splashed across them in the stifling heat.

There were Indigenous rock paintings, previously unseen by white eyes, in far reaches where our wanderings took us. The drilling rig was able to be put into operation once the missing chief field assistant was discovered on a second trip to Darwin and brought out to camp to cold-turkey the effects of an LSD bender. The rig brought mineral core samples up in perfectly rounded strata for packaging up and sending off to Adelaide for assaying.

On days when I was alone in the remote camp preparing food, I washed clothes and bedding in the nearby creek and ran the gauntlet of the stifling pre-Wet-season heat. The air was pregnant with unfulfilled expectation as the blackening cumulonimbus clouds gathered, and scattered, and gathered again. The humidity rose and the heat grew, but the weather refused to break. It was building up to the northern Suicide Season, when those who are going to crack, do, and those who can't take it exit the place to retreat to kinder climes.

Sometimes the Indigenous owners of the land would arrive at our camp with a shot kangaroo slung over their shoulders, bartering for our kind of food, jabbering in their lingo which left me quite taken aback that English was not (of course, why would it be?) their first language.

Bandicoot, buffalo and brumby footprints circled our camp in the mornings. One memorable early morning there was a ruckus in a nearby tent as an inquisitive buffalo stuck its massive horns in the open flap; incumbents James and John fled with undignified haste in one direction, while the buffalo blundered around the camp in a panic and left a trail of destruction in its wake.

I was conscious of how lucky I was to have the opportunity to see this raw and beautiful part of the world. When necessity took us further afield in early mornings, such as visiting the neighbouring Pancontinental mine to borrow equipment, crystal-clear air backlit with the morning sun created an almost supernatural glow around surreal vistas of pelican-laden waterholes and thirsty plains waiting for the Wet. There was an air of eerie moodiness around the pandanus swamps that so resonated with radioactivity and tribal secrets.

Sometimes my dreams were infiltrated with strange forms, bogey-men and Mimis, the fairy-like beings of Arnhem Land. I would wake up sweating and trembling in the middle of the night, feeling like the interloper I undoubtedly was in this land so filled with spirits.

The field workers all had stories to tell of lives spent moving around from place to place, working at whatever was offering. They belonged to a transient world I had thought only existed for the young adventurers I had met (and been) during my time overseas, but I realised that there is an echelon of society that lives somewhat lonely lives 'on the wallaby', impelled by both inner and outer motivations to keep moving, abhorring the thought of putting down roots.

Many of the field assistants belonged to this itinerant class of wanderers. They were reliable only from pay cheque to pay cheque, answering some call to constant motion that belied an ability to settle down in one place, much like their forebears the swaggies. There was a joke going round that when *Australia's Most Wanted* came on TV, the pub at Humpty Doo emptied in a flash. Our field assistant Murray succumbed to his craving for LSD and absconded with the Toyota and a few loose bits and pieces—including his tent-mate's pay cheque—to feed his addiction. The 'old' Irishman James (he was 57) stayed the course for a few weeks, but soon his inner marching music called to him and he moved along to greener pastures.

My final bout of wanderlust reached its climax in a drive with Mike across the continent from the Territory to Adelaide. The desert was hot and arid, as deserts are wont to be, although 1976 had been a good season and the countryside was greener than usual.

Our journey took us through the centre of Australia, past deserted Indigenous wurleys in the parched landscape, across an isolated flatness that went on for mile after mile of mystical and picturesque nothingness.

We passed through the underground opal town of Coober Pedy, out of sight in the high heat of summer. The dugout caverns (Coober Pedy means 'White Man's Hole in the Ground') where its inhabitants lived and worked created another world, a cool world, peopled largely by Italian immigrants seeking their fortunes in this arid and forbidding place.

Soon it was Christmas time again and another new year—the turning of another page in the book of my life, always a restless time, for me, of endings and new beginnings. The calling of my cultural heritage and my own people was too strong to compete with the offering of a permanent lifestyle in an unfamiliar place with Mike, my companion of the last couple of years. I returned home alone to the Darling Downs to start afresh.

In Toowoomba, close to the bosom of my family, I struck out on an independent path. I ended up staying there for 13 years, concentrating on developing my administration skills and consciously settling in one place. Perhaps it was a response to my own years of wandering; perhaps it was a need to make something of myself, for myself. While I rued the absence of a mate, I had no wish to be a kept woman. That seemed to me to offer a stultifying existence. I had no stomach for boredom at the hearth of domestic responsibility; I felt life had something more for me before I truly settled down.

Nonetheless, in answer to my restlessness I moved house in Toowoomba 12 times in those 13 years, eventually owning my own sunny little cottage opposite the creek.

My first job was with a solicitor, John Robinson. He had seen a need for a secretarial service and engaged me to set up the business. That kept me occupied for close to a year, and I learned the intricacies of legal support administration in the process.

Then I moved on to an architect's office, Durack, Brammer and Stekhoven. It was interesting and I was trained in the fundamentals of drafting, as well as enjoying a great social life with a wide group of friends in Toowoomba. But as another year started to wind down my internal calendar started to calculate the passage of time once more; my wanderlust resurfaced. Thoughts of moving on, open spaces and horseflesh pervaded my dreams again.

That's when R.M. came into my life, and another world opened up to make use of my accumulated skills, loves and pent-up energy.

We bounce over the unmade road out of Oenpelli, three of us jammed gaily into the front of the Toyota.

It's a tight squeeze, and I have to straddle my backside across the gap between the bucket seats for 250 miles, but youth is nothing if not indomitable. I've been more uncomfortable in my time and no doubt will be again.

Besides, we're off to Darwin and it's worth the inconvenience. It will be a six-hour drive.

Mike is driving; I'm in the middle; Irish James, one of the field workers, has the passenger seat—or what's left of it. He chatters to us brightly in his Irish brogue as we bounce along. We exchange travel tales, homeland tales, and tall tales about the bush.

Ours about meeting the tiger snake on this same road just last week is not a tall tale, though. It was a shocking experience. We ran over it first— it was so well camouflaged against the dirt of the track that I didn't see it, but Mike did. Then he couldn't see it in the rear-view mirror.

Conscious that it might have flipped up into the undercarriage of the vehicle, where it would give us a nasty shock when we arrived at our destination, he backed up to find it. It was there all right—but it came for the Toyota and attacked the tyre, striking again and again and chasing us down the road with incredible speed as we watched with morbid fascination.

We were dumbfounded at its bravery—and more than a little glad we were safely ensconced in the cabin of the vehicle. Imagine if we had been running down the road to try to escape those lethal fangs! I shudder again at the memory.

A buffalo suddenly rushes across in front of us, raising dust on the road, startling a group of parrots. They wheel around in the glare of the sun, crying out, and then alight in a tree behind us when all has quietened down. A cliff rises out of the mist in the distance.

After a long haul we reach the boundary of Oenpelli and cross the East Alligator River. A crocodile slips soundlessly into the water from its sunbathing spot on the muddy bank; soon a pair of reptilian eyes emerges from the water, watching, watching, waiting for an opportunity to garner an easy meal. Ugh. I shudder. Always these canny creatures make the hairs rise on the back of my neck.

Past the Border Store with its alcohol and its patrons lying in the dust, still catatonic from last night's bender. Then the road offers bitumen, a bit of a smoother ride. The road takes us through swamps laden with magpie geese, pandanus and huge tropical trees with the odd boab putting out fresh new leaves in expectation of the coming rain. Eventually we sail triumphantly into Darwin in the late morning, in good time for Mike to conduct his business.

We drive down the Esplanade, where a patch of red paint is still visible many floors up the brick wall of the Travelodge. The fact that it was made by a flying car is a poignant reminder of the power of nature in this place—Christmas 1974, Cyclone Tracy.

CHAPTER 21

R.M.

It was October 1978 and a humdrum summer's day in the offices of Durack, Brammer and Stekhoven architects in Lindsay Street, Toowoomba.

Outside on the corner of the street, the leaves on the giant red cedar tree, towering over our busy little world, rustled in the sultry breeze. Sue and I sat in our little workspace near the front entrance to the lovely old house that contained the architects' rooms. Heads down, we busied ourselves attending to the secretarial demands of our four busy architect bosses. One of those duties, for me, included taking shorthand dictation for regular letters to Bill Durack's beloved sisters Mary and Elizabeth in Western Australia.

'My dear sister Mary,' he would begin, or 'My dear sister Elizabeth'. And then would follow the news of the doings of the eastern branch of this famous family, peppered with responses to theirs, mentioning names like 'Perpetua' and 'Patsy', his letters to Mary mentioning 'Bob Dodd', 'Reg Saunders', 'Reg Williams' and 'Bob Katter' in the context of something he called 'The Stockman's Hall of Fame'. He always ended with his hope that his letter found her well, and the assurance of his fondest love.

One day some months before, Bill Durack had called me into his office to dictate a letter to 'My dear sister Mary'. With it, he included the blueprint of a brochure for which he sought her blessing. The poem she had selected to go on the back, he said, Ian Mudie's 'Australia Day 1942', expressed their goals well.

The painting Hugh Sawrey had done especially, of his 'Vision Splendid', in muted colours and in typical Sawrey style, was particularly striking on the front cover and said it all. The wording put together by 'Reg' expressed the project's aims succinctly and all in all, Bill believed, Mary would approve of their efforts.

I read the aims laid out in the brochure that sat on my desk:

The Australian Stockman's Hall of Fame and Outback Heritage Centre was formed out of the conviction that, as the unique history of Australia's pioneers was fast disappearing, an effort should be made by the nation to establish a monument to the people who created this history. Such a place would be a national repository for the Australian culture, lore, writings, art and history; a museum, art gallery, theatre and historical library where facts relating to the outback will be preserved and illustrated for the education and entertainment of Australians and visitors to Australia.

A wonderful ideal indeed, and I hoped that whatever they were planning, they would succeed. But I was young and powerless and it had nothing to do with me.

As I worked that October day I toyed with the growing idea of moving on. It was time to head back to the bush; town life—sitting, constrained within four walls—had served its purpose for the last 18 months. By now I had set aside enough savings to get going again. I put a good face on it, but on the inside my thoughts were once again like Clancy's with his vision splendid of the sunlit plains extended. I was longing to get my backside into the seat of a Barcoo poley saddle once more, to smell the incomparable smells of horse sweat and saddle grease, to feel the wind in my hair and the sun on my face.

My reverie was interrupted when the front door opened. In came a small, bow-legged old bloke, smartly dressed in his town clothes, and wearing a narrow-brimmed brown hat.

'Can I help you?' I asked, standing up and smiling a welcome across the counter. He looked shy, and when he spoke, he did so through lips that were set in a way that I later learned was a sign of self-consciousness.

He held his hat nervously by the brim. 'Arum Williams to see Bill Durack.'

Did I hear right? Had he said 'R.M. Williams?' I looked at Sue, who had registered nothing untoward. Bill Durack's door opened and swallowed him up.

The name 'R.M. Williams' was synonymous with the bush. It was there on the pull-up tags of our elastic-sided boots; an R.M. Williams mail-order catalogue was on a shelf in every bush home, an essential reference for bush equipment and clothing of every imaginable kind.

The distinctive R.M. Williams longhorn logo stood out on the front of the magazine *Hoofs & Horns*, which in turn was on a shelf in every Australian home that valued horse sports. It was emblazoned in leather on the back pocket of the moleskins all bushmen wore, as well as the working jeans and familiar brown or green cotton trousers that were the 'going to town' clothes of the consummate bushie.

But the boot tag read 'Prospect, S.A.'; this was Toowoomba, Queensland. Besides, to my 25-year-old mind, any name that had achieved such widespread recognition must be at least a hundred years old. This person could surely not be 'the' R.M. Williams?

It was. His story is a remarkable one. I later came to know that stories such as his do not just happen. They are appended to extraordinary human beings. Like the poem by R.M.'s father-in-law

Joseph Cummings, 'The Men Who Try and Try', I was to observe and learn the never-say-die attitude that had brought R.M. to this place in Australia's history; that Dame Fortune does indeed lay her treasures at the feet of those who try and try.

And soon enough, I was to be swept up among people of this ilk.

After some time he emerged from Bill Durack's office, tipped his hat without making eye contact, and left. I hurried into Bill's office to confirm my suspicions.

Yes indeed, he was 'the' R.M. Williams; he was one and the same with the Reg Williams who had been referred to in letters I had typed. And, said Bill Durack, he was here to discuss an idea which had been mentioned from time to time in Bill's letters to his 'dear sister Mary' and that had caught my imagination—the Australian Stockman's Hall of Fame.

Those references of late had been somewhat fraught. There was something about the voting process in selecting the site that had raised the ire of the very punctilious Bill Durack and foundation committee member Bob Dodd. But, Bill had told his sister Mary, while Bob had opted to retire from the committee in protest, for her sake he, Bill, would continue to act as her proxy in the east. The idea was bigger than the man.

Not long later R.M. called in again. This time he hovered at the desk, obviously wanting to chat. Chat we did, and in no time he learned of my yearning to return to the bush and, above all, how much I missed riding and longed to be in the saddle again.

The next time he called in, he hung about at the desk again, shuffling his feet. Removing his brown hat, he took a small flower from the hatband and shyly handed it to me. With a muffled 'I thought you would like this' he disappeared again into Bill Durack's office, leaving me somewhat stunned with the token in my hand.

I later learned that the committee—not without some angst about the selection process—had settled on Longreach in Central Western Queensland as the site for their Stockman's Hall of Fame from many nominations. It looked exciting and interesting, if a little 'pie in the sky' in terms of the probability of its completion. What an enormous undertaking! I wished them well, but the fact remained that I was tired of town life, and so I handed in four weeks' notice to Durack, Brammer and Stekhoven, applicable Christmas 1978, and started planning for my return to the bush.

Meantime, R.M. had been delegated by the management committee to establish an office with a full-time secretary. The job of secretary, previously filled by Joy Katter, had been an honorary one. The project was now at a point where, if it were to move forward, it required an office and a paid executive secretary to work under the direction of the council.

Somehow R.M. caught wind of the fact that I was available. He sent an emissary to approach me. Bill Cooper was an independent stock and station agent who had been doing contract work for R.M. Williams Pty Ltd, which included piloting his aircraft. He came to see me and offer me the job.

I was dumbfounded. Had R.M. not understood that, much as I appreciated the ideals they were striving to honour, the last thing in the world I wanted was to move from one office job to another! I said, 'No, thanks.'

Thinking money was the issue, R.M. sent Bill back to me offering a higher wage: $60 a week sounded like a lot of money, but money was not the point. And besides, where was the money to come from? I reasoned that I would just as likely give this mob weeks of my time only to find myself unpaid for it. Bill was sent back with another resounding 'no', and an explanation that what I was looking for was fresh air and life in the saddle; that was certainly not what was being proposed here!

This time the offer came back in different terms, and it was made by R.M. himself. He invited me to visit him at Rockybar, his Arabian horse stud at Hodgson Vale, outside Toowoomba, and to go for a ride with him. I went out there on a Saturday, dressed smartly in anticipation that the great man would live in a fabulous house as befitted his status and likely wealth. In my bag was a change of clothes for the ride.

I was more than a little taken aback, then, when I arrived at a humble white timber farmhouse with lino on the floor and plain and serviceable furniture. R.M. greeted me at the door while I took in my surroundings with some surprise. Lesson No. 1—trappings do not the man make. It was a lesson R.M. had learned some time ago, and not before he had tried out living in grand style. He was now at that stage in his life, at the age of 70, sufficiently beaten up by life's vicissitudes, when he had decided with vivid clarity what was important.

Some time later he showed me his most treasured possessions: a small bag containing a few lumps of gold taken from the Nobles Nob mine at Tennant Creek in the Northern Territory from which he had made his fortune, and a whip plaited by Alec Scobie, the best (in R.M.'s educated opinion) whip-plaiter of all time. These were treasures of the heart and mind that transcended household grandeur for him.

After a simple lunch I kitted myself out for our ride; I was a walking advertisement for R.M. Williams by virtue of my well-worn riding workwear. Duly mounted on a pair of feisty Arab horses, a storm hit us unexpectedly when we reached the bottom of the hill below his house. My horse took fright, shied and leapt across the creek in one bound; R.M. was impressed with the way I sat my mount and brought him under control. I didn't know it, but I had passed a final test. Thoroughly drenched, we sat at his kitchen table and he made me the offer that convinced me to give his job a go—a least for a few weeks until I saw if the pay was forthcoming. And for longer if it proved to be so and the deal was satisfactory.

I was to ride his endurance horses for the first half of each working day; the office work would occupy me for the second half. If I didn't turn up at work for a week at a time, he would ask no questions. I was to start immediately I finished my other job. No, there was no question of my taking leave between jobs, not even a few days between Christmas and New Year—well, all right then, I could have Christmas off, but I was to start the day after New Year's. Time was of the essence. We had to get going on this thing and there was not a day to spare.

Disappointed I wasn't to get a decent break between jobs, and more than a little perplexed about the rush, I worked out my final week or two with Durack, Brammer and Stekhoven and took my leave, as usual not qualifying for the gold watch and long-service acknowledgement. Christmas was once again a family affair, by now with a clutch of baby nieces and nephews adding colour to this special time.

It was over in no time. Barely changing stride from one workplace to the next, I drove my beaten-up Toyota Corolla out to Hodgson Vale to start my new job as soon as the New Year's holiday was over.

All was quiet at Rockybar. R.M.'s German shepherd dog, Marcus, came out and barked at me. Apart from him, not a soul was in evidence. The sound of silence echoed in my ears as I searched first at the house, then the sheds, for R.M.—who was, according to our arrangement, so anxious to begin work that he must surely be waiting for me somewhere, ready to launch into work on the project as soon as I arrived.

Eventually I came across his son Peter down at the yards. When I told him I was there to start work with R.M. that day, he seemed surprised that I was looking for him.

'Dad's in hospital,' said Peter.

What shocking news! Surely something awful had happened?

'No,' replied Peter, perplexed. 'He's had his hernia operation. It's been planned for ages.'

Thus began the crazy roller-coaster which was life working with R.M.

January 1979. Rising early, dressing carefully, I drive the 20 or so kilometres south from Toowoomba along the main highway to Hodgson Vale, where Rockybar is located on the northern slope of a picturesque valley.

It's an old dairy farm, run-down, treeless except for the bottlebrushes that line a mostly dry creek running in a crazy zigzag pattern, finding its way along the lowest contour in a gently undulating landscape. It's a beautiful part of the country.

R.M. has built a huge shed just below the house, in which are generous stables for his working endurance horses, with enough room in between the two rows to carefully work a fractious young horse before venturing out through the huge roller doors into the rectangular working arena adjacent.

A short distance away, a smaller shed houses his extensive collection of riding tack; another corrugated iron building, the hayshed, holds the lucerne hay which is fed to the stabled horses in hay nets slung from hooks high on each stable wall.

I pull up outside the simple white farmhouse and survey the panorama before me. R.M.'s prodigious rose garden sends me wafts of fragrance on snippets of breeze; the rose blossoms' colours are as vibrant as they are varied.

I shift my gaze to the young Arabian stallion, Parada, who has followed me down the 100-metre driveway and now snorts impatiently in the corner of his small paddock. He lifts his tail and adds a generous contribution to the pile of dung on his dung heap, letting me know that this is his territory, and he knows I am a stranger.

A German shepherd dog stands in front of the house and barks at me. I approach as far as I dare and call out, but no one comes to the door. No one there.

It's my first day at my new job. I would have thought, considering the urgency with which R.M. had insisted that I begin at once, that he would have been there to meet me and get me started with whatever important task he had in mind! I turn my attention back to the sheds and set off in search of him.

Silence. A few leaves skitter across the kikuyu lawn in front of the stables. I have the distinct feeling that I am the only person here.

Suddenly a young man emerges from the hayshed. Bespectacled, with black wavy hair, he looks like a taller, younger version of R.M. He introduces himself as Peter. Obviously used to unexpected visitors, he doesn't inquire as to my reason for being there, but I tell him anyway.

He explains that R.M. is in St Vincent's hospital in Toowoomba for his scheduled hernia operation and would likely be there for a few days.

Not to be deterred, but more than a little stunned at this rather weird turn of events, I return to my car and turn it around, heading back to Toowoomba to take my instructions for my first day at this unconventional job.

On the way I stop off at a newsagent and buy a dictation pad, an eraser and a pencil. I'm obviously going to need something to write on, and with.

At the entrance to St Vincent's Hospital is a bank of frangipani trees bursting with my favourite flowers. I stoop and pick one up; a return gesture, it is my offering to a man lying in the men's ward in striped hospital pyjamas, a man who is proud, humble, famous, intensely private, reliable, unreliable, enigmatic beyond measure, infuriating and lovable in equal parts, and my new boss—R.M. Williams.

CHAPTER 22

GENESIS—HALL OF FAME

AUSTRALIA DAY 1942

If ever it were time for the dead to ride
then surely that time is now:
From the Leeuwin's cliffs to the roar of Sydney-side
From Wyndham to the Howe
call up your ghosts, Australia, call up your many dead,
your Kelly and your Lalor and the shirted men they led;
call up your brave, your Stuart, your Wentworth, your Bennelong,
your men who dared the Hashemy, with its bitter slavish wrong.
Call up your quietened singers from the silence of the grave,
who sang your latent spirit to the complaining wave.
                                                    —Ian Mudie

I entered a story that had been going for four years.

In December 1974, bush artist Hugh Sawrey and his wife Gill were visited at their quarter horse stud, Bangtail, at Boonah in South East Queensland by expatriate American pastoralist David Briggs and his wife Maryrose.

David had immigrated in 1966 after bringing to Australia the 31 quarter horses that formed the basis of Cloverleaf Quarterhorse Stud at Murrurundi in New South Wales, in which he was a partner. By 1974 he had a number of pastoral interests in Australia and travelled extensively through the outback. As a guest at many historic stations he had come to appreciate the rich culture of the bush and lament the probability of its disappearance, since there seemed to be no effort being made to collect and preserve it.

That December day as they visited with the Sawreys, David revisited a conversation they had often had. Why does Australia not have a place, he said, where the stories of your bush heritage are told, a place like our Cowboy Hall of Fame and Western Heritage Centre at Oklahoma City? Surely your outback heritage is every bit as rich as America's? And being a younger nation, surely much of that pioneering has taken place in living memory! Is Australia going to let those old-timers quietly disappear, taking their stories and memorabilia with them?

This time, though, David had brought a magazine with him to illustrate his point. *Persimmon's Hill* was a regular publication of the American Cowboy Hall of Fame, of which David was a member.

Hugh Sawrey was a bush artist whose popularity was on a trajectory to fame. He had knocked around the bush all his life and knew it from every angle. He loved it only as someone who knows it intimately can, and his evocative paintings were a true portrayal of the hardship, horsemanship and humour he knew so well.

As he had during their previous discussions, Sawrey agreed that something should indeed be done in Australia. But what? How to go about it? Who might take up the cause?

David had met R.M. Williams as a neighbour near Eidsvold, in Queensland's rugged Burnett region, some years before. In 1972 they were involved together with the establishment of the Australian Trail Horse Riders' Association. They had met again during

Hall of Fame Chairman Hugh Sawrey, 1981, at Rockybar, Queensland.
His inscription reads, 'To Jane, who always comes to my assistance!!'

Hugh Sawrey's painting 'Vision Splendid', which now hangs at the Australian Stockman's Hall of Fame & Outback Heritage Centre in Longreach.

Hugh Sawrey's personal vision: the Stockman's Hall of Fame as he saw it in 1982.

Slim Dusty, watched by R.M. Williams, lays the first stone for the Bruce Yeates Memorial Cottage in 1981. The cottage was built by R.M. and friends.

Architect Feiko Bouman with Hugh Sawrey as the Hall of Fame rises out of the ground in Longreach.

The five Paull sisters in 1987, the year Dad died. Standing: Nicola Paull. Sitting (from L to R): Sally Wright, Tina Merriman, me and Prue Graham.

My wedding to Robert Grieve, 25 June 1988.

The board enjoying a celebratory dinner at the Crest Hotel in Brisbane. (From L to R): Dr Bruce Yeates, Sir James Walker, me, R.M. Williams, Hugh Sawrey, Jill Bowen and Ranald Chandler.

ENTREE CARD

It is requested that on completion of the Official Opening by Her Majesty you proceed at once to take your place at the Afternoon Tea before the arrival of the Royal Party.

Please note the following is the Itinerary for the visit by Her Majesty —

    Friday, 29th April, 1988: 2.00 p.m. — Arrive Longreach Airport;
    2.10 p.m. — Arrive Hall of Fame, followed by a tour of inspection;
    2.30 p.m. — Official Opening followed by afternoon tea which will be held at the rear of the building, in both the eastern courtyard and the temporary exhibition area.

Immediately Her Majesty completes the Opening Ceremony and leaves the balcony, please make your way down the ramp to the right of the main entrance from where ushers will direct you.

THIS ENTREE CARD MUST BE PRESENTED FOR YOU
TO GAIN ACCESS TO THE AFTERNOON TEA.

1788-1988

Afternoon tea with the Queen at the opening ceremony of the Australian Stockman's Hall of Fame & Outback Heritage Centre 29 April 1988.

The Queen and I—with Sir James Walker at the opening ceremony. Unfortunately, it is a poor photograph of Her Majesty, who was in fact wonderful company and most interested in her surroundings.

A crowd gathers outside the Hall of Fame for the opening ceremony.

H. M. YACHT BRITANNIA

At Brisbane

29th April, 1988.

Dear Sir James,

When we reached BRITANNIA tonight, The Queen commanded me to write immediately to thank you for an afternoon at Longreach which she will always remember.

The extraordinary welcome which the people of Longreach and the surrounding area gave Her Majesty and The Duke of Edinburgh was warmer than could have been anticipated, even for the visitors who had experienced an Outback welcome before. The Queen was truly moved to find that so many had come from far and wide to see her again eighteen years after her last visit.

Now to the Stockman's Hall of Fame. It is nothing short of a triumph for you and all your colleagues that, in the heart of the Outback, you should have created a monument of these dimensions to the qualities that have made Australia great. Her Majesty was delighted to have opened it and greatly enjoyed her tour of the exhibits.

The Queen hopes that her thanks will be passed on to all those immensely deserving people who helped you over the months and years of preparation, and especially mentioned Miss Paull, one of the hosts who, like you, made the whole event such fun.

I have been asked by Her Majesty to send you the enclosed photogravure, which you may like to hang at the Hall of Fame, so that future generations can look back on a great day for Longreach and its visitors in Bicentennial year.

Meanwhile, the charming bronze of the ewe and lamb will be treasured by The Queen. It gave enormous pleasure, and it was most kind of Dame Mary, on this day of days for her, to have presented it.

Yours sincerely

Robert Fellowes

Mentioned in Despatches—the Queen's thankyou letter from her secretary, Sir Robert Fellowes. I was thrilled to read how much she enjoyed her visit and that 'Miss Paull ... made the whole event such fun.'

COUNCIL AT INAUGURATION
28TH JULY, 1985
CHAIRMAN—SIR JAMES WALKER, K.B., M.B.E., LL.D.
DEPUTY CHAIRMAN—DAME MARY DURACK—MILLER, D.B.E.

MISS J. BOWEN   SIR FRANCIS MOORE
MR W. R. M. CHANDLER   MR W. F. MUNRO
MR K. E. COWLEY   DR T. J. MURPHY
MR L J. M. CUMMINGS   MR W. C. K. PEARSE, C.B.E.
MR E. HAYES   MR H. C. SCHMIDT, C.B.E.
HON. R. C. KATTER   HON. R. M. STEELE
MR D. KEFFORD   MRS T. M. STROUD
HON. SIR JAMES KILLEN, K.C.M.G. MR R. M. WILLIAMS, C.M.G.

EXECUTIVE DIRECTOR—MISS J. O. PAULL
FOUNDER
MR HUGH SAWREY

The commemorative plaque set in stone outside the Hall of Fame, as unveiled by the Governor General Sir Ninian Stephen on 28 July 1985.

The Australian Stockman's Hall of Fame & Outback Heritage Centre in 2011, with Eddie Hackman's symbolic 'Ringer' statue taking pride of place.

the merging of the Australian Cutting Horse Association and the Australian Quarter Horse Association, and were on the board of the Australian Quarter Horse Association together.

David had observed that R.M. was a man who was not afraid of taking up a cause, especially to do with horses and the bush. Moreover, he had a bulldog's tenacity and made things happen. He suggested to Hugh that they approach R.M. Williams.

Hugh and David and Maryrose visited R.M. at his Hodgson Vale home near Toowoomba in January 1975. Over lunch they enthusiastically discussed the idea. Each of the three men threw $50 down on R.M.'s kitchen table towards the costs associated with registering the name throughout Australia and taking the necessary steps towards incorporation of a company. It would be called, they agreed, 'The Australian Stockman's Hall of Fame and Outback Heritage Centre'.

The registration of the name was a task delegated to David Briggs. He approached Cannan & Peterson Solicitors, signed the application for the registration of the name in every Australian state, and began the process of incorporation.

Until the end of 1975 the team of Briggs, Sawrey and Williams continued to meet and follow the process through. Then David returned to the States, leaving the project in good hands.

Hugh and R.M. pledged to put together a team of like-minded people to join them in their mission. They brainstormed a list of prominent Australians who might join the enterprise. At that time, almost every second- and third-generation colonial Australian could trace lineage back to the bush, one way or another. Much of the wealth in the cities was directly linked to the bounty to be had from investment in outback properties. There were still very strong city links to Australia's bush heritage, even though they might in some cases have been forgotten or ignored, and in general there was a strong nostalgic feeling for the perceived (and very real, to those who knew and loved it) romance of the bush. It was a matter of tapping into them.

Bob Katter Senior was the federal member for Kennedy in Queensland, the second-largest electorate in Australia, and a good friend of Hugh and Gill Sawrey. Involving Bob and his new wife Joy from the outset was a stroke of genius; both willingly supported the project and worked hard to get it off the ground, with Bob staying on the board to take it to its successful conclusion. Bob became the first chairman, and Joy was the first honorary secretary.

Hugh's doctor in Boonah, Bruce Yeates, was a savvy man much respected by Hugh, and with contacts in high places. He, too, joined the committee—and was ultimately responsible for the greatest coup in the project's establishment, its inclusion on the list of major projects for Australia's bicentennial in 1988.

Mary Durack Miller, historian and academic who had been raised in the Kimberley region, was the author of the iconic book *Kings in Grass Castles*. This was the story of her forebears' epic pioneering overland trip to the Kimberley. She willingly accepted an invitation to come aboard, nominating her brother Bill, who lived in Toowoomba, as her proxy since she lived in Perth.

Rupert Murdoch's star was well and truly on the rise. Through his company News Limited, *The Australian* newspaper had united Australians via a national daily newspaper since 1965. The CEO of Murdoch's News Limited, Ken Cowley, willingly took on a role which was ultimately to become a pivotal one.

Bob Katter conscripted a Central Western Queensland grazier from Barcaldine, Ranald Chandler, to the cause. Ranald was a raconteur of prodigious memory, a most entertaining man, with a profound commitment to his bush roots and Australia's unique story.

R.M. cast the net a little wider and included his brother-in-law and business partner, Mike Cummings, a member of the board of R.M. Williams Pty Ltd and based in Adelaide.

Hugh approached Jack Hillis, from Victoria, widening the scope of the network by continuing to seek support from further afield. Jack Hillis's involvement was brief in the greater scheme of the project, but significant, as he travelled to attend meetings leading up to the selection of the site and was a signatory to the original Articles of Association. In this same category of brief but significant contributors were a couple of others: Captain Reg Saunders, the first Indigenous Australian to gain a commission in the army during the Second World War, represented Indigenous Australia; Bob Dodd, a Toowoomba businessman, offered financial acumen.

Bob Cheesman, of Cheesman, Applegarth & Partners accountants in Toowoomba, when approached by Bob Dodd, agreed to act as honorary auditor for the company. This role was generously and expertly performed by Bob Cheesman for many years.

Gradually an eclectic team was building, each person bringing different strengths, contacts and skills to the project, each committed to the cause and determined to bring it about.

Hugh Sawrey donated a painting, the sale of which at $4500 helped to cover the inevitable costs. His agent, John Cooper of Eight Bells Gallery in Surfers Paradise, added a personal donation of $1000.

The Memorandum and Articles of Association of the Australian Stockman's Hall of Fame and Outback Heritage Centre were registered in the office of the Commissioner for Corporate Affairs in Brisbane on 28 June 1977. Its signatories were Hugh Sawrey, Bob and Joy Katter, Bob Dodd, Bruce Yeates, R.M. Williams, Ranald Chandler, Reg Saunders, Jack Hillis, Mike Cummings and Mary Durack Miller.

*

In August 1977, through *The Australian* and courtesy of Ken Cowley, an ad was placed calling for tenders for the siting of the Australian Stockman's Hall of Fame and Outback Heritage Centre. The comprehensive ad was put together by the very thorough Bill Durack. It called for submissions that stated historical interest, suitability of siting in terms of backup services in the way of motels and other points of interest, but citing a 'country atmosphere' as imperative. Communications, roads, rail and air transport were essential requirements, as were tourism potential and scope for future development. A key requirement was an indication of the degree of local assistance and support that might be anticipated in the establishment and maintenance of the centre.

R.M. later told me that more than 40 places throughout Australia registered their interest. Only a few, however, met the criteria and were deemed worthy of the exhaustive and expensive business of inspection visits by a delegation of committee members. Those places included Albury–Wodonga, Rockhampton, Toowoomba (and relatively nearby Boonah and Warwick), Charters Towers, Alice Springs, Cloncurry and Longreach. Canberra was also on this shorter list, with talk of a possible siting at Black Mountain although red tape proved this impossible to negotiate.

Ranald Chandler, using his family's Cessna aircraft, flew board members to inspections; R.M. Williams used his company aircraft flown by Bill Cooper to ferry others.

It seemed, however, that Longreach was ticking more and more of the required boxes.

Mrs Nancy Button, a Longreach grazier, had seen the ad in *The Australian* in August 1977 and thought, 'Why not Longreach?' She approached Sir James Walker, chairman of the Longreach Shire, who put the idea to the next shire council meeting. They agreed. Why not Longreach?

Longreach was in the wide brown land, the land of the min min light, strategically situated on the Tropic of Capricorn. The district positively vibrated with Australian history. It was the birthplace of Qantas, and the birthplace of the Australian Labor Party was just down the road at Barcaldine. As well, at Alice Downs Station, Blackall, not far away in outback terms, Jackie Howe had created an Australian legend in 1892 by shearing a world-record 321 sheep in seven hours, 40 minutes, using hand shears.

Capping it off in historical terms, relatively nearby (once again in outback terms), at Dagworth Station near Winton, Banjo Paterson had written Australia's unofficial anthem 'Waltzing Matilda'; a little further afield, Burke and Wills in 1861 marked their lamented Dig tree at Thargomindah, thereafter to die wretchedly and earn an everlasting place in the history books.

Longreach was rich in sheep, rich in cattle, a quaint classic outback town rich in outback tradition. It offered endless water from the artesian basin and the Thompson River. It was on the crossroads of the west, the main road from the south to the Northern Territory, and was a major centre for government, education and rural enterprise. It had a large (for a rural centre) aerodrome, had a regular flight service and was situated on the Central West railway line.

As well, it offered the essential ingredient: strong community and local government support with Sir James Walker at the helm. There was an unmistakable air of civic pride about the place, starting with the fig trees that lined the wide streets, offering an oasis of shade in an otherwise literally wide brown land.

So, why not Longreach?

A steering committee of interested citizens was put together. Later they became the unstoppable Central Western Queensland Branch of the Hall of Fame. Local medico Dr Tom Murphy chaired the committee (and later, the branch) and together they tackled their first brief, to prepare a submission; it was the start of 12 years of dedication to a cause for Tom and his devoted team, which naturally included Nancy Button, the instigator of the Longreach initiative.

The submission was lodged. Longreach quickly made its way to the short list. By 1978 it was a close contender for selection, but (unbeknown to the committee) there was diversity of opinion in the selection team, and what was needed was some concentrated lobbying to finally win them over to the Longreach cause. This arose from an unexpected quarter.

A woman in a lolly-pink cowboy hat came to town.

Jill Bowen had bush roots and relatives living in Longreach, and although she identified with, and loved, country people, time and tide had washed her up on the shores of city life. In 1978 she was a senior journalist with the Australian Consolidated Press flagship, the *Women's Weekly*.

She and *Weekly* photographer Ernie McQuillan arrived in Longreach in August 1978. They had been sent by editor Ita Buttrose to cover the story of a wild-pig race that was scheduled as a major event for Longreach's much-touted Starlight Stampede.

They arrived to find that because of rain the race had been called off; nothing was in the offing to justify two return air tickets from Sydney to Longreach, which meant uncomfortable recriminations from Ita should they return home empty-handed.

Jill proved herself to be made of stout stuff. With what we all came to know as her trademark determination, she set about organising the wild-pig race herself. Fresh from Sydney though she was, she headed into the pub and found a roo shooter, Frank Hatton, who promised to find her the wild pigs—by tomorrow. She borrowed and polished up a trophy from the local golf club; acquired timing gear from the local race club; fashioned a neck garland for the winning pig; wrote out a set of rules; and informed the local radio station that a wild-pig race would be happening in Longreach the next day.

And so it did. It was a remarkable feat.

Jill got her story, Ernie got his photos, the *Women's Weekly* got its article, and Sir James Walker realised that in this iron-willed woman was an ally worth having. He approached her and gained her support in the matter of lobbying to get Longreach over the line with respect to hosting the Australian Stockman's Hall of Fame and Outback Heritage Centre. She took her commission to heart. Armed with the names and contact details of the members of the selection panel, when she returned to the south Jill Bowen lobbied for all she was worth.

Sir James was a canny man. Not without undue attention to civic duty over the years had he gained his knighthood; not without good reason was he the chairman of the Longreach Shire for more than 20 years. He was also chairman of the Longreach Pastoral College, and for many years chairman of the Capricornia Electricity Board. His Santa Gertrudis stud, Cumberland, was a huge Australian success story. Sir James was a fierce advocate for the town he led and loved. He knew that being the home of such a monument would be a wonderful thing for Longreach and the Central West, so he and the shire council set about consolidating the offers that would ultimately clinch the deal.

In addition to 100 acres of land from the pastoral college on the eastern edge of town—which they assured the Hall of Fame would be deeded over as freehold as soon as the paperwork was able to pass through the necessary channels—Sir James added the offer of some of his own land, which happened to be adjacent. Sir James's land was in two adjoining freehold parcels of 5 acres each.

By November that year a postal vote had been taken by the signatories to the Articles of Association, as well as Bill Durack and Bob Dodd who had been involved in the site inspections. The vote was overseen by the shire clerk at Charters Towers, and Longreach was selected as the site.

Meanwhile, support was being garnered from the other side of the nation. Dame Mary (Mary Durack Miller was made a dame in the January 1978 New Year's Honours) had presented the concept to her academic colleagues. Professor Geoffrey Bolton, an eminent historian at the time engaged by the Murdoch University in Western Australia, was on side; Roy Hamilton, director of Western Australia's Office of Regional Administration and the North West, attended several meetings and offered advice and support.

R.M. Williams had not been idle, either. He was honorary treasurer of the Australian Rough Riders Association (ARRA); in May 1978 they pledged a donation of $50 000 over a period of time. President of the ARRA, Jim Bailey, was appointed to the board.

Bob Katter had been successful in approaching Qantas management with a request that they sponsor a deputation to the US to inspect the Oklahoma City Cowboy Hall of Fame to gain ideas for the Australian counterpart. Qantas pledged three return fares to the States; in January 1979 Sir James Walker, his brother Owen Walker, Jim Bailey, Ranald Chandler and Jill Bowen undertook this trip, returning full of ideas and enthusiasm. Bob Katter, on parliamentary business, also inspected the cowboy centre around the same time.

The ARRA contribution provided the wherewithal to engage a person to act in a paid secretarial role. Unbeknown to me, R.M. had been on the lookout for such a person. He had spotted one. He was anxious to tie me to the bronco rail and brand me with the Hall of Fame logo. If I went on holiday I might change my mind.

The ball was rolling. I had a tiger by the tail. It was to lead me a merry dance for ten long years, almost swallow up my child-bearing years, and dominate my life.

I find the bed the ward nurse has indicated he will be in, and stand nervously at its foot, holding aloft my frangipani flower token for him to see. My dictation pad is under my arm. The sharp new HB pencil nestles in my lime-green handbag.

He takes the flower, pleased, and waves his arm. 'Ah, it's you. Sit down,' he says in that self-conscious, tight-lipped way he has. I don't know him well enough yet to recognise it, but in retrospect I realise that this is an indication that he, too, is aware of the incongruity of the situation.

We exchange pleasantries. I explain that I have already been out to Rockybar and found him not there. No apology is offered, and no explanation. A nurse comes in and stands at the foot of the bed.

'Have your bowels moved yet?' she inquires.

Rigid with embarrassment, I look out over the next bed to the window that overlooks the brick wall of the hospital chapel. I examine the bricks in minute detail and hum a little tune in my head to block out the sounds as the nurse proceeds to do her obs, the old man just another body, and me, his 25-year-old visitor, as far as she is concerned no more in need of protection from this personal probing than the chair on which I am sitting.

At last she leaves.

My first instruction from the great man lying in the bed is as obtuse as the great man himself. 'Ring the Women's Weekly, will you, and ask them when they are sending us the money they promised us.'

What?

He seems to think that this is a completely rational request—as indeed it would be, if I knew what money, how much, who at the Women's Weekly, when, why, how they had offered us the money and to what written offer I might refer. But nothing more is forthcoming. That's all he has to say on the matter.

'Right then?' he says, his mien indicating that the conversation is over, and that he has expressed his intention perfectly.

'Right,' I reply.

Utterly out of my depth, utterly perplexed, I bumble across the road to the hospital gift shop and buy a Women's Weekly. I search the first few pages until I get to the editorial information, and to my relief there is a phone number there.

At home I dial the interstate number. A receptionist answers, and I pass the monkey from my back to hers. 'R.M. Williams asked me to phone and ask you where the money is that the Women's Weekly promised to the Stockman's Hall of Fame.'

'What?' she says. 'What?'

I couldn't agree more.

CHAPTER 23

HEAD OFFICE: ROCKYBAR, HODGSON VALE

Once he came out of hospital at the end of the first week and was able to get about, R.M. showed me the small office near the front door of his home which was to be my workspace. A nice old desk on turned table legs sat under a picture window overlooking the stallion's paddock. There, the lovely grey Arabian stallion Parada pirouetted and played for his own amusement and mine, and that of any mares who caught his eye.

It was a nice backdrop, although once I began the work I didn't get to look out at it much.

I sat down at the desk. 'How's the height?' said R.M.

'It's a bit high, actually,' I replied. 'But it'll be right.'

R.M. disappeared, reappearing in a few minutes with a small saw. 'How much too high?'

I indicated that it was about a handspan higher than I found comfortable, whereupon R.M. cleared everything off the desk and, soliciting my help, tipped it onto its back. Then he made a mark on each of the elegantly turned legs and without further comment sawed the bottom 4 inches clean off each one.

I watched him, open-mouthed. It had been rather an attractive desk. Here was a man for whom no obstacle stood in his way. I was to learn that if you couldn't go through it, you went round it, over it or under it. Or, you simply ignored it or pretended you didn't realise it was there.

During the first few weeks it was a matter of learning to decipher R.M.'s obtuse way of communicating. I was a typical daughter of the 50s—polite, obedient and at pains to please. On no account did I wish to appear rude or to question what he said, but a million doubts elbowed for room in my mind.

I had never met anyone like him! He waved his hands and spoke in expansive terms about the grand monument that was going to be built in Longreach, an enduring memorial to the heroes of the outback. Every story of every one of them would be on display there. From the humblest drover's cook to the greatest landowner of them all, Sid Kidman, they would all be honoured in this magnificent building.

It would be built in stone; it would be a cathedral where beauty of form was dedicated to magnificence of action.

It would bridge the gap in understanding between urban and rural Australia.

The Australian Stockman's Hall of Fame at Longreach would one day be as well known as the Sydney Opera House or Ayers Rock (now Uluru), he assured me, and as sought-after as a destination. The Hall of Fame would be a mecca for all Australians.

'One day,' he would say as we plied the weary outback miles between Toowoomba and Longreach on one of our visits there, 'one day, all these tired, sad, dusty little towns will be painted and prosperous because of what we are doing out here.

'What we're doing will bring people out here in droves; it will open the outback. It will bring it back to life.'

I had my doubts about this fantastic scenario he painted, but I humoured him. His enthusiasm was contagious, without a doubt. It just defied all logic when I knew that all we really had was an idea, a few people who were enthusiastic, very little money and not much else. Certainly not the makings of a national monument, built in stone, according to his vision, on the western plains in the middle of nowhere.

The task was breathtakingly enormous. R.M. did not appear to have a doubt in the world that it would happen. I was weighed down with them, but I hid my thoughts.

Another lesson—believe in your vision, and set about making it happen.

There was an enormous, heavy document on R.M.'s kitchen table.

'First,' he said, his voice taking on an evangelical note, 'we have to get the support of the nation. We have to get people to join up as members. Like-minded people will be the foundation stone on which this monument will be built.'

Lady Rupert Clarke had generously inveigled for us a complete printout of the members of the New South Wales Royal Show Society. It contained thousands of names and addresses in alphabetical order, courtesy of a dot matrix printer on striped continuous paper, the ultimate in 1970s technology.

'These are our membership base. We're going to write a personal letter to every one of these,' said R.M., waving his hands triumphantly. 'You're going to do the letters!'

I looked at the printout. It was massive. It was the days of the electric typewriter, with a ribbon through which each individual character was imprinted by a striker. A good typist might average 60 words per minute; typing mistakes were printed over (rather obviously) with white chalky paper, or covered (more obviously) with special white paint. Copies were made using carbon paper between the original and the copy, or multiple copies, each of which had to be corrected in the event of a mistake and each of which copy was unmistakably exactly that—a copy.

I'd been in the job less than a week, and this was my second impossible task.

Perhaps I turned white. I was certainly looking for the door to make my escape.

R.M. disappeared into the office, and soon the sound of a type-writer clacking made its way into where I sat in the kitchen, flicking through the enormous tome of addresses with a heavy heart. Soon he returned and without a word put a letterhead on the table in front of me. On it, he had typed Rudyard Kipling's 'If'.

I still have it today, his dubious typing skills evident throughout. The intent in R.M.'s gesture was as clear as the intent of this wonderful poem's creator. It gave me the strength to take up the cudgels, just as R.M.'s encouragement taught me that I had what it took to wield them.

'Don't worry. I've ordered a memory bank typewriter. You'll be able to do hundreds of letters a day,' he said.

Well, not quite hundreds a day, as it eventuated. But lots. Over time we managed an unbelievably enormous number of letters in 1979 terms.

Two weeks later I went to Brisbane to collect an Olympia Memory Typewriter 6101 and undertake the training in its operation. Pre-PC, laser or bubble-jet printer, it was a fantastic piece of technology and, using a magnetic tape with memory, could pump out a one-page letter in a few minutes, faster than anyone could possibly type. It cost $12 000.

R.M.'s letter began, 'You have no doubt heard about a movement to build an Australian Stockman's Hall of Fame in Longreach, Central

Western Queensland . . .' and went on to emphasise the importance of this project to every Australian, and invite membership.

Each letter was personally signed by R.M.

The letterhead, which had already been printed by Braeside Press in Toowoomba, featured a painting of a horseman with a backdrop of cattle, which Hugh Sawrey had created especially in his distinctive style. The same painting is the centrepiece of today's Hall of Fame logo.

This letterhead sported the rather spectacular address 'Box 1, Brisbane, 4001'. R.M. had acquired Queensland's No. 1 address through a contact in the post office. The Hall of Fame enjoyed the use of GPO Box 1 for many years. Mail was onforwarded to the Toowoomba head office—it was worth the day's delay to have such a distinctive address.

We managed up to 60 letters a day, and signed them every afternoon on R.M.'s kitchen table; I became as adept at signing R.M.'s name as he was himself. A Vision Splendid brochure with a membership application card was included with each letter, and a stamp (no self-sticking stamps in those days) fixed painstakingly to the envelope.

It was essential that each letter be personal, said R.M. A personal signature, with an actual postage stamp rather than a printed post office bulk-postage annotation.

The membership applications with their $20 cheques attached began to come in; just a trickle, they were indeed the foundation of what has now become, if not a place that everyone has seen, at least a place most Australians have heard of.

By the end of January we had printed off and sent hundreds of letters. The noise of the clacking memory-bank typewriter rocking the rafters of R.M.'s house was starting to wear very thin indeed, and we were yet to reach the end of C in the alphabet. I calculated that I would be doing this job alone for at least two years, if I did nothing else.

By March our wonderful high-tech typewriter had the first of many breakdowns, and had to be sent to Sydney for repair; there were so many moving parts in this valiant progenitor of the PC that it was bound to suffer from its huge workload, and it did. Frequently.

But there was a great deal more to do besides sending letters to potential members. Communication was the linchpin, and the pot had to be constantly stirred to keep building up the burgeoning momentum of the project. And of course, for me, there was the promised riding which had to be slotted into days that were becoming more and more occupied with the business of the Hall of Fame.

While the membership numbers were quietly building up, thanks to R.M.'s letters, the board needed to be consolidated and developed to create an Australia-wide focus. The first full board meeting that I attended as the new secretary was on 3 March 1979. The minutes I created, the first of many such records of Hall of Fame meetings, were long and detailed, as were the meetings!

The meeting was held at the Crest International Hotel in Brisbane, where it was resolved to expand the size of the board to 20 members so that representatives from every Australian state could be included.

The *Women's Weekly*, which—via Jill Bowen—had played a significant role in lobbying for Longreach as the site and subsequently promoted the project extensively through prominent feature articles, was represented at this meeting and many subsequent ones. On this occasion Marjorie McGowan from the magazine formally pledged a donation of $10 000 towards a prize for a design competition. The *Weekly* would publicise the competition and announce the winner.

Bob Katter resigned as chairman, and Joy Katter as secretary/ treasurer. They had played a huge part in the beginning days. Their departure heralded the start of a new era, a ten-year epoch during which the administration of the project was conducted from our office in Toowoomba. There it grew from the contents of Joy's briefcase to a non-profit public company with thousands of members and a multi-million-dollar major bicentennial project. For the first 2½ years this office was in R.M.'s home at Rockybar, Hodgson Vale; then I moved with it into Toowoomba.

On Bob Katter's retirement Hugh Sawrey took on the role of chairman; Charlie Palmer, commissioner for main roads and former shire clerk of the Longreach Shire, temporarily took on the role of honorary secretary; later R.M. moved into this position and remained in it for the duration of my tenure.

Sir James Walker, appointed to the board in December 1978, took on the responsibility of honorary treasurer.

Dr Bruce Yeates was a personal friend of Queensland's treasurer Sir Llew Edwards. Bruce left the March meeting with a brief to lobby Edwards and Premier Joh Bjelke-Petersen for Queensland government funding and support. His role in this capacity was invaluable. It resulted in the Queensland government's matching the *Women's Weekly*'s $10 000 contribution towards the design competition, and set in train a $500 000 contribution towards capital costs. Most significantly, Bruce Yeates's efforts paved the way for the ultimate success of the project through the Bicentennial Authority.

The Longreach branch under the chairmanship of Tom Murphy was moving into full swing. Lloyd Walker, Sir James's brother, encouraged Longreach Rotary to organise a fundraising auction that resulted in a donation, in June, of $12 500 to kick-start the funds of the Longreach branch. Local interest was becoming an unstoppable force. Soon Tom's ingenuity would run to a series of Challenge Dinners which accounted for many fundraising dollars and a great deal of publicity, not to mention memorable good times that became part of the fabric of the Hall of Fame ethos.

It seemed that the obvious support of the Longreach district well and truly vindicated the faith placed in it by the Hall of Fame board.

Cannan & Peterson solicitors in Brisbane made representations to the justice department and the taxation department to secure the tax-deductibility of donations. Changes to the constitution were registered to make this possible.

Offers of practical assistance tumbled in as the idea caught people's imaginations. The Queensland chapter of the Royal Australian Institute of Architects (RAIA) agreed to conduct a national design competition and prepare a brief for this purpose. Rupert Murdoch offered to print four tabloid newsletters a year. Ansett Airlines, approached by Dame Mary Durack Miller, sponsored travel for directors from Western Australia. Trans-Australia Airlines (TAA), approached by Don Davies of News Limited's *Mirror* newspapers, upped the ante and offered free flights for all directors to attend meetings.

Life went on, though, with all its ups and downs. Dame Mary was hit by a car in September and had both legs broken, which put a dampener on everyone's spirits until it was evident that she would recover fully.

In October I travelled to Longreach for the first time with R.M. and a delegation of architects to inspect the site. RAIA design competition assessors Bill Durack, Daryl Jackson and John Morton looked out over the expanse of nothingness; goodness knows what they thought. On an endless flat landscape on the edge of Longreach, our promised 110 acres sat, empty and treeless, a palette from which our masterpiece was to arise. It was hard to imagine.

Longreach itself was a lovely, prosperous-looking town. It wasn't dusty and down-at-heel like some of the other places we had passed through on the long drive up. On the basis of its plentiful water supply the expansive streets were tree-lined and the front lawns green, with subtropical gardens lit up with brilliant flowering bougainvillea and the occasional waft of frangipani or mock orange.

We were entertained by Sir James Walker in the Longreach Club. Interested local luminaries lined up to meet R.M. and the architects; some were sceptical, some were enthusiastic. All were interested to hear what they were planning for their quiet outback town.

A prominent and highly respected stock and station agent, Gordon Reid, of Longreach, joined the board in August. Lady Rupert (Kathleen) Clarke, or 'Lady Kath', a Melbourne socialite from one of Victoria's most prominent families, joined the board in November, at the same time as the irrepressible Sir James Killen, federal politician, staunch Queenslander and raconteur.

In November we had the first of many meetings in Rupert Murdoch's boardroom at News House, the News Limited head office, in Holt Street, Surry Hills, in Sydney. I found it particularly thrilling that I had an opportunity to use Rupert's personal loo. But of course much more serious business was at hand. Later that month R.M. had a visit from Rob Neville, an emissary of the United States Embassy, sent to discuss the possibility of cultural exchanges between the Australian and US halls of fame.

Nineteen seventy-nine was a big year. Gradually each facet of the diamond that was the Hall of Fame concept began to shine and coalesce into a brilliant thing. It was a very exciting time—and very exciting to be involved.

*

I rise before the sun and snatch a quick breakfast. Thanks to endurance horse training, I'm used to early starts.

I have made sandwiches for the trip the night before. I sling the last few toiletries into my overnight bag and throw it into the hatchback of my gleaming new yellow Mazda 323. Already it knows the familiar route through Toowoomba, along the New England Highway to Rockybar where R.M. waits impatiently, exhaust fumes rising from his huge old white Fairlane and wipers noisily scritching the dew from the windscreen.

Early starts always have an air of anticipation that I love. My luggage stowed, we set off into the early-morning darkness. Destination Longreach—1111 kilometres away, a one-day trip with two drivers and not many stops.

The kilometres whiz by as we slip past Toowoomba and set our course to the west. After an hour, we pass my old stamping ground, Bowenville, almost the suburbs of Toowoomba. Dalby disappears in a flash and in no time Chinchilla looms. Miles is next, then a few small towns that look half-deserted and shuttered; still we travel west, barely making an impression on the map of our vast state.

Five hours since leaving Rockybar the Roma watertower rises above the undulating horizon lined with brigalow, belah, the odd bottle tree and sundry scrub. Roma has more of an air of prosperity than its predecessors along the track; but after Roma, where we change drivers and fill up the car in anticipation of longer distances between petrol stations, the countryside levels out and the road narrows.

It goes on and on and on, the black ribbon unwinding before us, its dotted white line inexorably drawing us westward.

At Mitchell we pause to eat our sandwiches beside the Maranoa River. We stretch our legs and drive on. At Morven we turn right off the Warrego Highway, onto the Landsborough, and our course changes to north-west. We are a little more than halfway and still it looks like nothing on the huge expanse of our Australia road map.

There are only four towns for the next 400 kilometres until we turn west. The countryside changes. At first the land is red sand with twisted sandalwood scrub; the dry creeks are lined with stunted coolibah trees with trunks of the purest white. Then gidyea trees appear. 'Wonderful firewood,' says R.M.

The pungent smell of gidyea permeates the air.

Kangaroo and emu carcasses dot the roadsides. Emu families—dad and the kids—silhouette against the blue, blue sky.

The bitumen narrows to not much more than a single lane.

When we meet an oncoming vehicle we have to share the road; this means negotiating a shoulder of bitumen which is 6 inches high in places, ragged and sharp, running the gauntlet of a puncture, or a hail of stones which will break our windscreen if we are unlucky. Our luck holds. We keep moving.

First Tambo, then Blackall, emerge from the haze of heat. The countryside is by now blacksoil plains, rich with a waving sea of grass. The towns are dusty and quiet, with a slightly forlorn air of dilapidation, but their beautiful, ornate timber civic buildings speak of grander days.

'One day,' says R.M., 'you will drive up here and all these towns will have had a fresh coat of paint. There will be businesses here and shops to attract the tourists. The road will be fixed up and there will be cars heading out to Longreach to see our Hall of Fame.'

Yeah. Right.

At Barcaldine, home of the Tree of Knowledge, birthplace of the Australian Labor Party, we turn left. We drive into the setting sun along the Capricorn Highway, through one more tiny town, Ilfracombe. Our destination is now a mere 106 kilometres away. There, a welcome awaits us, Sir James Walker and the people of Longreach ready to greet the weary travellers at the Longreach Club, that last bastion of squattocracy. There, they will show us and the three architects who have

229

already arrived by plane the hospitality that underpins the reason why Longreach was chosen as the site for the Australian Stockman's Hall of Fame.

CHAPTER 24

ENDURANCE RIDING

THE DROVER'S COOK

The drover's cook weighed fifteen stone,
He had one bloodshot eye,
He had no laces on his boots,
No buttons on his fly.
His pants hung loosely round his hips,
Hitched by a piece of wire,
They concertinered round his boots,
In a way that you'd admire.

He stuck the billy on to boil,
Then emptied out his pipe,
And with his greasy shirt sleeve,
He gave his nose a wipe.
With pipe in mouth he mixed a sod,
A drip hung from his chin,
And as he mixed the damper up,
The drip kept dripping in.

—from *The Drover's Cook and other Verses*
by Tom Quilty

R.M. was a stalwart of the Australian Endurance Riders' Association, and a keen endurance rider himself, although his gammy knee somewhat stymied his enjoyment of riding. Nonetheless, he was still able to tack a shoe on a horse, was game for anything and uncomplaining about pain.

It was a matter of pride for him, for example, that he always refused anaesthesia at the dentist, whatever was in the offing. 'I just hold the nurse's hand,' he said with a twinkle in his eye.

Training for the 1979 Tom Quilty Gold Cup 100 Mile Endurance Ride began soon after I started working for R.M. He had been the instigator of this event and named it for his friend Tom Quilty, a character of renown in the Kimberley. Its origins were typical of the way such things come about.

As told to me by their son, Basil, many years later, some time in 1966, Tom and Olive Quilty stayed with R.M. at Rockybar, his Arabian stud near Toowoomba. They had an animated discussion about the merits of the bush horses from the early days in comparison with the stockhorses of the modern day.

Tom, strongly in favour of the opinion that old-time horses had more stamina, cited his frequent rides from Eureka Spring on the Flinders Highway to Cloncurry—a distance of a hundred miles—in order to contact his father in Sydney by telegraph. He rode the distance, he said, on one horse, overnighting in Cloncurry and riding back to the station the next day. It was quite a remarkable feat of endurance on the part of the horse!

The upshot of their discussions was that R.M. was deputised to organise an endurance ride of one hundred miles, and Tom Quilty offered to provide a gold cup as a perpetual trophy for the winner.

The Quilty Endurance Ride has been an annual event since that time; the cup—which cost Tom $1000 in 1966—had more gold in it than the famed Melbourne Cup. It now resides in the Australian Stockman's Hall of Fame. The Quilty was touted as—and was—the longest and most gruelling one-day endurance ride in the country. It is still considered the pinnacle of endurance riding in Australia today.

I was allocated a purebred Arabian gelding from R.M.'s stable, Rockybar Somali, to train and ride in the July event. The woman who managed R.M.'s stud, Marianne, was training Somali's half-brother Granite. Both were greys; Granite was as solid as his name, while Somali was a rangier animal. Both were by R.M.'s purebred stallion Shieke; both were big horses, strong and stoic in the Arab style.

Training had to take place in the cool of the morning so it was a case of rising well before the sun and saddling up, half asleep, to work our horses at the trot, up and down the hills to the south of Toowoomba. It was beautiful countryside crisscrossed with roads and tracks through the wooded ridges at the top of the Great Dividing Range.

From the top of the range the view went on seemingly forever. In the heat of the day a thick haze of eucalyptus gas hovered above the trees—although it was only on weekends, when office work was not calling me, that we had longer training rides and were abroad later in the day.

The forest was wild and rugged, teeming with wildlife, alive with the sounds of birds waking to one lovely morning after another as we trotted or galloped uphill and walked or trotted down dale. Our quest for fitness for our horses, preparedness for the gruelling 100-mile epic around the mountains and valleys of Colo in the Hawkesbury region near Sydney, pushed us on and on, ever further, carefully monitoring their recovery rates and progress as we went.

Somali and Granite gradually settled into the routine. They were fed a diet of oats mixed with oaten and lucerne chaff, a little linseed to oil and brighten their coats, and supplements to increase their stamina. Hay nets with lucerne hay hung in their stables for grazing throughout the day. Their feet were regularly shod and carefully monitored for the corns that would put paid to all our training efforts. Sore feet, sore legs, sore anything, no riding.

The horses were hosed and rubbed down and left to dry while they supped a well-earned breakfast when we got back from our early-morning ride. They were rugged against the cold in their stables every night. Their coats began to glisten and their muscles to ripple. Bit by bit, as they became fitter and their regular meals of oats made them feel cheeky, they became more feisty and harder to manage.

We got to respect each other, as horse and rider do. Somali was a sensitive horse; Marianne told me that he'd had an awful experience as a youngster and an air of sadness had hung over him ever since. His best friend was his brother; one day on an excursion into the national forest at Goomburra, Somali's brother got into a nettle patch and flung himself down in fright—right into the nettle patch. The nettles stung him more as he rolled in terror and before the thrashing mass of horseflesh could be coerced into standing up, he died of shock. Somali witnessed this and, it seemed to Marianne, was forever something of a tragic figure. He made other friends among the herd at Rockybar, but never again a best mate like the one he had lost.

Horses have good days and bad days just like anyone. I came to know Somali's every mood. Ever adept at sitting a shy, I learned to anticipate the signals that set him to taking a mighty leap to the side in mid-stride—usually a kangaroo startled by our sudden appearance out of the mist, or a topknot pigeon taking off in fright from a low branch with a loud rush of wings, its distinctive tinkling alarm call an excuse for Somali to snort and leap sideways as if he was a newly broken colt.

Despite this tendency, I rarely rode him with a bit in his mouth. A halter with a pair of rope reins looped low on his neck was all I needed, my signals the merest shift in posture or squeezing of the legs. At an extended trot Somali overstepped by a spectacular amount. He was a delight to ride, flying along with barely a bump, his proud Arabian tail held high and slightly to one side. He was a beautiful horse and I loved him dearly.

R.M. taught me to make a leather bridle that first year, and to plait a set of gaucho knots as stays.

It was like beautiful music watching R.M. work with leather. He cut the length of thonging for a set of gaucho knots from a complete kangaroo hide. Using a special blade for the purpose, he cut the hide around and around, holding the thonging firmly as it dropped down beside him in a perfectly even solitary piece.

Then he honed his homemade knife on the small whetstone for the next part of the process. Sometimes the knife he used was one made from a hacksaw blade as the most resilient material for the job—he made me one of these. When his knife was sharp enough to shave the hairs on the back of his hand, which he did by way of illustration, he began to bevel the edges of the thonging.

He made a notch in a piece of pine board that matched exactly the width of the thonging he had just cut. Deputising me to hold the end—'and don't let go whatever else you do, all right?'— he held the knife firmly against the notch in the pine board at such a precise angle that when he began to step backwards out the front door and down the road past the rose garden, the very finest sliver of leather poured over the top of the knife. With perfect precision, without stopping in his gait and only vaguely aware of where he was going, watching the thonging feed through the notch and the tiny overflow spill out above it, he backed down the road until he reached the end of it.

Then he returned to the house, gathering up the strand of thonging as he went, and bevelled the other side.

R.M. had a small amount of horsehide which he used for the base for the gaucho knot. It was strong, he said, and made a firm base, but was not as bulky as cowhide, so it made a lovely flat knot. Somehow he had calculated exactly the right width to cut the thonging. Fashioning another piece of pine board to the size of the bridle's cheek strap that was to hold the gaucho, he stitched the horsehide with an invisible knot using waxed saddler's thread.

Then he began the over and under, over and under, of the knot itself, weaving it round and round its horsehide base, back through itself, over and under, until it fitted snugly in a masterpiece of perfection.

After thoroughly wetting the completed article with water mixed with wood glue he rubbed it fiercely into a shiny patina with a piece of pine board. The final knot, painstakingly prepared, was a work of art.

A set of gaucho knots on a plain bridle was lovely. I made a perfect set for Marianne.

I made several bridles under R.M.'s direction. One had a double headstall, a stockhorse bridle. Another was of red leather double-stitched with waxed white saddler's twine with a full set of gaucho knots. Yet another was double-stitched from white leather, with red gaucho knots. I bought a set of saddler's 'beetle ears', long, curved pieces of plywood which held the item being stitched in an iron grip, yet was able to be released easily every couple of stitches.

With an awl I made an angled hole for every stitch as I went. Using two threaded needles I pulled one waxed thread through first, then the other back through the same hole, pulling the threads tight.

It was backbreaking work, and painstaking, especially as I finished the bridle off with a full set of gaucho knots. But as R.M. said, it was a thing of beauty and I have, as he predicted, cherished it for a lifetime.

As winter took hold on the Downs the sun rose later. The ground was thick with frost and the mist often impenetrable when we set off on our training rides early each morning. My workload in the office meant that I still had to keep the same draconian training hours of 4 a.m. rising. Often it was still pitch dark as we crested the top of the ranges several miles from Rockybar.

Riding in the dark was good training, as I was to discover. The Quilty was a 100-mile (160-kilometre) endurance ride, competed over 24 hours in midwinter; obviously many of those hours were going to be in the dark. It started at midnight. We planned to average 16 kilometres per hour over the distance; factored into our calculations were the obligatory three hour-long rest stops during which a team of vets assessed the progress of each horse according to a strict set of criteria.

The vets measured the horses' heart rate and respiration on arrival at each of three checkpoints as well as the finish, and checked them for dehydration, lameness or discomfort of any kind. Half an hour later they measured the heart rate and respiration again and checked the horse thoroughly for any soreness. Horses were allowed to proceed only if they were comfortable and had recovered to within the given parameters; horses deemed unfit to continue were 'vetted out'.

Riders were weighed in and out again at each checkpoint; rider and tack had to weigh between 73 and 91 kilos. If not, lead had to be carried. Marianne carried lead; I didn't.

In July we drove the long distance to Colo Valley in R.M.'s truck, laden with horses and horse feed and camping gear.

For the Quilty ride in 1979, 54 horses and riders lined up for the race's first shotgun start; only 29 completed the ride.

After a midnight start before the moon came up we had a wild ride through pitch darkness across the most rugged portion of the course. I felt like the Man from Snowy River with a blindfold as we slid down vertical inclines and splashed across frigid creeks we could barely see.

R.M. and Marianne's friend Linda were our strappers, meeting us at each checkpoint, whisking our horses off for a rub down, a feed and carefully meted drinks of water. They walked them around with a rug over their backs so they didn't stiffen up, while we collapsed in a heap, rubbing aching knees and sore spots.

An hour later, fresh and raring to go, we set off again.

In one of those weird twists of fate, four of us approached the finishing post together, vying for what we believed was to be third place. We all started to race each other, but realised that if we kept it up all four of us would ruin our horses and 'vet out' at the finish after our tremendous effort in covering 160 mountainous kilometres at an average of 16 kilometres per hour.

We made a pact that we would stay together until we were a hundred or so metres out, then make a mad dash for the line. And that's what we did. Apart from demolishing a cameraman who was making a television documentary about the ride and was standing too close to the action, we all arrived uneventfully within seconds of each other. It just happened that Somali stretched his long neck across the line fractionally ahead of the others.

With a time of nine hours, 36 minutes and 11 seconds, I was placed ahead of the other three; the winner was vetted out when the vets declared his horse lame. I was declared the second-placegetter. I received a silver Quilty No. 2 belt buckle and a somewhat unfair place in the annals of the Tom Quilty 100 Mile Endurance Ride.

It is my tribute to Marianne that she husbanded me through what was the most gruelling undertaking of my life. I was a new chum at endurance riding. Marianne had wonderful expertise with horses and rode with an ease that belied the harrowing nature of the sport for the rider.

I did endurance riding as part of R.M.'s team for three years. The sport has become in my mind, especially after the two subsequent rides I entered which were considerably longer, an analogy for life. For the sake of the team, and for the sake of the horse who willingly puts his heart and soul into the job (and believe me, if he doesn't want to, there is no way he will), you continue through barriers of pain and exhaustion that would normally pull you up.

You learn that it is possible to go on.

In each of the following two years I successfully completed the 260-kilometre Stockman's Hall of Fame Winton to Longreach endurance ride. Then I knew about heart and nerve and sinew! And as it progressed, hanging on in the face of the growing demands that were placed on me in the administration of the Stockman's Hall of Fame project took all the heart and nerve and sinew that I possessed.

I reach the door of R.M.'s house at about the same time as the winter sun.

Stamping the dampness off my boots and clapping my hands against the cold, I turn around and look across the bare rose garden at the valley below. The last tendrils of the morning's mist are lifting away from the ragged trees down at the creek; a crisp, cloudless winter day is dawning.

Piccaninny dawn two hours earlier had found us shrouded in the stuff as we made our ghostly way along the lanes and gravel roads of Hodgson Vale. Our two grey Arab horses, Somali and Granite, had paced each other doggedly along, their rhythmic breathing the only sound that kept up with our chatter in the strange, muted silence.

The clip-clop of their shod hooves striking gravel was quickly muffled by the fog and left behind in the silence.

With a sigh, I open the door and step inside onto the mat. My Santa Fe elastic-sided riding boots will stay by the door; my saddle-stained jeans and sweat-stained jacket will be my office attire for the day. The scent of horse-sweat will be my companion. The view of the stallion Parada and the rural hills of Hodgson Vale through the picture window above my desk will be an occasional reminder of a life outdoors—when I remember to look out.

I leave my outside identity with my boots at the door, slip into the office and seat myself at the desk with the vandalised legs. My alter ego kicks in. Soon the morning disappears. I am utterly absorbed in the business affairs of the Australian Stockman's Hall of Fame and Outback Heritage Centre.

CHAPTER 25

HITTING THE GROUND RUNNING

This to express our gratitude
For interest you have shown
Friendship and hospitality
Stressing the solidarity
Of your land with our own.
The prospect of your leaving us
We all regret so much:
But may the vision that we share
Provide a link of lasting care
God Bless! Let's keep in touch.
                    —Mary Durack Miller, 6 December 1980
        Written for Philip Alston Jnr, US ambassador to Australia

To say we hit the ground running would be no exaggeration. R.M. had had four years dreaming about how this thing would come about. Now that he had the wherewithal to make things start happening, he plunged on with a vengeance.

The wherewithal came from the ARRA—Australian Rough Riders Association. Every couple of weeks its general manager, Jim

Stuart, came up to Rockybar from ARRA headquarters in Warwick with accounts payable and the cheques for R.M. to sign as treasurer.

They sat at R.M.'s kitchen table and discussed the affairs of the rough riders, who was on top of the ratings and how well McPhee's bulls were bucking, who had punched whose lights out and how plans were going for the World Cup Rodeo.

Jim was a bull-rider himself, the boldest of the bold (or the silliest of the silly, whichever way you looked at it), and often limped in with a gammy leg or a few broken ribs for his trouble.

My pay eventuated from each of these meetings.

Meantime, it was essential to keep up the momentum of the Hall of Fame. The people of Longreach were bursting with enthusiasm, and wanted to see things happening. Each person who had so far taken up a place on the board was busily networking, seeking out support and contributions, and suggesting prominent people who might be willing to come aboard.

Because the project was to have an Australia-wide focus, the number of board members was increased to 20. A policy was adopted that there be at least two directors from every state. In 1980 another six directors were added. They were Jill Bowen of the *Women's Weekly*; Eddie Connellan of Conair Airways in the Northern Territory; Wallace Munro of Weebollabolla Shorthorns in Moree, New South Wales; Colin Pearse of Western Australia; Tess Stroud, also of Western Australia; and John Ayers Senior from South Australia.

With sponsorship from Trans-Australia Airlines (TAA), it was possible to hold board meetings around the country to garner support and promote branches. Branches were formed in Western Australia, South Australia, New South Wales and the Northern Territory, while a Victorian/Tasmanian branch came into being in 1982.

During 1980 we met in the News Limited boardroom in Sydney,

at Murdoch's Southdown Press in Melbourne, at the shire council chambers in Longreach, at the Parmelia Hilton in Perth, and at the US Embassy at Yarralumla in the nation's capital, Canberra.

Under the guidance of Bill Durack, the Royal Australian Institute of Architects (RAIA) undertook the enormous task of conducting a two-stage design competition. It had been Bill's son Michael's suggestion that the competition be run in two stages—Stage 1 being the preliminary design, and then six finalists being invited to produce working drawings.

The RAIA nominated three assessors from within their ranks to judge the competition. They were W.A. (Bill) Durack FRAIA (Queensland chapter), John Morton FRAIA (Queensland chapter), and Daryl Jackson FRAIA (Victoria chapter).

In November 1979 the assessors Bill Durack and John Morton presented their architectural design brief to the board. It was based on a construction cost of $2.5 million. The competition offered a first prize of $5400, second of $3000 and third of $1300, with an additional $1300 to go to each of the six finalists.

The *Women's Weekly* published the story of the upcoming national design competition in January 1980. More than 200 architects registered their interest. Thirty-seven took up the challenge and lodged preliminary designs in June 1980.

The professional side of things notwithstanding, Hugh Sawrey and R.M. met in R.M.'s kitchen one day and over a cup of strong black tea (R.M.'s laced with butter and honey as was his wont) expressed their scorn for the modern need to go about things in such a complicated way.

'I could design the thing in minutes,' said R.M., waving his hands expansively.

'Exactly!' said Hughie. 'So could I!'

Exasperated with their constant stream of bold rhetoric, I challenged them both. 'All right then—I've got a few minutes to spare. Do it! Design your Hall of Fame!' I said to them.

So they put their heads together over R.M.'s kitchen table and Hugh drew a magnificent classic Grecian façade, complete with columns and bas reliefs, grand staircase and enormous portico, built, of course, from stone.

Having worked in an architect's office myself, I couldn't help but notice that there were one or two rather major omissions. Such as a floor plan, elevations other than the façade, anything in the nature of working drawings. Anything in the nature of anything, for that matter, but the sketch of an idea not unlike Hugh's 'Vision Splendid' shrouded in campfire smoke in the painting on the front of our brochure.

But it was no use explaining this to two old bushmen who were used to making do, and building everything they needed with their own bare hands.

Stage 2 of the design competition began with six finalists in July 1980. While the entrants stretched their imaginations to try to come up with the winning design, we were comfortable in the knowledge that at least they had no competition from the landscape to hinder their ideas. Apart from a couple of small gullies lined with occasional stunted trees, the 110-acre site was as bare as the top of a billiard table.

With the design competition ticking away in the background, there were other matters to keep moving along from our office in R.M.'s house at Hodgson Vale. Planning had begun for a promotional book, *The Stockman*, to be published by Lansdowne Press. A limited edition of 1000 copies, with 250 signed, of a Sawrey painting 'Reining the Near Leader' was to be printed and sold from head office. Mike Cummings had organised 5000 poster-quality prints of Sawrey's 'Vision Splendid' painting, also to be sold at promotional events.

Rupert Murdoch had phoned R.M. with the offer to print material for the project. Don Davies, the manager of News Limited's *Sunday Sun* newspapers, arranged the printing of 10 000 of the Vision Splendid brochures at cost price, a huge saving.

But the newsletter was their pivotal contribution. News Ltd offered to print four editions of 20 000 copies of an eight-page tabloid newspaper for the Hall of Fame per year. This it did, at first from its *Sunday Sun* printing house in Fortitude Valley, and later at the *Warwick Daily News* in Warwick. Jill Bowen took on the huge role of editing the publication in a voluntary capacity. This labour of love cost her dearly. While eventually, after a number of years, she was paid an honorarium, it was a pittance in comparison to her contribution to this vital organ of the developing project.

The newsletter became our voice; 20 000 copies per edition enabled us to spread ourselves unimaginably widely in the days before the internet. It was just a matter of distribution, and that became our logistical problem at head office. It created a huge workload. When, in April 1982, Jill Bowen suggested that the newsletter be published with 16 pages and only twice yearly, I'm sure we breathed a sigh of relief that our distribution of 20 000 newspapers was to be only a twice-yearly event.

While the design competition was in progress, R.M. in his inimitable style was concocting another plan.

It had been over a year since Longreach had been selected as the site. Like a duck paddling upstream, a great deal had been happening behind the scenes to move the project along. But like that duck, not much was showing in the way of effort above the waterline—or in this instance, on the flat piece of western plain that was the site for the Hall of Fame.

In mid-1979 the Longreach branch had used some of its hard-earned funds to construct an impressive sign—'This is the Site for the Australian Stockman's Hall of Fame'. It was undoubtedly an eyecatcher in its prominent position adjacent to the Landsborough Highway as people drove into Longreach from the east. But behind it was an expanse of nothingness—not a sod turned, not a ruffle on the undisturbed acreage behind it.

R.M. took me with him when he visited the premises of JH Wagner & Sons, stonemasons, next to the cemetery in Toowoomba. We walked around their noisy workshop where stone of every description was being cut, polished and inscribed. R.M. obviously had something in mind.

We were shown a huge block of granite being split into portions to make headstones. Granite was not cut with a saw, Wagner explained; rather, it was split along its perfect plane with a series of small chisels.

Sandstone, though, was another matter. Its make-up was altogether different, not along perfectly formed lines of crystal like granite. Sandstone was a random material, a sedimentary rock composed of whatever had been washed to the place where it was laid down millions of years ago. To cut sandstone a diamond-tipped saw was required.

R.M.'s interest in his favourite building material, stone, had become a possibility when he visited Warwick and Rosemary Champion at their property Longway, near Longreach. They drove out to the Herbert Range and surveyed the magnificent vista spread before them.

'There's sandstone in this range, R.M.,' said Warwick. 'We have a small quarry of it. Perhaps you should think of building your cottage out of sandstone.'

While sandstone had never been used as a building material on the unstable blacksoil plains, and was not considered either feasible or viable, R.M. believed that a fitting monument should be built in stone.

He began to fight a quiet one-man battle. Word got around that he was on the lookout for sandstone deposits and soon he was also approached by local grazier Barty Deane. Barty had a large sandstone deposit on his place, Goodberry Hills, which was also on the Herbert Range. R.M. was welcome to try it and see if it was of building quality.

The general consensus, however, was not wildly positive. 'Never been used up here; never do the job. Impossible on blacksoil. Too crumbly. Too costly. Won't work.' Such talk was like water off a duck's back to this tough old codger.

R.M. inspected the deposits. They were good. He became quite fixed on the idea of using stone.

At the board meeting in February 1980, R.M. quietly mentioned that he had found suitable sandstone, and that at his request Bill Durack had drawn up a plan for a simple stone 'cottage' to be built on the 10-acre block of land donated by Sir James Walker, to trial the use of the local material.

People didn't take a great deal of notice, what with all the excitement of the design competition, new directors, new branches being formed, the newsletters, the membership base growing rapidly, talk of fundraising ideas, and offers of support coming in from every angle.

But other things were happening as well on something of an informal basis. R.M. was having meetings with Toowoomba mechanical engineer Ray Hagan of Hagan Machinery.

In December we had our board meeting as guests of the US ambassador, Philip Alson Jnr, and his wife Elkin, at the magnificent US embassy at Moonah Place, Yarralumla, Canberra. R.M., my new office assistant Peggy Filmer and I drove down from Toowoomba in R.M.'s Fairlane.

Eleven directors attended, including the much-loved Dr Bruce Yeates who had recently been diagnosed with leukaemia and would, to our great sadness, lose his battle with the disease just over a year later.

The three architect assessors, Bill Durack, John Morton and Daryl Jackson, arrived in a cloud of secrecy with armfuls of architectural drawings. After the meeting's preliminaries had been dealt with, they unveiled the much-awaited secret of the winner of the competition and—more excitingly—the design.

Feiko Bouman was a Sydney architect in his late 30s. He had been a member of the design team for the High Court in Canberra. He had also been a finalist in the design competition for the National Archives.

With Hugh's vision of the classical Grecian monument firmly etched in our minds, we greeted Feiko Bouman's extraordinarily imaginative design with a mixture of emotions. A series of curved roofs was joined by walkways and terraces.

The Australianness of his design, he said, was assured by the extensive use of the ubiquitous corrugated iron. The rounded shape was indicative of storage silos or water tanks, its generous overhangs and pergolas reminiscent of homestead verandahs.

The large central hall with supporting minor halls gave the form of a woolshed with a central space and lean-to's, and was similar also to the shape of the aircraft hangars on so many station properties.

Most of all, however, its internal void space bespoke that commodity which was found most generously of all in the outback, but not in the city—space.

One small detail was that Feiko had not envisaged that his

building—or series of buildings, as originally designed—would be constructed from stone. That was not part of the design brief.

The competition had been won on the basis of a projected cost of construction of $2.87 million at December 1979, plus 12 per cent for other expenses such as surveyors, engineers and architects. Construction time was estimated at two years, with a lead-up time for documentation of nine months.

The board accepted the recommendation of the RAIA assessors, and the *Women's Weekly* published their Australia-wide exclusive announcement of the winner of the design competition on 17 December 1980.

The original design incorporated a series of similar buildings. Magnificent though it was, it almost immediately became evident that its construction would cost way more than the projected amount. This took several years to sort out before the first sod for the building was turned in 1985.

There was also the pressing matter of funding. At that stage, even the $2.5 million on the basis of which the competition had been staged was not in the bag. The board was confident that it would get the money, but just when and how were matters which required urgent consideration.

Bruce Yeates had mentioned that Dr Llew Edwards, Queensland treasurer and a medico friend of Bruce's, had suggested that the project consider tapping into Australia's upcoming bicentennial celebrations in 1988. A bicentennial authority was being formed, he said, which would be seeking out projects to fund. We should keep an eye out for what was happening, and be ready to apply.

The bicentennial year seemed like a terribly long time away. But as it eventuated, the way these things go, the timing was rather perfect.

This suggestion became one of Bruce Yeates's enduring legacies. His other was the securing of a one-off special grant of $500 000 from the Queensland government for the establishment of the Australian Stockman's Hall of Fame.

It's 1.55 a.m. on 11 July 1980. Rugged up to the eyeballs, mounted on our horses, we mill around on the main street of Winton waiting for 2 a.m. and the starter's gun.

The crowd of 35 horses includes three from R.M.'s stable; R.M. himself is on Somali; Marianne rides Granite, and I am riding a beautiful brown Anglo-Arab called Rockybar Dusk, or Dusky.

We are facing a very different outlook from last year at the Quilty. We have travelled every bit as far to get here but in the opposite direction this time. We've been camped on the flat plains of Winton in Central Western Queensland, 180 kilometres further on from Longreach, for a few days now to get the horses acclimatised.

One of the major acclimatising factors is enticing them to drink the artesian water. It smells like rotten egg gas and I suspect tastes a bit like it, too. At any rate, our showers at the showgrounds have been nice and warm—boiling hot, actually—straight from the artesian basin. They smell like the water, but the soap lathers so well that it's hard to wash off.

This endurance ride is touted as the longest two-day ride in the history of the sport. It's the first annual Winton to Longreach Golden Horseshoe 250-kilometre endurance ride, organised as a promotion by the Central Western Queensland Branch of the Stockman's Hall of Fame.

We have come prepared for the high diurnal temperature range in the desert-like conditions of the Australian outback. The winter days are hot, up to 30 degrees Celsius, while the nights are below freezing. My swag, out of which I have removed myself reluctantly not an hour since, is liberally lined with a sheepskin I tanned myself, with the wool still on, and a mohair rug knitted by my mum.

Now I am feeling the cold. But the excitement is intense.

Someone makes an elaborate speech as we try to hold our excited horses in check. Then the shotgun blast and we're off into the pitch.

A horse bolts past us in the darkness, and we struggle to hold our own mounts. 'Hold them! Walk!' calls R.M. We walk awhile, or should I say our horses dance a merry jig as we hold their heads into their chests, and then when everyone has gone ahead we let them stretch out and settle into a steady pace. We have just over 100 kilometres in which to catch up with the rest of the field, so there's no panic.

Some of the riders have miner's helmets, a great idea. We haven't caught up with that technology so tout torches, which aren't really that much help. It's best to just let your eyes get accustomed to the darkness. I thank my lucky stars that R.M. and Marianne are riding greys; otherwise I can barely see a thing. It's a pity, as the most picturesque portion of the first day's ride is in the dark, before a reluctant moon eventually rises. Then by the time the morning sun comes over the horizon, we are onto the flat plains for an interminable jog across an empty horizon strewn with gibber stones.

One by one the checkpoints loom, and we go through the rigorous process of vet checks. One by one horses vet out; by the time we reach the overnight stop at Maneroo Station well after dark the numbers are depleted to 14. Marianne is in second place; R.M. and I have stuck together further back in the field and husbanded each other along.

Our horses are tired, but spry. I am feeling quite spry, too, except that one of my knees seems to have taken on a life of its own. I kick myself in the backside with every laborious step I take on the way to the shower block to bathe off my sweat in the steaming stream of artesian water.

In the morning, amazingly, our mounts are quite frisky. We have 52 kilometres to go. It's a lovely ride along the Thompson River with a triumphant lap down the main street of Longreach. We arrive at the finishing point under the newly erected sign announcing the site for the Australian Stockman's Hall of Fame. Marianne takes second place; R.M. and I share equal seventh.

Our horses are tonguing for a drink of water—but, in a perfectly synchronised and quite magnificent effort at a first-ever endurance ride by Dick Law, Rosemary Champion and the Longreach team, someone has forgotten to supply water for the finishing line.

Without it, and quickly, our horses will overheat, dehydrate and vet out after all that effort. Someone finds a hose, but I have to line up for a bucket. I snatch off my hat and fill it to overflowing. Dusky drinks gratefully. A camera flashes. A tender moment between rider and horse is captured, to be cherished forever.

CHAPTER 26

THE COTTAGE

Ian, R.M.'s son, had warned me that R.M. would be very likely to lose enthusiasm for the day-to-day running of the Hall of Fame head office; this was backed up by R.M.'s frequent assurances that 'one day you will run this thing by yourself'.

The thought horrified me. I couldn't imagine how I would ever find the courage, let alone expertise, to deal on my own with a company that was progressing at the rate at which it was doing, growing exponentially, and creating a faith that couldn't be broken with so many people.

Then there was the matter of dealing with the personalities on the board. There was so much at stake, so much to do! I was so young and inexperienced.

I didn't want to do it on my own.

By this time Peggy Filmer, who worked away at the introductory letters on a second memory bank typewriter from R.M.'s house, and I were kept absolutely flat to the boards with the workload. The correspondence was increasing; the membership roll grew steadily; subscriptions and donations required receipting, recording, thankyou letters; and with the guidance of Bob Cheesman I learned to put in place the transparent accounting procedures required of a non-profit public company. Branches needed direction and support. Every few months another 20 000 tabloid newsletters arrived at the door to be distributed, and in the first instance the newsletter had to be proofread by me at the printers, in the early days in Brisbane, then in Warwick.

Directors' meetings needed to be arranged, attended and recorded, their travel organised. Reports needed to be written, before and after meetings, and detailed minutes taken. Everyone had to be kept happy and informed. Letters of thanks, letters of request, branch by-laws—a huge PR machine was growing up around me as I felt my way.

I breathed and lived every small detail. The technology we used to do our work, while we thought it was state-of-the-art at the time, was very primitive. Everything was hands-on; at that stage there was no such thing as fax, let alone the internet. All our communications were by letter, and there were many of them. The corporate responsibilities weighed heavily with me; I had to learn the stringent corporate requirements as I went.

I wasn't great at creating boundaries; the Stockman's Hall of Fame took over my life. But at least I still had R.M. between me and ultimate responsibility.

But that changed in April 1981.

R.M. had attended a board meeting of R.M. Williams Pty Ltd in Adelaide. Chairman John Swain agreed the company would pay for the construction of a stone-cutting saw. So R.M. went back to see Ray Hagan of Hagan Machinery in Toowoomba. 'I need a pretty big saw, Ray, to cut this sandstone,' said R.M.

'How big, R.M.? What exactly do you need?'

'You'll work it out, Ray,' said R.M.

Ray worked it out. He went to the Ziglers, of Monumental Masons in Mort Street, Toowoomba, for help. They were very generous with their advice. Gradually and with consummate engineering exper-tise, Ray constructed a huge saw. It weighed 4½ tonnes and had a 30-horsepower electric motor, which together with a 56-inch diameter diamond-tipped saw provided a cutting rate of 3 inches per minute.

In April 1981 it was loaded onto the back of R.M.'s body truck. R.M., his son John and granddaughter Debbie drove to Longreach with their teetering load. Sir James Walker met them and with substantial assistance from the shire council they unloaded their cargo.

Once the building of the cottage was underway, R.M. realised that he needed another saw, one with a moving tray for ease of handling the huge rocks that were eventually forthcoming from Longway Station. He had Ray Hagan build him a second saw, larger than the first, and I got my truck licence so I could drive it to Longreach on the back of R.M.'s truck. John Williams was co-driver. It was heavy going, my short career as a truckie.

R.M.'s building of the cottage made good sense. There were mutterings beginning to be heard that nothing was happening, the Hall of Fame was all a furphy; not a sod had been turned and it was over a year since the site had been declared. Without a doubt something had to be done in a practical sense to keep faith with the project.

Besides, R.M. wanted to prove that the local stone was a viable building material.

In typical R.M. fashion, he took one step at a time—pretty major steps, to be sure—without looking too far into the future or at the possibility of failure. He had not blundered altogether into the unknown; Sir James had promised support and assistance from the shire council in provision of utilities and carting of the stone. But further than that, the actual sourcing of the timber needed for posts and trusses, the acquisition of the stone, its blasting from the quarry at Longway and later Goodberry Hills, and who was to cut it once landed on the site, let alone pay for all this, were still to be determined. It was a measure of R.M.'s unparalleled faith and vision that he firmly believed that all would fall into place. And it did.

A Longreach character, a nuggety, knockabout sort of bloke with a chequered history, Bob Sadler, happened by not long after. R.M. had set up a camp near the saw, using discarded ironbark sleepers from the nearby railway, and 44-gallon drums, with canvas stretched across as a roof. Bob called in to see what he was up to. They shared a cup of billy tea and exchanged yarns.

'I'll help you, old feller,' Bob declared, when R.M. told him his vision. So Bob was sent to Helidon in southern Queensland to do a dynamite course and get his blasting licence.

Keen to defray naysayers' concerns that a stone building would never stand up to the movement of blacksoil, R.M. dug footings to bedrock at 13 feet, and filled them with concrete. Then a concrete floor slab, 30 by 50 feet, was poured.

It was a busy Longreach Show week for R.M. that May in 1981. Settling into the site, he arranged for the concrete base for the saw to be poured. It was the day Ita Buttrose, editor of the *Women's Weekly*, came to the Longreach Show, and she made a fortuitous impromptu visit to the site. She arrived just in time to sign her name in the wet concrete of the saw base.

Still wrestling with the problem of securing the hand-adzed timber he envisaged for his stone building, R.M. sat in the crowd at the show and watched the wood-chopping. One contestant stood out. His name was Cyril Dahl.

'Some old bloke wants to meet you,' someone said to Cyril. Once he heard it was R.M. Williams, whose gear he had used in his rodeo days, his ears pricked up. Cyril and half a dozen axemen mates went down to R.M.'s camp on the Hall of Fame site to see what he wanted. Over a cup of tea they yarned; Cyril sharpened R.M.'s chainsaw. He told him his grandfather had been a bullocky, his father a bridge builder.

R.M. knew bridge builders to be the best adze men of their kind. 'Can you use a broadaxe and an adze?' he asked.

'Most certainly; bred to it,' was the laconic reply.

'I need timber door- and window-frames for the stone cottage I'm going to build here. Think you can do it?'

Cyril gave his assurances and returned home to Bundaberg. R.M.'s faith was well-placed; Cyril was a man of his word. A couple of weeks later R.M. received word from the Longreach railway station that there was a load of timber for him. It was the promised frames, cut from spotted gum and hand-adzed to perfection.

In the ensuing months Cyril cut all the timber R.M. needed for the job. While he included some ironbark, Cyril used mostly spotted gum, as its natural oil prevented the timber from splitting. The 9- by 9-inch, 60-foot long centre beam of spotted gum was spectacular.

To quote Cyril 31 years later, 'R.M. was as pleased as punch.'

Slim Dusty came to Longreach the day the first stone was ready to be laid, the first Monday in July 1981. With a flourish R.M. offered Australia's most beloved country singer the honour. A photographer from the *Longreach Leader* captured the moment.

In October, Sole Bros circus came to town. Their 4-tonne, 85-year-old elephant Lena lent a trunk to lift one of Cyril Dahl's doorframes into place.

An untold story was that of a building inspector from Rockhampton who happened to be passing along the Landsborough Highway on his way into Longreach. He called into the site to see what was going on. He couldn't believe his eyes when he saw the scaffolding for the by-this-time 8-foot high stone walls, on which R.M., helped by his sons Peter and John, worked. It was nothing but 44-gallon drums perched one on top of the other, with lengths of timber slung between, with an oddly teetering quality here and there that didn't fit anywhere within the Building Inspector's Handbook. Somehow R.M. talked him round.

As a morale-boosting exercise, building the cottage was a stroke of genius and well worth its $150 000 price tag. So, too, as a promotional exercise. The story of the old man (R.M. was 73) camped on the Hall of Fame site at Longreach appeared in dailies and magazines around the country. Kenyon Castle from ABC's *A Big Country* featured the story in a documentary. Something tangible was happening on the site; not something that could be picked up and moved away if things didn't go ahead—but something in solid stone, immovable, visible, beautiful, a bold statement of intent.

While all this was happening in Longreach, I remained at head office in Toowoomba and ran the business side of the Hall of Fame. This was the start of my management of the company.

Happy camping in the bush and working with stone with his sons beside him, R.M. still managed to attend the four board meetings that were held that year.

We met in Adelaide in February and formed the South Australian branch, and in Alice Springs in June, where Queensland Tourist and Travel Corporation chief Frank Moore (later Sir Frank) took a seat on the board. In September we met in Sydney and at the end of the year, in Brisbane, where Laurie Muller and Anne Wilson of Lansdowne Press presented their offer to publish a book to raise funds and awareness for the project.

At the end of the year, Dr Tom Murphy, stalwart of the Longreach branch, agreed to take a place on the board. And during the year, John Ayers Senior died and was replaced on the board by his son John Junior, who retired from this position in December.

There were feints at getting a major fundraising program off the ground, but more groundwork was needed. A professional fundraiser was engaged only briefly. It quickly became evident that fundraising was a job best tackled from within. There needed to be more of a story to present, and some scores on the board. The board wrestled with the modus operandi for this.

Bruce Yeates died in December after a valiant battle with leukaemia. Bone marrow transplantation was a new medical procedure that was undertaken in the hope that it might save him. It didn't. At the Alice Springs meeting in June, as Bruce and I strolled down the pretty streets of the centre of town and looked at the sights, Bruce reached up and plucked a red gum blossom from one of the small flowering trees in the civic centre.

'Look at this!' he said, cradling it against the palm of his hand. 'It's only when you realise that you won't . . . um . . . that you won't be around much longer to see things like this that you really learn to appreciate how beautiful they are.'

Mid-year, I moved the Hall of Fame's office out of R.M.'s home at Hodgson Vale and into Toowoomba. The very grand front room of one of Toowoomba's historic homes, Vacy Hall, became my office. I left R.M.'s dainty-legged, vandalised desk at Rockybar where years later his son John wondered at its strange architecture and placed blocks under the legs to raise it back to its former height. My neighbour Bill Gunn acquired for me the loan of a grand oak desk with a surface the size of a ping-pong table, which I had placed in the bay window of my expansive new office.

Peggy had moved on so I advertised for a replacement assistant. Carol recalls the day she came for her interview at Vacy Hall. She knocked nervously at the door to my office. A voice called to her to come in. When she opened the door, all she could see was a vast cloud of cigar smoke emanating from a place by the window. A voice from behind it bade her come in, and when the smoke cleared, she saw me sitting there with a Wee Willem cigar in my hand.

Nicotine and adrenalin were my constant companions during those years, and Carolyn Price (later Crist), bless her loyal, hard-working heart, was my constant support and champion. Years later, when everyone was lining up for accolades—including those who had looked on with scepticism in the early days—Carol, who had worked side-by-side with me for seven years as we frantically dealt with the unstoppable avalanche of demands that were placed on our small office and young shoulders, whose strength and sense of humour kept us going many a long day, wrote a letter to the paper. 'Jane Paull is the backbone of this organisation,' she wrote. 'She is the strong silent force that unites the many and varied people who make up the Stockman's Hall of Fame.'

Carol's tribute meant more to me than she will ever know.

February 1981. We gather in Dame Mary's room in Adelaide. It's been another marathon meeting, this one held at the Educationalist Centre in Flinders Street. It's been a huge couple of days, in fact, and we are justi-fiably exhausted. Nonetheless, with Ranald Chandler's usual banter and fruitful exploration of the minibar, we have found another burst of energy at the bottom of our glasses.

R.M. tells us about how he met his mate Eddie Connellan, our newest board member. Not a bad story of two bucks of the same ilk coming to blows. It goes like this:

'It began badly,' says R.M. Eddie, perched on the edge of Dame Mary's chair, jiggling his brown hat by the brim, nods sagely, and chuckles at the memory.

'I suppose you could say I was a bit brash in those days,' adds R.M. Another nod from Eddie, more enthusiastic this time. 'Well, it was 40 years ago!'

R.M. continues: 'Conair Airways was in its fledgling stages, and Eddie was flying the plane that was taking delivery of merchandise for Alice Springs. I was waiting at the Adelaide airport for him. I had a pile of hatboxes with an Akubra inside each one. It wasn't a big plane. Eddie loaded everything else in and then stood looking at my hatboxes.

'"Those hatboxes won't fit in the plane," he said. "You'll have to take the hats out and stack them inside each other."

'"That won't be happening," I said grandly. "The hatboxes stay. You sort out how you fit them in the plane."

'"You sure about that?" said Eddie.

'"Absolutely. The hats stay in their boxes," I replied. I was quite adamant.

'Well, Eddie thought about it for a little while. Not for long, though. Then he lifted one hatbox off the pile, put it on the ground and stood on it. "That should about do it," he said. Then he took the next box and put it on the ground beside the first one.

'"You win!" I said.

'Well, that's the sort of bloke we're dealing with here,' says R.M., smiling wryly. Eddie nods his handsome head and takes another sip of his drink.

Good story.

Eddie has just told us about his Rolls Royce. He's converted it into a farm vehicle complete with fencing-wire dispenser and a full toolbox.

'Very handy at Narwietooma,' he chuckled. Narwietooma was his vast cattle station near Alice Springs.

When the axle broke, he told us—an inevitable consequence of driving a road vehicle across bore drains—he wrote to Rolls Royce in England and asked the cost of a new one.

'Rolls Royce axles don't break,' was the reply. 'A replacement has been shipped out to you, free of charge.' Another wicked chuckle from our Territorian as he spun his hat around on an axle constructed from his fingers.

Someone says, 'Our table should be ready, better go downstairs,' and we stand up to leave. Dear old Dame Mary, solicitous darling that she is, turns to Eddie and says, 'Eddie, dear, would you like to use my bathroom?'

'No, thanks, Mary,' Eddie replies. 'I've got a long-range tank.'

CHAPTER 27

A TIGER BY THE TAIL

Men I have known many
And loved but a few
It should be no surprise to hear
That one I loved was you.

Although our paths don't cross now
—a practicality—
Just knowing we tread the self-same earth
Often comforts me.

I don't forget the things we said
Though time has passed us by
I don't forget how our minds touched
And what we did, and why.

I answer other drummers now
My love is vested here
But often still I think of you
And still, I hold you dear.

—Jane Paull

I was very much at the front line now in the management of the business, just at the time that the pace picked up.

Many of my friends had married by now and moved into that world of family that did not accommodate single career women. The life I was leading, and in my mind (rightly or wrongly), the success of the project, demanded a choice from me; I made the choice in favour of the Stockman's Hall of Fame. The rest could wait. The man I had in mind didn't.

R.M. and his cottage-building were wonderful for the project. He loved living in a camp again, and everyone dropped in to see him and have a cup of tea around his campfire. He was quoted as saying that as he lived in a humble camp, everyone came to visit; if he lived in a mansion, no one would visit.

R.M. was never short of a feed; it became something of a local competition among the Longreach wives to take the most appetising stew or casserole down to R.M.'s camp to feed him and his workers. And his dog. Ray Hagan flew himself up to inspect his saw; Ray's wife Gavina cooked a delicious apricot chicken casserole for him to take to R.M. They heated it in the camp oven over the open fire and it was a triumph, absolutely delicious. Ray was pleased to note that there was enough for another meal.

That was not to be; with a grunt R.M. raised himself to his feet, grasped the handle of the camp oven, and whistling his dog, placed the offering at his feet. The dog ate a fine tucker that evening.

'That old R.M. was a scallywag!' chortled Ray many years later.

With 18-inch thick sandstone cut to random size, Cyril Dahl's hand-adzed timbers, and an interior floor of black marble from Marble Bar in Western Australia acquired at a cost of $5000 donated by R.M. Williams Pty Ltd, the 'cottage' was a triumph.

The third Golden Horseshoe Endurance Ride was held in July 1982. The Queensland governor Sir James Ramsay and Lady Ramsay, in company with their aide Vicki Walker, were special guests. After-wards, on 24 July 1982, Sir James formally opened the cottage, the Bruce Yeates Memorial Administration Centre. A flour bag was used as the curtain the governor pulled back; no velvet or tassles for this outback memorial.

The construction of the cottage was a fantastic diversion from pressing concerns that were bogging down the project behind the scenes. There was the matter of finance—significant finance. Millions of dollars in funds were needed.

And there was the matter of the building; we had a design, but it was much too expensive in its present form.

Eddie Connellan was to attend a meeting of the newly formed Australian Bicentennial Authority (ABA) when it met in Darwin in May 1982. He would present a submission on behalf of the Hall of Fame. Who would prepare it?

Colin Nichols, a marketing professional in Toowoomba, was engaged to prepare the ABA submission. One was to be presented to the Queensland body of the ABA in May, one to the Darwin meeting later that month, and a formal submission for the federal body in June. Eddie and I were to oversee the content of the submission. Practicality determined that the task fell to me. The submissions were duly lodged. Round One.

Sir Frank Moore, in his role as chairman of the Queensland Tourist and Travel Corporation (QTTC), met John Reid, federal chairman of the ABA, and discussed our project. More detail was needed; concerns had been expressed about future viability. Sir Frank organised a viability study of the project.

Richard Bramley of Pannell Kerr Forster Chartered Accountants prepared a comprehensive market study. It was presented to the board in March 1983, and then handed to the Queensland government, the prime minister's department, and the ABA to support the application for funding.

The study was very positive about the prospects of the Australian Stockman's Hall of Fame project; it did bring to light, however, the fact that 'outback tourism was almost non-existent'. Sir Frank Moore had voiced this opinion to the board in October 1982 and added that 'the QTTC sees the Hall of Fame as a potential fulcrum for this untapped resource, and that potential exists to set up the Hall of Fame as a management scheme for tourism in the outback'.

In the 30 years that have elapsed since that time, the roads of the outback are, if not bumper to bumper with traffic, certainly substantially filled with travellers wanting to see the 'wide brown land'. Sir Frank's words, and R.M.'s, were visionary and prophetic. The faith placed in the project by the ABA has had far wider repercussions than for the establishment of the Stockman's Hall of Fame alone.

In October 1982, supporting the bicentennial submission, Bob Katter Senior arranged a visit by Sir James Walker, Hugh Sawrey and me to Prime Minister Malcolm Fraser at what is now Old Parliament House in Canberra. He listened, and offered his backing.

In the meantime, there was the matter of the development of Feiko's conceptual design. When they were put together, the design competition guidelines had been as comprehensive as to the requirements of the centre as was possible. Before working drawings could proceed, however, it was imperative to bring the design back within budget and prepare a detailed design brief.

Sir James and R.M. approached Claude Wharton, the Bjelke-Petersen government's Minister for Works and Housing. In November

Mr Wharton gave his response—his department would prepare a pre-design brief to assist with planning and coordination of the project.

Roman Pavlyshyn, director of the building division of the State Works Department, instructed his staff to prepare a pre-design brief which would, he assured us, place the project on a firm basis. Under the direction of Hugh Somers, senior planning officer of the building division, a study was to be prepared including a time schedule, a list of accommodation requirements, a functional brief, a selection of building options, and construction options.

To me fell the somewhat lonely role of link between the department and the Hall of Fame. I didn't think twice about it, actually. It had to be done to progress the project.

First, they needed the Hall of Fame's projected budget. I was at something of a loss as to how to prepare it. Ken Cowley, who had taken on the role of honorary treasurer, offered me the advice and support of Don Davies and his team at News Limited's *Sun* newspapers in Brisbane. Their guidance was invaluable. I presented the budget to Roman Pavlyshyn, and work started on the pre-design brief.

Over the ensuing months I wore a track down the bitumen between Toowoomba and Mineral House, George Street, Brisbane. There were certain days on which I couldn't arrange meetings at the department owing to their regular interdepartmental ping-pong tournaments; on these days the desks were moved to accommodate the ping-pong table and work ceased, the sounds of electronic devices replaced by the hollow thud of the ping-pong balls and the encouragement of the onlookers.

As far as the Hall of Fame was concerned, I was 'It' in terms of nominating the accommodation requirements and for that matter, all the requirements, of the building complex. 'How many toilets will you need?' Hugh Somers would ask. 'How many galleries? How much space in the servery? What sort of counter? Will you be having a gift shop? You'll want a turnstile, won't you? What about security? Power points? Comfort air conditioning or atmospheric control? How about control of natural sunlight?'

It went on and on. I answered as best I could. I rang galleries, spoke to Alan Bartholomai of the Queensland Museum, found suppliers in the Yellow Pages and asked their advice. Hugh pointed out that an ideal art gallery was really a square box in which lighting, atmosphere and space could be manipulated to suit the art.

I rejoindered that this building had to be spectacular, and a fitting monument. I still hold that view, and it is indeed spectacular, and a fitting monument.

With the new title of executive secretary, I now reported to a smaller administration committee—consisting of the Queenslanders, Sir James Walker as chairman, R.M., Ranald Chandler and Dr Tom Murphy—as the board had become unwieldy with its 20 members; and Trans-Australia Airlines, having reached a budget crisis of its own, had presented us with an amendment to our carte blanche travel arrangements for all directors to attend meetings. It was no longer an open-ended arrangement—we had to stick to a budget of $6000 worth of travel per year.

Our office in Toowoomba had moved to new premises at an old house, not nearly as grand as Vacy Hall, at 24 Hill Street. A junior clerk, Wendy, joined our head office team to manage some of the workload. Carol learned the intricacies of a new gadget, a Canon CX1 computer which now managed our huge mailing list. Despite its simplicity in modern terms, it was then the newest of the new and cost $13 250. With it came a dot matrix printer that (noisily) (and slowly) cranked out its offerings on striped continuous paper. There was no potential for personal letters from this machine, so the bulky old memory-bank typewriters still acted in this capacity.

And by this time the newsletters were once again being published four times a year, this time in quantities of 15 000 per issue. In that way we gained the advantage of the reduced rate for regular registered publications sent through Australia Post.

By June 1983 the Queensland Department of Works' pre-design brief was completed. I was sorry to see the last of Hugh Somers and the gang at Mineral House. I had spent such a lot of hours there that I felt like part of the team. The brief cited a projected cost for Feiko's amended building of $11 million. This was made up of a building budget of $6.5 million, and non-building costs of $4.5 million.

We had work to do!

Feiko made one of his many visits to Longreach to visit the site and discuss the historic qualities of the larger Longreach precinct. He went to the cottage to visit R.M., hard at work building.

R.M. persisted in calling Feiko (pronounced 'Faiko'), 'Feeko', and even spelling his name that way, till the day he died. A conversation would go like this:

R.M.: 'Well, Feeko, what do you think of the cottage?'

Feiko: 'Feiko. It's good, R.M.'

Feiko was able to bear witness to the successful use of sandstone as a feasible building material in Longreach. He was particularly taken with some of the lovely local buildings, especially the timber railway station which was built in 1916 in an ornate style. There was talk of replacing it with something more modern and functional; Feiko was horrified. In the strongest possible terms he pointed out the aesthetic value of its architectural charm, and that of remaining similar buildings in the town such as the beautiful old post office.

The Queensland government confirmed their special grant of $500 000 towards the construction costs. We had the means to proceed with working drawings. In mid-1983 Feiko was instructed to proceed with schematic design drawings, incorporating local sandstone wherever possible in favour of his proposed brickwork.

In October that year Feiko pegged out the spot where the future building would stand. A Longreach local, Charlie Harris, who had an earthmoving business, had offered to construct a dam on the watercourse that ran from the highway across the middle of the site.

Once Feiko had pegged the building site Charlie built the small dam for which, later, Kenny Scott donated a Comet windmill with a sail diameter of 35 feet and a 4-tonne motor for pumping water into a turkey's nest dam. Comet ensured that the windmill was functional.

Charlie Harris's dam became the first sod of earth turned on the then-treeless main site. It formed a crucial part of the landscaping adjacent to the future building.

Sir Frank Moore as head of the Queensland Tourist and Travel Corporation was well positioned to follow the progress of the Australian Bicentennial Authority. Being in with the inner circle, he was able to pass on a great deal of advice direct from the coalface. He advised the board that the project should seek part of the projected $166 million national funding under the category of 'National/State Commemorative Projects'.

Eddie Connellan was hot on the trail of the bicentennial funding requirements and offered advice at every meeting. The ultimate success of the Hall of Fame's application was due in no small part to his representations and this became Eddie's enduring legacy to the project, as well as Bruce Yeates's. Eddie became ill midway through 1983 and to our immense regret, as he was a colourful and extremely lovable character, he died on Boxing Day 1983. It was two years almost to the day after the untimely death of his co-conspirator in the ABA application stakes, the equally respected Dr Bruce Yeates.

Two new directors joined the board in 1983. Ted Hayes of Undoolya Station in Alice Springs strengthened the Northern Territory representation and Charles Schmidt from South Australia, former CEO of Elders, came aboard with an impressive business pedigree including current chairmanship of the Commonwealth Savings Bank.

At a meeting in Townsville in July 1983 Ken Cowley handed the treasurer's role to Charles Schmidt, remaining on the board as a powerful force. Charles Schmidt's wisdom and financial acumen were an enormous help to me in the role that was winding itself around me at head office, and of course of immense value to the Hall of Fame.

Also at that meeting the details of the sale of a set of limited-edition Sawrey prints were finalised. The *Sunday Mail* promoted the sale of the signed and numbered prints, which featured the Winton to Longreach endurance ride, Diamantina Lakes, the quart pot that Hugh nominated as his inspiration for the Hall of Fame, and 'The plainsman and his wife', being Bill and Edna Kelly. There were 250 of each print and they sold for $125 each or $400 for the set of four.

The board decided to set up a finance advisory committee consisting of the members of the administration committee as well as Charles Schmidt. Fundraising ideas were being collated, names of business luminaries for a fundraising committee were bandied around the table. Sir James looked to the brotherhood of knights for membership of this committee. Groundwork was being laid for a fundraising program to kick into being as soon as the bicentennial announcement was made.

Bit by bit, jigsaw pieces were being constructed to fill the gaps in the puzzle.

There was a change of federal government. Labor took the reins as the bicentenary loomed. In September 1983 we made another visit to the same office in the lovely Old Parliament House building in

Canberra that we had visited just less than a year previously. This time there was Sir James, R.M. Williams, Ken Cowley and me in the deputation, and we met with a different prime minister in the same office.

Bob Hawke assured us of his personal support for our bicentennial application.

I sit at the top table beside my chairman, Hugh Sawrey.

Hughie's a good chairman; he listens to everyone, lets everyone have their say; if anything, he's a bit too generous with that part—letting everyone talk on and on. But he understands, as do I, that everyone has to feel involved.

They've each made a huge commitment of time and money to come to these meetings. They've each put in a lot of energy between board meetings, too, attending branch meetings and functions, spreading the word, approaching government. There is a feeling of one big family around the board table that is immensely heartwarming—everyone united with a common goal, and everyone feeling so strongly about the importance of preserving our unique Australian outback culture.

The price for Dame Mary's commitment is higher than any of us realise. The Hall of Fame has taken so much of her time that she has had to put her new book idea on the backburner, where it stays and stays until it is too late for her to write it. What a selfless contribution!

Darling Dame Mary. Last night before we all met up for dinner at the dining room at the Windsor, she started reading everyone's palms. She took my hand and said in her lovely lisping voice, 'Jane, dear, you're going to be a writer one day! I can see it written here.'

That is my secret dream. I wonder how she tapped into that?

A good chairman he might be, Hughie, and more than capable of waxing lyrical about his vision when he's on the podium, but he needs a lot of support and prompting during meetings. Sometimes he gets preoccupied and I have to nudge him and remind him where we're up to on the agenda. Then there are so many reports that I have written for him, that I have to elbow him in the ribs and hand him the right one. He is always so ready to laughter, and so good-natured, it really makes it a pleasure to work with him.

He gets impatient though, sometimes, with the long hours sitting presiding over meetings. He's a typical bushman in that respect.

Hugh loves words, just as he loves his art, but unlike his art the words sometimes come out wrong. Like just now, for example. Everyone was going on and on and on about something on the agenda, and I knew something was about to happen because, sitting beside him, I could feel Hughie starting to fidget with impatience. Suddenly he'd had enough.

'Come, gentlemen,' he said, his voice rising into something of a petulant quaver in that way he has. 'And ladies,' with a nod at the ladies.

'Let's not perambulate any longer.'

Of course he meant 'preamble'. No one else seemed to notice anything untoward though. I had trouble keeping a straight face. I suppose I'll never know if he said it on purpose.

He's obviously feeling his oats today, though. These meetings do go on and on, sometimes. And some of the suggestions can be a bit—well. Someone says, 'Why don't all directors have name badges showing they are directors of the Hall of Fame, so we can wear them when we come to meetings and things and people know that we are on the board?'

I feel Hughie stiffen beside me, and here comes something else I suppose. Sure enough, he's grabbed a pen and turned his agenda over, and he's scribbling away. Another drawing, perhaps? He's always passing me drawings during meetings. Anyway, he passes me one now. What's this? Oh! He's designed the badge! It says in large letters, 'ME IMPORTANT'!

He's a dag, that Hughie.

CHAPTER 28

CONSOLIDATION

Sub-committees were formed to develop the project's three main thrusts—building, funding and acquisitions. My role absorbed the organising and recording of those committees' meetings, along with following up on many of their tasks. The basic corporate administration and membership development continued apace. I felt a bit like Atlas carrying the world on his shoulders.

In October 1984 my title changed to executive director. My pay packet remained the same.

Minister Wharton kept good his verbal promise to follow up the preparation of a pre-design report with continued monitoring and quality control of the building's progress by his department. The department had declared they were confident, now, with amendments to the original design, that it was on track according to the revised budget—now $6 million in July 1982 figures. In this respect the department took on the role of project managers. Each stage of the preparation of drawings was submitted by Feiko to Roman Pavlyshyn's team at Mineral House before it progressed to the Hall of Fame board for its approval—based on the recommendation of the Department of Works. Minister Wharton promised to see it through to a successful conclusion.

Sir James, in thanking the minister's department, estimated their contribution of expertise at a value of $60 000.

At the end of 1983, a timeline had been set in place for construction, and by now Feiko was convinced of the value of using the local stone. Gathering and cutting was a slow process, so in order to generate a stockpile of the required 790 square metres of 18-inch thick random cut stone, Bob Sadler was put back to work on R.M.'s stone-cutting saw around the start of 1984.

Feiko had made his first visit to Longreach in January 1981, just after he won the design competition. He travelled up in a small plane with R.M. and Bill Durack to inspect the site for his proposed building. They'd organised to leave at 4.30 a.m. to beat the thermals that would build with the heat later in the day.

Feiko was not keen about small-plane travel, and his lack of enthusiasm for this mode of transport was exacerbated when he and Bill Durack arrived at the Toowoomba airstrip to meet R.M.

R.M. greeted them in his usual way. 'Morning, Bill. Morning, Feeko.'

'Feiko. Good morning, R.M.'

Feiko noticed a huge lump of cut granite sitting on the ground beside R.M. 'It's the foundation stone,' said R.M.

The 'foundation stone'—which Feiko recalls (and perhaps it has grown over the years) was 'as big as a person'—was manhandled in and deposited on R.M.'s lap in the back seat. It was a nerve-racking six hours for Feiko. The stone teetered on R.M.'s lap as R.M. slept peacefully, while Feiko, from his seat in the front, watched it anxiously, expecting it to drop off and fall through the floor of the plane at any moment. It didn't. But by the end of that plane trip Feiko had been thoroughly initiated into the laissez faire world of working with R.M. Williams.

The completed cottage was attracting a lot of visitors with its volunteer staff. It was lacking somewhat in amenities, though, so R.M. took great delight in returning to his campsite and, with Cyril Dahl's help, building what is probably the most solid toilet block west of the Great Divide.

Built in stone in the same style as the cottage to which it is adjacent, it is certainly not in danger of blowing away in a sudden willy-willy such as the one that lifted some unsecured tin, and Ray Hagan with it, from the roof of the cottage during its construction the year before.

In February 1984 I was able to report to the board that the Queensland government had nominated our project as one of only two major Bicentennial National/State Commemorative Projects. The other was the Great Barrier Reef World in Townsville. The matter was now 'in the hands of the Prime Minister'. We had done all we could do in the way of lobbying, and now just waited. But while we waited, we continued to move forward.

Later that year, in 1984, the Northern Territory branch staged the first of a number of Bronco Branding Days. Bronco branding had not previously been a competitive sport, not officially anyway. It is a method of managing stock for branding that takes place in the absence of a set of cattle yards.

Cattle are individually lassoed by a stockman riding a clumper, or heavy horse, equipped with a special saddle. Each beast is then dragged across to a bronco branding rail where it is manhandled and branded by a couple of stockmen; then it is released and the next one brought up. Bronco branding includes the practical application of the sport of campdrafting, taking it one step further and using skills very much required on large cattle stations.

I was determined to fly the flag for head office and support this endeavour of the Northern Territory branch which was being held in Alice Springs. The sculptor Eddie Hackman and his wife Maureen were intent on going, too. Eddie had a caravan that had been tailor-made to his requirement of displaying his magnificent solid bronze statuettes at field days and shows. It had large glass windows with display shelving for the figures.

Here was an opportunity for Eddie to showcase his art and, at the same time, attend this world-first event in his old Territory stamping ground. Eddie was an expatriate Englishman who, as new chums seeing it with fresh eyes are often able to do, had grown to love the lore and culture of the Australian outback. This he expressed through his sculpture and, later, his poetry; there were small solid bronze tableaux of horses and cattle, and evocative individual pieces in a pioneer series of outback characters, all produced by the lost-wax method of casting.

One of these was 'The Ringer', a perfect miniature representation of a Northern Territory stockman complete with every small detail of his kit. He wore spring-sided leggings and Cuban-heeled elastic-sided boots, carried a poley saddle over his shoulder, and a Barcoo bridle hung from his other hand. His Log Cabin tobacco tin was in his pocket, his bull straps around his hips. His belt carried his knife pouch and a watch pouch. He wore a tall Akubra hat with a Territory bash in the crown.

Later, when Jean Battersby was looking for suggestions for an iconic bronze image which might be commissioned to 'say it all' at the entrance to the Hall of Fame, I showed her my edition of Eddie's 'Ringer' which I kept on my desk, and suggested that Eddie be prevailed upon to produce a double-life-sized reproduction of this piece. It now stands in the place of honour at the entrance to the Australian Stockman's Hall of Fame.

Eddie and Maureen and I set off in their truck towing the caravan, from Toowoomba, early on the morning of 3 May 1984. At Oakey— half an hour down the road—we had a flat tyre. That small problem rectified, we reached Winton the next day without further incident but with a great deal of driving.

At Winton we sailed off west into the desert along the Donohue Highway en route for the famous Plenty Highway. It was a remote and unsealed road but a shortcut to Alice Springs. Eighty kilometres along the road there was an almighty bang under the bonnet and the engine stopped dead; Eddie investigated. The con rod had come adrift and thrust itself through the engine block. We were going nowhere.

No mobile phones, no communications. We sat and looked at the clumps of spinifex and the endless horizon. We speculated as to whether a min min light would emerge after dark. We waited for a miracle, and tried the ignition again—perhaps there had been a mistake. But, nothing doing. And no passers-by, either.

After many impatient hours, during which time I tried to contain my anxiety about missing out on the Bronco Branding Day, a vehicle happened past, heading east. The driver offered to send out help from Winton; I threw my swag in the back of his four-wheel drive and went back to town with him, determined to continue my journey.

Back at the small town of Winton I took the only course open to travellers heading for the Territory without a vehicle of their own; I called on my New Zealand past and stood in the main street with my thumb out and my blue swag on the traffic island behind me.

That's how it was that I arrived in Alice Springs two days later in the cab of a Kenworth truck.

The Bronco Branding Day was a highly successful event. All the Territorian characters turned out in force.

I travelled by plane for the return journey.

The beautiful publication, *The Stockman*, a lovely coffee-table book, was launched at the splendid old Commonwealth Bank premises (the old moneybox) in Martin Place, Sydney, on 27 July 1984. The authors, Dame Mary, Hugh Sawrey, R.M. Williams, Ron Iddon and Marie Mahood, lined up and signed copies while Colin Munro of the ABC performed the honours as MC. Contributors Olaf Ruhen, who had also written R.M.'s biography *Beneath Whose Hand*, and Keith Willey were not able to be there. Lansdowne Press contributed $5000 from this book to the Hall of Fame; the authors contributed their time and expertise as a donation not only to the burgeoning Australian Stockman's Hall of Fame, but also as a start to recording the ideals that were to be preserved within it.

In 1984, two more directors took their places on the board. Doug Kefford of Kefford Transport in Victoria began a tenure that has endured for more than 27 years. Roger Steele was the former speaker of the Northern Territory parliament, and Minister for Tourism.

Then in 1985 the Hon. Kevin Newman joined, representing Tasmania, and Peter Sleigh took up the cause for Victoria. Bill Norton, general manager of the Stanbroke Pastoral Company, and Roger Vale of the Northern Territory parliament, both elected in 1986, were the last two new directors on my watch.

Barty and Kate Deane of Longreach, who had already contributed so much in the form of the stone, offered to donate—and were authorised to commission—a bronze bust of Dick Skuthorpe. The bust was created by Ester Bellis, cast by Alan Crawford, and was put on display in the cottage. It was the first formally accepted artwork to be put on display.

Dick Skuthorpe was known for his extraordinary horsemanship. He embodied the bushman qualities the Hall of Fame was setting out to record. Born around the turn of the 20th century, Dick and his brother Lance were consummate horsemen. While Lance was more of a showman, and had a 'wild west' show which travelled around the country, Dick worked for many years for Rowley Edkins and his son Beau (Kate Deane's father) at their property Bimbah near Longreach. They had 1000 horses there which Dick broke in and trained. Kate herself, born in the 20s, has no recollection of learning to ride. 'It was always just something we did,' she said.

The Longreach Shire Council, realising that they were on the cusp of a huge influx of visitors that would change the shape of their district forever, began planning for an upgrade to the Longreach airstrip. While it was a major stopover on the flight path to the outback, it still only accommodated the relatively small Fokker Friendship. Obviously, larger planes were going to have to be able to land there.

Two hundred metres were added to the airstrip, creating a more serviceable runway of 1960 metres. In years to come this would just manage to accommodate—within a nerve-racking hair's breadth—the landing of a Boeing 747 Jumbo, with a crew of five pilots but empty of passengers, which took up residence as another tourist attraction at the Qantas museum across the road from the Hall of Fame.

As R.M. had predicted, since that time many more tourist attractions have burgeoned in the outback, capitalising on the opportunity created by the establishment of the Australian Stockman's Hall of Fame. This undoubtedly opened up the outback to tourism.

On 28 September 1984, the long-awaited announcement came from the Australian Bicentennial Authority; our project had been selected as a major National/State Commemorative Project; funding of $6 million adjusted to July 1982 costings was to be made available for the capital cost of the building. The other costs—displays and fitout—were to be met by the Hall of Fame itself.

Over the past few months the modus operandi for a corporate fundraising campaign had been nutted out. Mike Evans, who had recently retired as the much-vaunted director of the National Party in Queensland, had agreed to take on the role of coordinator and chairman of the Queensland push.

Sir James Walker MBE was chairman of the national finance committee, and Sir Robert Mathers OMRI the deputy.

A prominent citizen had taken on the chairmanship of each state committee. They included: Sir Brian Massy-Greene for New South Wales; Sir Laurence Muir for Victoria; Sir Charles Court AK, KCMG, OBE for Western Australia; Charles Schmidt CBE for South Australia; Harry Giese MBE for the Northern Territory; Lieutenant-Colonel the Hon. Kevin Newman for Tasmania; and Mike Evans for Queensland.

The list of 44 committee members was top-heavy with knights, CEOs and chairmen of the boards of Australia's major companies.

The groundwork had been laid. Now it was time to get down to the tin tacks of the business.

I sit at my humble pine desk at the Hall of Fame head office at 45 Hill Street, Toowoomba; no more fancy desks for me, we're on a serious budget here.

The smell of Angelo's Italian cooking wafts through the open window from the restaurant next door. My dog, Harry, shifts in his sleep under the desk, scratches himself briefly, looks at me balefully as I push my chair back and peer into the cool shade of his cosy possie, and closes his eyes again.

'Nearly lunchtime, Haz,' I say. His eyes open briefly at the mention of his name, then close again.

I lean back and rub my eyes. It's been a long morning. There was, as always, plenty to do. A 'to-do' basket that never empties, an in-basket that fills up every day with the arrival of the mail in the large letterbox outside on its post in the middle of the front lawn.

Today was a bit different from the usual routine. A visit from R.M. It was quite funny, really—well, very funny. I heard him arrive. He opened the front door cautiously and threw his hat into the middle of the front office where Carol and Wendy sit, working away. Then he peered around the door and said, 'Has the boss settled down yet? Is it safe for me to come in?'

A good question, considering the last time we met. Yesterday he came storming in like King Pin and demanded to know where all the money was going. He had my financial report in his hand—of course he had only read the bottom bit—and he could see funds coming in by the hundreds of thousands, and then going out and where were they going, he wanted to know? Could I explain myself, please?

At first I thought he just wanted to know—the funds were bank bills being rolled over every three months. Treasurer Charles Schmidt being the chairman of the Commonwealth Savings Bank, I have a direct line to a bloke called Merv at the banking centre in Sydney who gets us the best possible rate.

Then I realised R.M. was accusing me—accusing me!—of tickling the till! What? I was wild! I rolled the report up, hit him around the ears with it first, then chased him out of the office with it. I was ropeable.

Anyway, he came back today and had the grace to apologise. I'm glad because I love the old bloke, I love him to bits.

I stand up and stretch, ready to go out to lunch. In the front office, there's no sign of Carol and Wendy. They went to collect the newsletters from being packaged at the Endeavour Workshop hours ago—wherever could they be?

Carol suddenly rushes in and, looking very sheepish, scrabbles in her desk drawer. She rushes out again holding a screwdriver.

A screwdriver? I look out the bay window. Carol's car is parked halfway across the lawn; she's been backing up to the other front door to disgorge her load of newsletters. But why has she stopped halfway? She and Wendy are fussing around one of the car's back windows, shrieking with laughter.

I go outside to take a closer look. 'What the . . . ?'

They turn around, see me, shrug their shoulders in unison. Carol waves the screwdriver helplessly as they fall into fits of giggles again, and points at the letterbox.

Somehow—God only knows, but somehow—Carol has managed to get the large letterbox on its post in the middle of the lawn wedged firmly inside her back passenger window. After a certain amount of fruitless manoeuvring, which has only made matters worse, there is only one way to solve the problem. The letterbox has to be removed altogether from the post.

That's certainly one for the annals of the Stockman's Hall of Fame!

CHAPTER 29

TOPSY'S SNOWBALL

When he wasn't confusing us by declaring that 'many a mickle makes a muckle', Hugh Sawrey often referred laughingly to 'Topsy's snowball'.

'This thing's growing like Topsy's snowball,' he would say. And when it wasn't growing like Topsy's snowball, it was 'going like a Bondi tram'.

Well, once the Australian Bicentennial Authority (ABA) announced their support, and 1988 became the goal for the completed building fitted out with displays and landscaped as far as possible, we were indeed going like a Bondi tram. And Topsy's snowball (whoever Topsy was) would have melted with the sheer momentum of our progress.

Each of the various teams worked well together. While it was a busy time, it was also a wonderful time, an exciting time. It was like awaiting the birth of a child, all anticipation and none of the disagreement that must inevitably arise once the child has arrived and must be raised, and then proves to have a mind of its own anyway.

Mike Evans had accepted the position of fundraising coordinator. Sir Robert (Bob) Mathers, being deputy chairman of the National Finance Committee, offered to be available to meet with Mike and me at his office in Mary Street, Brisbane, on Monday afternoons at

4.30 p.m. There, usually finishing off our meetings with a comforting glass or two of the Glenfiddich whisky which Sir Robert kept by the case, and with a great deal of good humour and laughter, we planned the trips that took us around the country to follow through with the corporate fundraising plan.

The goal was to raise $4 million in tax-deductible donations from Australian corporations by personal approaches. Bob Mathers led the charge with a commitment from Mathers Enterprises for a donation of $100 000 over four years.

Many of the chairmen of Australia's major corporations were knights; the mention of Bob's knighthood on our introductory letter, and his position as a scion of the Queensland business world with Mathers Shoes, opened the doors to the top boardrooms.

The might and power, and combined acumen of all those on the fundraising committee, created a highly effective campaign of promotion, awareness, publicity and word-of-mouth that resulted in a very successful fundraising campaign over the space of a year.

By now, I was wearing a pathway on the bitumen from Toowoomba to Brisbane airport as I travelled around the corporate head offices in company with one or other of my finance committee members, soliciting donations. I had the drive to Brisbane airport down to a fine art so as not to waste a precious moment of my time. It was a 1½-hour trip by car, at the end of which I glided into the long-term carpark and sprinted to the Trans-Australia Airlines (TAA) terminal just in time to catch my plane.

On one occasion I had a flat tyre a couple of suburbs short of the airport. It was pre-mobile phones, but I rushed into the nearest house and borrowed their phone to call a cab. The time spent waiting for the cab was saved at the other end when I didn't have to park my car; I left my car on the kerb and got to the plane with seconds to spare.

Once airborne my heartbeat settled and I was able to look back over the events of the last hour. It occurred to me that I had absolutely no idea where I had left my car. On the return trip I phoned my friend Tim Ferrier who kindly drove me up and down the streets in the vicinity of where I thought I had left it; we found it eventually, and Tim helped me change my tyre and set me on my way safely home.

Sir Brian Massy-Greene, chairman of Dunlop Olympic (later Pacific Dunlop), was my Sydney fundraising committee chairman. I got to know him well as we were chauffeured around Sydney city in his limo, to find that he, as too the others of his ilk, was human and a lovely person and just like anyone else. I don't know what I had expected, but it was a pleasant surprise.

Likewise in Melbourne where I accompanied Sir Laurence Muir, chairman of Liquidair Australia and one of nature's gentlemen, around Melbourne's top boardrooms soliciting support.

During 1985 the site was registered as freehold. But most significantly, at the end of March tenders were called for construction of the Hall of Fame. Ten of the 17 contractors who registered their interest were invited to tender; in the event, eight quotes were received for a fixed-price tender with a two-year building period.

In June, the contractor T.F. Woollam and Son was selected as the builder. Their quote was a lump-sum fixed price of $6.397 million, fixed for two years.

About a month later R.M.'s lump of granite that had caused Feiko such grief on its journey to Longreach came into its own. Cut into two large stones, they were engraved with the words 'This foundation stone was laid on 28th July, 1985, by the Right Honourable Sir Ninian Stephen, AK, GCMG, GCVO, KBE, Governor-General of the Commonwealth of Australia', on the first, and the names of the chairman and board, executive director and founder on the other.

The stone was laid by the governor-general at a sunset ceremony. The backdrop was a brilliant blue outback sky emblazoned with the incomparable red of the setting outback sun. The unique local smell of gidyea permeated the air. Just after the official proceedings a million or more corellas flew overhead to their evening roost, bestowing a blessing and confirming the authenticity of the site. It was an enchanted evening.

In September, Irvine Heesom was appointed as clerk of works for the project. We were extremely lucky to catch this very competent veteran of building project management at the end of his formal career, who was not quite ready to retire and was willing to make this project the last of his working life.

Under Irvine's watchful and practised eye the building progressed apace. Woollams were conscious that penalties would apply for overrunning their two-year deadline. They completed the enormous building task ahead of schedule.

Stonemason Michael Bullock created the stonework which is undoubtedly a hallmark of this remarkable building complex.

Meanwhile the vexed question of how to present the story of the bush through the displays—the whole point of the exercise apart from creating a memorial—was debated and tossed around the board table. Professor Barrie Reynolds, head of the Material Culture Unit at the James Cook University, agreed to assist in the definition of a plan and guidelines for the collection. It was no easy task. Up until now, there had been no occasion to get down to the nitty-gritty of putting on paper each director's personal vision.

On behalf of the Hall of Fame, Professor Reynolds called for registrations of interest from exhibition consultants, their submissions to be received by November 1985. The level of interest was high; more than 80 firms submitted written submissions by the due date.

In August 1986 the design and fabrication group Acumen was selected to prepare the displays.

It had become rather painfully obvious that everybody had a fixed idea of his or her own in the matter of the content, and that those did not necessarily coincide. It was going to take a very strong person to run the gauntlet of the various personalities and somehow please them all. Under Barrie Reynolds' direction, a curator was appointed early in 1986. He was experienced, having worked at the Australian War Memorial, but very young, and definitely not familiar with bush culture and lexicon, not to mention the somewhat idiosyncratic way of getting things done that flourished around the board table. When he tried to make any progress with actual design of the displays, he continually came up against the strong personalities on the board, who were quite adamant about the many and varied ideas they envisaged although they didn't have the technical skills to bring them into being.

In October 1986 Ken Cowley struck a master blow for the cause. He managed to engage the services of Dr Jean Battersby AO, the founding chief executive of the Australia Council in 1968, as a display consultant. Jean Battersby was a formidable achiever in the world of art, and a formidable force in the battle of wits required to sort out how to incorporate the combined visions of the founders and directors, and within the tight timeframe to opening in April 1988.

Jean performed miracles. She charmed everybody with her eloquent wit and self-confidence. She called in favours from museums and art galleries throughout the land, and her coup de grace was to prevail upon Australia's leading artist Sir Sidney Nolan to do a dedicated painting as a contribution to the Hall of Fame. She prepared a comprehensive display report for the board. Then she set about following through with the practical aspects of filling the voluminous spaces in Feiko's building with such varied displays that they created an impression of completeness from the day the doors opened to the public.

There was so much going on during the last mad couple of years leading up to the opening of the Stockman's Hall of Fame by the Queen in April 1988 that it is impossible to gather the different strands of the various stories into a cohesive tale.

Everybody was at their wits' end raising money, preparing displays, building the building, landscaping, promoting, and variously pulling the whole thing together.

The amount of publicity that was generated in the printed press was really quite astonishing; obviously the project and the personalities involved, not to mention the concept of creating a place in which to portray such a romantic aspect of Australia's unique character, held a lot of appeal for the media.

The Queensland Merino Stud Sheepbreeders' Association's offer to donate a sculpture of a merino ewe and lamb, cast in solid bronze, for the displays, was accepted. Sculptor Bodo Muche created and cast the sculpture, which is 1¼ times lifesize, and he and his wife Robbie delivered the lovely piece to Longreach in time to be put in pride of place for the opening.

Bodo also created two maquettes of this sculpture: a one-off piece with hoofprints on the base was presented to the Queen; the other was sold at a fundraising auction on the evening of the opening celebrations, for $10 000, to John Chandler (brother of Ranald) and his wife Maree.

Landscaping of the site commenced early in 1987 with the appointment of gardener Bob Kelly to begin planting trees. Landscaping had also been part of Feiko's brief. On one of his many trips to Longreach to gather information for the plans he was developing, he consulted with the Longreach Department of Primary Industries' Dick Law on the selection of a range of inland flora that was not familiar to the Sydney-based architect.

Tom Murphy's Challenge Dinners raised a spectacular $250 000.

And Ranald Chandler and Gordon Reid spent several years organising a droving trip touted as the Last Great Cattle Drive, from Newcastle Waters in the Northern Territory, across the Barkly Tableland to Longreach. The drive left Newcastle Waters in May 1988, arriving in Longreach in September. This huge project generated a great deal of media interest, and raised a profit of $150 000 for the Hall of Fame.

A librarian, Gunela Astbrink, was engaged and began collating the documentation and collections to create an archive. Gunela introduced us at the Toowoomba office to the technology of laser printing and at last we jettisoned our faithful dot matrix printer.

An executive director of administration, John Jenkins, was installed at Longreach to look to the future running of the Hall of Fame. John's tenure was brief, and he was replaced by Bill Gair who managed the Hall from within for several years from the time of its opening.

Ken Cowley, who over the previous few years had been more than a little preoccupied with a very busy life as CEO of News Limited, brought his strength to bear in the crucial last year of the Hall of Fame's development. Realising there was a shortfall in funding for displays, he approached Prime Minister Bob Hawke and John Brown, then Minister for Tourism, and secured the balance required.

He also convinced Dr Bob Edwards, Director of the Museum of Victoria, to act as managing agent for the display program. The fortuitous acquisition of Team Edwards and Battersby ensured that the displays were on a sound professional footing from the very beginning; between them they secured enough display material on loan from other museums to fill the hall with an impressive line-up of material by opening day, April 1988.

In a fever pitch of excitement, as 1988 dawned the spotlight was well and truly on Longreach, Central Western Queensland, and the extraordinary monument in stone that had emerged from its flat plain, its huge curved corrugated iron roof now glittering in the outback sun like a beacon—the Australian Stockman's Hall of Fame and Outback Heritage Centre.

For me, at a personal level, 1987 ranks as one of those years not to be repeated.

I was exhausted after more than nine years of almost nonstop work and as the project reached its crescendo I was under immense pressure.

In February my Uncle Sandy died.

And then on 10 July 1987, Dad died suddenly. He was 69.

I had known grief but this was something else altogether. I found that as I was going about my daily business I would suddenly realise that my face was wet with tears. I was angry and sad and could not hold it in. Irvine Heesom took me aside and counselled me about the indignity of the colourful language which began to pepper the outbursts of frustration that started to creep into my working life.

I was utterly spent, but the finishing line was in sight, thank God. I had met Robert Grieve through mutual friends. Robert, a stoic bushman, became my rock as I struggled to fulfil my personal commitment to see the project through to the conclusion of its gestation, and the beginning of its life.

EPILOGUE

VALE

Council at inauguration
28 July 1985
Chairman—Sir James Walker, KB, MBE, LLD
Deputy chairman—Dame Mary Durack Miller, DBE

Miss J. Bowen

Mr W.R.M. Chandler

Mr K.E. Cowley

Mr L.J.M. Cummings

Mr E. Hayes

Hon. R.C. Katter

Mr D. Kefford

Hon. Sir James Killen, KCMG

Sir Francis Moore

Mr W.F. Munro

Dr T.J. Murphy

Mr W.C.K. Pearse, CBE

Mr H.C. Schmidt, CBE

Hon. R.M. Steele

Mrs T.M. Stroud

Mr R.M. Williams, CMG

Executive director—Miss J.O. Paull
Founder—Mr Hugh Sawrey

What a team effort! The time had come to hand over what we had created together. Everyone wanted a piece of it now, and rightly so; it belongs to every Australian.

But the legacy of those names on the foundation stone goes on and it goes both ways. It reaches back into the past, to the forebears it was created to honour.

And also, it reaches out into the future, to those Australians born and unborn since that time, from every origin, those bringing with them ancestries of their own, histories of their own, to implant here alongside those who have been here longer; some much, much longer.

It belongs to all of you. It was done for you.

There was Hugh Sawrey, the acknowledged founder, his name engraved as such in the foundation stone in front of his 'Vision Splendid', now a splendid reality on the wide brown plains.

R.M. Williams, the builder, who saw only success and doggedly refused to entertain—even for a minute—the possibility of failure. He has left his indelible footprint at Longreach.

There was Dame Mary Durack Miller, writer and historian, whose wisdom, loyalty and tenacity bore us all through many a tough time.

Jill Bowen, the self-proclaimed 'little brown dog' in her lolly-pink hat, who gave more than most and received less, and made the Hall of Fame her life's work.

Sir James Walker, who dedicated his life to public causes and was the tower of strength that made things happen wherever his considerable influence extended.

Ken Cowley, who generously shared his position of power through News Limited to open doors and contribute fundamental practicalities.

Ranald Chandler, raconteur and funny man, who never missed a meeting, whose enormous personality brought celebrities into our small circle everywhere we went.

Wally Munro, cattleman, who quietly made things happen wherever he could from the cattle yards to the boardroom.

Tess Stroud, who looked after Dame Mary in her growing frailty as they crossed the country to bring the blessing of Western Australia and add their considerable combined strength to the project.

Mike Cummings, who was there from the outset and who continually stirred the pot in South Australia for the benefit of the Hall of Fame.

Bob Katter, who unhesitatingly brought his political influence to bear wherever he could, and who was the first chairman; Joy, his wife, the first secretary.

Doug Kefford, who stayed the course long after everyone else dropped away and is currently at 28 years on the board, and still counting.

Sir Jim Killen, politician and orator, his name a beacon for credibility and who unhesitatingly caused doors to open in the Halls of Power.

Charles Schmidt, who found himself sitting among a group of free spirits, dealt with their idiosyncrasies with gentlemanly aplomb, and astutely husbanded the finances of the Hall of Fame.

Tom Murphy, Dr Tom, beloved of his Central Western Queensland branch and tireless in his enthusiasm and dedication to the cause.

Sir Frank Moore, who clinched many a deal for the Hall of Fame and believed it would be the fulcrum for the outback tourism that was 'non-existent' in 1982, and that flourishes today as a direct result, in no small part, of what this team achieved.

Roger Steele, a Territorian who knew Australia from the saddle to the speaker's chair, and generously brought all in his power to bear when called upon to do so.

Colin Pearse and Ted Hayes, their names engraved on R.M.'s lump of granite at the entrance to the Hall of Fame in Longreach, forever bound to a most remarkable achievement.

Bruce Yeates and Eddie Connellan, gone but not forgotten as we stood in triumph in their Bicentennial National/State Commemorative Project.

Kevin Newman, Roger Vale, John Ayers Senior and John Ayers Junior, Peter Sleigh, Bill Norton, Ben Humphreys, who joined the cause too late to make it onto the foundation stone, but whose contributions were selfless and significant nonetheless.

And me, Jane Paull, also inscribed in stone. For ten amazing years I played a pivotal role in creating an extraordinary Australian monument. Those ten years almost—but not quite—stole away my child-bearing years. But they also presented me with opportunities, experiences, skills and achievements that most people don't find in a lifetime. They found in me a strength I did not know I possessed and a determination that surprised me.

What did it all cost me? A great deal. But who counts the cost? I did it; I reached the end. And I left our finished project, our slice of Australia's history, in capable hands. I changed my name two months after the grand opening in 1988. There was so much history, so much living, so much identity bound up in the name I had carried for 35 years. But I took Robert's name when we married on 25 June 1988, and bore his children, and created for myself another sort of family altogether.

We each give a little bob as we take the Queen's hand and exchange greetings. She looks exactly like her photographs, and not altogether unlike my aunt Peg Galwey. She is obviously delighted with the welcome she has received outside from the crowd of 20 000 excited visitors who have come from goodness knows where to take part in this day, and to see her.

The Prime Minister Bob Hawke, the Queensland Premier Mike Ahern, the US Ambassador Bill Lane, the Queensland Governor Sir Walter Campbell, and their wives, follow the royal party along our little welcoming line. Sir James Walker does the introductions.

Suddenly Jean Battersby and I are escorting the royal couple around the Stockman's Hall of Fame. Jean has the Queen; I have the Duke. At first we stroll in separate pairs but, when the Duke asks the details of a third artwork and I am once again at a loss for an answer because I only arrived in Longreach yesterday and was not able to get a proper briefing from Jean, we both opt to hang closer to Jean as she explains the displays to the Queen with unfaltering confidence.

I prefer it that way. The Duke is rather scratchy today; perhaps it's the heat, or perhaps his gruelling trip has made him tired. We pass a display featuring Sid Nolan's photographs of drought. 'We have been having a nasty drought lately,' I say.

'What will you expect if you cut down all the trees?' barks Prince Philip furiously. Quite. But I think this is perhaps not the time . . .

Robbie and Bodo Muche are standing beside the ewe-and-lamb sculpture Bodo created. The royal couple admire it, stop to talk to them, congratulate Bodo. In a little while, Dame Mary Durack Miller will present Bodo's one-off maquette of this statue to the Queen as a gift.

We reach the display about the working dogs. 'Oh, Philip, Philip, look!' says the Queen. 'Here are those dogs we saw! What are they called?' she asks, looking at me intently.

'Blue heelers,' I answer. Hooray! Got one right!

Then we are at the electronic map of the droving routes. I find myself walking along with my hands behind my back, unconsciously mimicking the Duke. Embarrassed, I quickly hold them by my sides, only to forget and put them behind my back again.

'When will we be meeting R.M. Williams?' asks the Queen, looking at me with such sincere intensity that I almost buckle at the knees. Her eyes plead with me to simply answer her, just talk to her.

The Duke wants to know, too.

Upstairs in the mezzanine galleries there is someone stationed beside each of the main displays. Brian Taylor, Marlboro man, looking handsome in moleskins and boots and full stockman's kit, steps forward and holds out his hand.

'How do you do,' says the Duke.

'G'day. Pleased to meet ya, Mister,' says Brian, grasping his hand and giving it a hearty shake.

We continue through the galleries, hanging close to Jean Battersby with all the answers. The Queen speaks to me a lot—I feel she has found an ordinary person among all the dignitaries, and wants to learn how one ticks. She is the most magnetic person I have ever met.

Hugh and Gill Sawrey, in the place of honour in celebration of Hugh's founder status, greet them and talk for a while. R.M. is standing in the top gallery, the Founders' Hall. He is flanked by two Indigenous stockmen, Wally Mailman and Charlie Chambers. R.M. introduces them to the Queen and Prince Philip.

'I understand the life of a stockman is a very difficult one,' says the Queen.

'Not half so hard as yours, Your Majesty,' counters R.M.

Appearing stunned by his logic, she looks at him for a moment; then the accuracy of his unlikely reply seems to hit her, and she turns her head to one side and laughs delightedly.

FUNDRAISING COMMITTEE

In 1983, a fundraising committee was put together on a state-by state basis. This list of committee members reads like a who's who of business and industry leaders of the 1980s and illustrates the level of importance of the Australian Stockman's Hall of Fame.

The inclusion of my name at the bottom of such an exalted list of men was remarkable for the times, and something of a triumph for me.

National Finance Committee
Sir James Walker, MBE (Chairman)
Sir Robert Mathers, OMRI (Deputy Chairman)

State Chairmen
NSW—Sir Brian Massey-Greene
VIC—Sir Laurence Muir
WA—Hon. Sir Charles Court, AK, KCMG, OBE
SA—Mr H.C. Schmidt, CBE
NT—Mr H.C. Giese, MBE
QLD—Mr M.G. Evans

Committee Members

Mr W.C. Adams

Mr D.J. Asimus, AO

Mr P.L. Baillieu

Mr L. Barrett, OBE

Mr B.A. Buckham, DSO, DFC

Hon. S.E. Calder, OBE, DFC, JP

Mr M.A.J. Cameron

Mr M.C. Capp

Mr R.K. Castle

Hon. Sir Gordon Chalk, KBE

Sir Rupert Clarke, BT, MBE

Mr C.F. Clements

Mr L.R. Connell

Mr J.K. Horwood, BE

Col. Sir Malcolm Macarthur, OBE

Mr D.I. Macarthur-Onslow

Mr D. Miller, AM, DFC

Mr G.M. Niall

Mr G.N. Nock, OBE

Sir William Pettingell, CBE

Mr F.A. Pratten

Mr P.W. Prior

Mr A.E.R. Coote

Sir Robert Chrichton-Brown, KCMG, CBE

Mr J.N. Davenport, AO, DSO, GM, DFC & Bar

Mr F.M. Davidson, OBE

Sir Ronald Elliott

Sir Vincent Fairfax, CMG

Sir George Fisher, CMG

Sir James Foots

Sir David Griffin, CBE

Sir William Gunn, KBE, CMG

Mr A.E. Harris

Mr G.F. Heaslip

Mr G. Higginson

Hon. Sir Wallace Rae

Mr J.A. Rickard

Mr R.A. Setter

Mr B.K. Smart

Sir Edward Stewart

Mr R.F. Stowe

Sir William Vines, CMG

Mr K.D. Williams, AM, BEC

Hon. Sir Edward Williams, KCMG, KBE

Executive Director
Miss J.O. Paull

ACKNOWLEDGEMENTS

My sincere thanks to my cousin, Dr Graham Mylne, whose welcome intervention in the up-and-down flow of my life brought about the series of events that led to my being 'discovered' by Claire Kingston of Allen & Unwin—to whom I am eternally grateful.

To my family, including the long list of those who went before, whose energy, vision, enthusiasm, humour, sense of honour, love of Australia and love of the written word came down to me, and whose love and support have sustained me all my life.

To the many teachers that life has put in my way—including my revered English teacher, Barry Hall, to whom this book is dedicated.

To Ben Maguire, CEO of the Australian Stockman's Hall of Fame, and his staff for their unfailing support and assistance.

To a plethora of dear friends who have accompanied me these many years.

To my husband Robert, the quiet 'rock' who is central to my busyness, and our children Sam, Lou and Jock, without whom life would be unthinkable.

Thank you.

Jane Grieve has been appearing in print media and on the radio as a voice of the countryside for years now. She has written a column on rural living for the *Courier Mail*, has had her blog read out on ABC radio, was featured in the *Australian Women's Weekly* and regularly speaks at various events. She is an honorary life member of the Australian Stockman's Hall Of Fame. Jane has also previously self-published a book of stories, *Slippin' on the Lino*, based around her *Courier Mail* columns.

www.janegrieve.com.au